"Rick Dunn's steady, measured hand in this book allows readers to draw from his many years of youth ministry experiences—as both a practitioner and a teacher. Youth workers and parents of teenagers alike will find his practical insights encouraging and challenging. I especially appreciated the 'Reflecting on Your Journey' exercises at the end of each chapter. A valuable resource for all who love kids and those who want to see more love Jesus."
DUFFY ROBBINS, *chair of the youth ministry department at Eastern College and author of* The Ministry of Nurture

"What a great time to be a youth minister! *Shaping the Spiritual Life of Students* is the latest indication that we're getting serious about this stuff. Rick Dunn's skillful storytelling and personal authenticity reveal a gifted and creative leader, grounded by his love for God and teens, pacing with us as he leads us into some of the deepest waters of youth ministry. This book draws efffortlessly from Rick's cultural savvy, theological acumen and expertise in adolescent development. And what a great new contribution! 'Pacing, then leading' will become a test of youth ministry literacy for years to come."
DR. DAVE RAHN, *Director, Huntington College Link Institute*

"*Shaping the Spiritual Life of Students* provides important insights to guide spiritual caregivers in successfully negotiating the turbulent waters of transformation for adolescents in the midst of our postmodern culture. Rick Dunn engages the reader with stories that teach, practical insights and thought-provoking questions in his perceptive look at the challenges inherent in assisting twenty-first century youth toward spiritual maturity. Reading this book brought me to a place of greater clarity and hope in my ability to affect students for Christ. The questions and suggestions at the end of each chapter both nurtured and challenged me. *Shaping the Spiritual Life of Students* will become required reading for our youth ministry majors and should be for anyone serious about ministering to students."
JANA SUNDENE, *Trinity International University*

"In a day when we need to do all we can to understand this changing culture— identifying the needs of this generation so we can effectively communicate Christ's love— Rick Dunn has composed a significant tool in this process! Student ministry leaders need tangible ideas to assist them in coming alongside students, to understand and communicate with them in a way that will ultimately point to God. This is a must-have resource to assist in training pastors and leaders in better reaching this generation for Christ."
BO BOSHERS, *Executive Director of Student Ministries, Willow Creek Association*

SHAPING
the Spiritual Life
of Students

A Guide for
Youth Workers,
Pastors , Teachers
& Campus Ministers

Richard R. Dunn

InterVarsity Press
Downers Grove, Illinois

InterVarsity Press
P.O. Box 1400, Downers Grove, IL 60515-1426
World Wide Web: www.ivpress.com
E-mail: mail@ivpress.com

InterVarsity Press® is the book-publishing division of InterVarsity Christian Fellowship/USA®, a student movement active on campus at hundreds of universities, colleges and schools of nursing in the United States of America, and a member movement of the International Fellowship of Evangelical Students. For information about local and regional activities, write Public Relations Dept., InterVarsity Christian Fellowship/USA, 6400 Schroeder Rd., P.O. Box 7895, Madison, WI 53707-7895.

Cover photograph: Richard Shock / Stone

ISBN 0-8308-2284-4

Printed in the United States of America ∞

Library of Congress Cataloging-in-Publication Data

Dunn, Richard R.
    Shaping the spiritual life of students: a guide for youth workers, teachers, pastors, and
campus ministers / Richard R. Dunn.
      p. cm.
    Includes bibliographical references.
    ISBN 0-8308-2284-4 (pbk.: alk. paper)
    1. Church work with teenagers. 2. Christian teenagers—Religious life. I. Title.

BV4447 .D86 2001
259'2—dc21

                                          2001016773

19	18	17	16	15	14	13	12	11	10	9	8	7	6	5
16	15	14	13	12	11	10	09	08	07	06	05			

For Jessica, Zachary and Benjamin.
May your adolescent journeys be shaped by
the faithful companionship of pacing,
then leading spiritual caregivers.

With love that springs from the deepest well of my soul,
Dad

Foreword

As an author of several youth ministry books, I found myself reading *Shaping the Spiritual Lives of Students* with a mixture of joy and jealousy. The joy came in absorbing chapters that I know will make a significant impact in the world of youth ministry. The jealousy came from the fresh insights and principles where I thought, *That's brilliant—I wish I had written that.* Bottom line: I was inspired and challenged as I read this book!

I don't know Rick Dunn, but I know of his work and reputation in youth ministry and I was honored to be asked to write this foreword. After reading every word, I feel like I know the heart of this influential author. Rick has a heart for God and a passion for youth workers to be used in the spiritual formation of students. He wants the youth worker's heart to know and focus on God as the foundation of leadership.

Shaping the Spiritual Life of Students is not an ideas book but a significant resource that gives us an idea of the importance of relationships in a program-saturated youth ministry world. It reflects the importance of significant adults playing the role of spiritual caregivers rather than program directors.

While it is academically challenging, it is also very practical and the type of book that I want my adult leaders to read. Rick encourages leaders to depend on God's power as well as the power of community. And the coaching he gives toward confronting, listening and affirming students is as solid as anything I've ever read. Leaders will be challenged to listen, learn, love and lead students to the Creator. I know that the leaders I work with are wonderful people who just need some vision for what a significant relationship "looks like" and some direction on how it might be achieved. *Shaping the Spiritual Life of Students* gives them what they're looking for!

In twenty years of youth ministry I've learned that programs are very negotiable. I believe most youth ministries could cut out half of what they're doing and they'd be twice as effective. We cannot program students to Christ or entertain them into spiritual maturity. Students need adults who are journeying with God themselves (pacing) to come alongside them and lovingly guide them (leading) to the Savior. Experienced youth workers understand that spiritual transformation is mysterious and can't be quantified in four easy steps. Yet, one of the transferable principles in any effective discipleship "strategy" is that discipleship involves life-on-life. Adult to student. Mentor to adolescent. Leader to learner.

The DNA within a healthy and effective youth ministry is quality relationships. *Shaping the Spiritual Life of Students* magnifies this biblical truth and challenges youth workers like myself to rethink the significance of strong relationships. I'm a different youth worker because of this book!

A friend and fellow youth worker,
Doug Fields
Pastor to Students, Saddleback Church
Author, *Purpose Driven Youth Ministry*

Acknowledgments

Thank you—

☐ to my best friend and wife, Teresa, for patience, persistence and passionate confidence that fueled my completion of this book. Above all, thank you for pacing with God's work in my unseen self. Your partnership in God's redemptive process in my life is his greatest spiritual gift to me.

☐ to my children for reminding me that being a godly father begins with being a child of God.

☐ to Jana Sundene for your friendship and collaboration in "outside-the-box" education for ministry.

☐ to Steven and Carol Hines for your companionship on the journey of real life with God.

☐ to Alan and Diane Ramsey and Chad and Lisa Ellenburg for being copilgrims with Teresa and me. I celebrate both our living together in authentic redemptive community and our learning together to pace and then lead the spiritual lives of twenty-first-century students.

☐ to Mark Senter for being the embodiment of an empowering servant leader in student ministries.

☐ to the pastors and staff of Fellowship Church for your loving embrace of the "broken guy." To the management team I express my joy in being "honest to God" with each of you.

☐ to Tim Shaughnessy for the years of being copilgrims in progress.

☐ to the members of Intern Community—I count it all joy to be a participant-observer as God fashions each of you into masterpieces of spiritual caregiving.

☐ to Angie Mueller Ward for contributing your time, thoughts and stories at a time when I needed fresh perspectives on the developmental process of adolescence.

☐ to Beth Utterback and Chris Carpenter for serving me along the long, winding road of calls, copies and changes in schedules.

☐ to the students, interns and student ministry leaders of Brainerd Presbyterian Church, Trinity College and Trinity Evangelical Divinity School, and Fellowship Church for all that you've taught me about spirituality as an authentic human experience.

☐ to Doug Fields for investing in this endeavor through the contribution of the foreword.

☐ to Cindy Bunch for not giving up on this project despite my incredibly challenging personal journey through the last three years.

Section 1

A Vision for Twenty-first-Century Ministry

Preparing for Your Journey

As you prepare to read chapters one to three, take a few moments to ask God to move the learning through your mind and heart into the very depths of your soul. Pray that God will speak truth and grace into your life concerning the following questions:

☐ What do the adolescents in my life need most from me as a spiritual caregiver?

☐ What is it like to be an adolescent on a spiritual pilgrimage in the twenty-first century? How do these adolescents experience their world? How do they process those experiences?

☐ How does my role intersect with God's role in the spiritual nurture of adolescents?

☐ What does it mean to be a spiritually whole person?

☐ How can God use the unique person I am to make a redemptive difference in the lives of the adolescents I love?

☐ How could an increasingly mature balancing of my spiritual life with God enable me to become a more effective spiritual caregiver for postmodern adolescents?

☐ What is a healthy relational style of spiritual caregiving? How can I grow in it?

Being a teenager can, as one youth put it to me recently, "turn into a long obstacle course." She is taking sex-education and drug-education courses in school. She knows about birth-control methods, and each of her boyfriends, she tells me, has known all there is to know about condom usage. She and they have lately heard plenty about AIDS—its channels of transmission and the necessary precautions.

She is nevertheless in jeopardy by her own description, and she needs much more than information, exhortation, and contraception, and dire television warnings about sex and drugs. She needs emotional and moral support. She needs the attentive, continuing concern of others—a community of caring individuals who will make up for what she lacked while growing up. . . . So she herself more than implied when she said that she wished she could "find one strong, good person to lean on—and the person wouldn't disappear."
ROBERT COLES, *THE LONG OBSTACLE COURSE CALLED ADOLESCENCE*

My secret is that I need God—that I am
sick and can no longer make it alone.
DOUGLAS COUPLAND, *LIFE AFTER GOD*

Youth ministry is a womb, an incubation ward for potential God-bearers as they ponder and struggle with the news that God is crazy in love with them, would die for them and, in fact, has. What youth need more than gung-ho adults are Godbearing adults, people whose own yes to God has transformed them into messengers of the gospel.
KENDA CREASY DEAN & RON FOSTER,
THE GODBEARING LIFE

But we were gentle among you, like a mother caring for her little children. We loved you so much that we were delighted to share with you not only the gospel of God but our lives as well, because you had become so dear to us. . . . For you know that we dealt with each of you as a father deals with his own children, encouraging, comforting and urging you to live lives worthy of God, who calls you into his kingdom and glory.
1 THESSALONIANS 2:7, 11-12

1

The Walk of Life

*T*oo fast, Dad."

Zachary and I were hiking an abandoned, decaying railroad bed carved out of the steep wall of a river gorge. What an ideal setting this was for engaging the heart of my adventurous and affectionate four-year-old. Walking hand in hand, we had exchanged thoughts about rocks, bugs, trains and each other. Along the way, however, I had taken an internal detour. Though my body was still close, my thoughts had drifted far from my little boy's side. Zachary's words caught me by surprise.

"I am sorry, Zachary. What did you say?"

"Too fast, Dad."

Though spoken softly, those three words were a resounding wake-up call. Striding at a pace that had overwhelmed the legs of my barely three-foot-tall companion, I had unconsciously changed the nature of our walk. What I had intended as a side-by-side journey had become a frustrating attempt on his part not to be left behind. No longer holding his hand, I had lost touch physically, mentally and emotionally.

I grasped Zachary's hand firmly, bent down to look him in the eye and said, "I am sorry, Zachary. I don't want to miss out on my walking with you."

Holding my son's hand, paying close attention to the pace of his steps, I reentered his world. In that world I found sticks, bugs and a sense of wonder that I would have missed had I stayed at *my* speed on the hike. More important, I discovered the joy of companionship with a little boy whose favorite part of the walk was simply my being present to share it with him.

Walking with a child whose strides do not match my own can be challenging. In spite of my best intentions, I find it difficult to maintain awareness and responsiveness to the gait of a four-year-old. Yet in the act of pacing with my son, life was shared, exchanged and invested. Journeying together at his pace, holding each other's hand, we embraced each other's hearts.

Zachary taught me a lot on that fall walk in the mountains. God used that time to shine light onto my tendency to be physically present but emotionally distant. Now when I spend time with my children that phrase "Too fast, Dad" echoes loudly in my heart. To love them well as a father is to learn to *pace* with their lives, not just physically but intellectually, emotionally, socially and spiritually.

Pacing: Entering the Walk of Life

Pacing is the language of love not only for effective parenting but for effective student ministry.[1] Pacing requires me to listen to the heart of an adolescent, seeing beyond words and behaviors. Pacing therefore demands time, the time it takes to go beyond the surface in a conversation or to enter the social turf of a student—a band concert, a dorm room. Pacing is costly. The payoff, however, far exceeds the cost. Choosing to listen or to engage personally an adolescent's world communicates, "Who you are matters to me. I care about what you think, how you feel and why you make the choices you do." Pacing builds trust. Trust produces relationship. Relationship conceives spiritual life exchanges. Such exchanges are the sacred places where the Holy Spirit reaches through the life of a Christian spiritual caregiver to change forever the life of a student.

Pacing is exactly what Dana, a college sophomore, and Melissa, a freshman in high school, needed most. Pacing is also what both had experienced least in their contrasting experiences with Christianity.

Dana's parents were missionaries. She had grown up in Christian boarding schools, was attending a Christian college and was hoping to be engaged one day to her Christian boyfriend. Dana dreamed of serving Christ in full-time vocational ministry. Melissa was a study in contrast. Her mere whisper of a frame suggested that she was not a day older than twelve. Her eyes, however, betrayed a lifetime of experiences that had robbed her of the innocence and play of youthfulness. Melissa was from a troubled home, was sexually involved with her boyfriend, and had no idea who God was, much less how he could make sense out of the mess her short life had already become.

What Dana and Melissa shared was the need to have someone pace with their worlds. For Dana, the absence of her parents for most of her life had left her feeling isolated, distant and angry toward the God her parents served. Try as she might, she could not find her way into intimacy with her earthly father—or her heavenly Father. The complications of Dana's pain included difficulties in her relationship with the young man she loved, guilt over her lack of passion for God, and fear that she would never be free of loneliness. For Melissa, the words I spoke were a foreign language. Her pain was sharpened rather than assuaged by my talks on what it means to have God as a Father who heals our hearts, including our sexual woundedness. Melissa was, however, drawn to the portrait of a caring, present Father. Her world had taught her that the life she had was all there was and hoping for more was just another setup for disappointment. By default, she had chosen denial and numbness over the more painful option of dealing with reality.

The Danas and Melissas of our worlds are familiar with teachings about what they should or should not be doing. Extensive knowledge of "what I should be doing" led Dana to try harder until she exhausted herself with failure and the corresponding guilt of feeling like a "bad Christian." Melissa just pushed those messages away. What was the point? Her life simply was a mess, and nothing, not even God, was going to change that.

Yet in both cases, just a few moments of pacing made a difference. Pacing with Dana and Melissa meant listening with a heart seeking understanding: "What are you feeling? What experiences are creating those feelings? What choices are you making? What relational commitments, personal convictions or processes of reasoning are behind those choices?" Pacing with their troubled spiritual journeys led to invitations for me to speak grace and truth into the dark places of both hearts.

Pacing created the relational environment in which Dana and Melissa could experience Jesus' love. What these young women needed most, however, was not a camp speaker who could spend a short time talking with them before they left for home. What they desperately needed—and lacked—was someone to pace with them when they returned home. Without this pacing, Dana will be left frustrated with her impotent spiritual life and Melissa will be left without a relationship with Jesus.

Overcoming the Urge to Tell

Pacing with an adolescent requires an intentional commitment to love. Being attentive to the internal experiences of an adolescent can be tiring, frustrating and overwhelming. Adolescents often appear to want to be left alone, to maintain a posture of independence, keeping their thoughts and feelings to themselves. Unfortunately, adults mistake this aloofness for lack of desire for relationship. Nothing could be further from the truth. In the depths of the adolescent's heart is a God-created longing for the embrace of an adult's understanding, affirmation and guidance. Being "cool" or "tough" is a façade; in fact the cooler or tougher students appear, the more desperate they really are to experience the pacing of a loving adult.

Rarely, however, does an adult discover a direct, unobstructed path to the hidden places of need in an adolescent's heart. With factors such as fear of rejection, self-protective relational styles, busy schedules, interpersonal demands and all the distractions that naturally invade adults' and adolescents' daily existence, it is no wonder that even the most well-intentioned spiritual caregivers default to *telling* rather than *pacing*.

Telling can be contrasted with pacing in the following ways:

1. Telling enters the relationship with an agenda: communicating what an adolescent should be experiencing, thinking or doing. Pacing's agenda is to understand what the adolescent *is* experiencing, thinking or doing.

2. Telling emphasizes the teaching and advice-giving abilities of the adult. Pacing emphasizes the listening and care-giving abilities of an adult.

3. Telling emphasizes the adult's expertise and knowledge about God's will for adolescent lives. Pacing emphasizes the adult's heart for hearing God's will at work in the life of a particular adolescent.

4. Telling has as its initial goals the student's assent to and application of godly advice. Pacing has as its initial goals a student's authenticity in relationship to God and the adult.

5. The primary delivery system of telling is controlled teaching times, ministry experiences and discussions. The primary delivery system of pac-

ing is dynamic, intentional yet informal interpersonal relationships.

6. Telling uses small groups to assist in application and accountability. Pacing uses small groups to build relationships that foster self-disclosure, affirmation, encouragement and challenge.

Telling appears to be much less costly, much easier to control and much more comfortable than pacing. And telling is more efficient. But after two decades of life among adolescents and the adults who love them, I am wholly sold out to this conviction: *For adolescents to grow into the fullness of the spiritual lives to which God has called them, a spiritual caregiver in their immediate, daily world has to be willing to pace with them.* There is no programmatic shortcut, no curricular alternative and no cutting-edge event that can address this God-created need. No one can *tell* a person into maturity.

Leading

A reactionary abandonment of speaking truth would, of course, violate the very commands of Scripture. Paul's instructions to young Timothy included the following:

> Command and teach these things. Don't let anyone look down on you because you are young, but set an example for the believers in speech, in life, in love, in faith and in purity. Until I come, devote yourself to the public reading of Scripture, to preaching and to teaching. (1 Tim 4:11-13)

Moreover, Jesus' Great Commission leaves all disciples with the responsibility to teach obedience.

How then do we reconcile the need for pacing with the call to teach? Isn't pacing a limiting approach that identifies where adolescents are but fails to show them where they should be going? If caring, mature Christians do not *tell* them what they should know and do, who will?

Jesus was a pacer. Whether with the rich young ruler whose heart was sold out to his accumulated wealth or the woman at the well whose heart was burned out by her lost loves, Jesus connected right to the heart. But Jesus' connection to the heart was not an end to itself. Jesus' love, like all true love, not only listens but leads as well.

Leading requires speaking truth, in love, into another person's life. For the wealthy young man, the truth confronted false gods of greed and pride. For the Samaritan woman, the truth challenged her failure to worship God "in spirit and truth," a failure that left her in religious death rather than spiritual life. In neither relationship did Jesus default to a telling model. He paced with them in order to offer to each of them a personal encounter with the truth.[2] To the young man Jesus spoke in terms of commandments and action—pointing out that the upwardly mobile heart must be bowed in submission to his kingship. To the woman Jesus spoke in terms of relationships—pointing out that social outcasts need not be spiritual outcasts in his kingdom. Jesus not only considered what needed to be said but also how it needed to be heard. Jesus' model of disciplemaking was simple: listen and learn (pace with), and then lead.

Communicating Truth Meaningfully

What are the implications for leading with the truth in the lives of adolescents? First, *adolescents need to hear the truth.* Our culture is flooded with deceptive messages about who God is, who we are and what is to be valued as truly meaningful. An adolescent can rarely watch a network sitcom, rent a popular movie or listen to the Top Forty without being deluged with lies about life. Failing to speak truth into the reality of young lives is simply unloving, unacceptable and irresponsible.

Second, *adolescents need to hear the truth communicated meaningfully.* To both the culturally esteemed rich young man and the culturally rejected Samaritan woman, Jesus communicated truth that was personally meaningful. He spoke the truth at their point of understanding. Here is where leading becomes much more than telling. Telling is primarily concerned with the question "Did I communicate truth?" Leading adds another dimension by asking, "Did I communicate truth meaningfully?"[3] Having paced with an adolescent, the communicator asks not only "Is what I am saying true?" but also "Am I saying the right things for this person's heart?" and "Will what I am saying be accurately and meaningfully understood?" Only by pacing (listening and learning) can the spiritual caregiver discover the answers to the latter two questions.

Pacing spiritual caregivers are well aware that what constitutes "meaningful understanding" to them may be a foreign language to students. The pacing-then-leading adult thus acts as a translator of truth into the vernacular of the adolescent's experience.[4] Leading does not seek to tell them what to think, feel or do. Leading rather translates and communicates truth in a way that is meaningful in the midst of the adolescent's thoughts, feelings and choices.

Third, *all adolescents need adults who will provide an ongoing relationship of pacing, then leading.* Stephen Covey has observed, "When you really understand someone, it's much easier to share, to teach, to confront with love. You know how to speak to others in language they understand."[5] Pacing is the relational entry point for a caring adult. Leading is the relational confrontation point for the adult to guide the adolescent toward a deeper relationship with Jesus Christ.

Some adolescents will follow the path of the rich young ruler. Their lives will be characterized by a profound sadness that seeks to medicate itself through consuming material goods, relationships or experiences. Other adolescents will mirror the response of the Samaritan woman. Their lives will be characterized by a profound love for Jesus, seeking to make meaning in relationship to him in spite of a culturally hostile environment. The adolescent's response is not the responsibility of the adults in her world. Pacing and leading are the responsibilities of the adults who serve as her spiritual caregivers.

Outside the Box

John told of participating in a communitywide outreach cosponsored by his church. Following a worship set led by the band, a pastor launched into a very confrontational message on the call to follow Jesus. He was loud and animated, and his words were stinging, indicting this generation for slipping from the truth. A few students from a huddled mass on the back row began to walk out of the packed sanctuary. John followed them, intending to ask them to at least participate respectfully in the event. When he finally stopped them, however, he decided to ask why they were leaving rather than tell them why they should stay.

One student spoke up: "That's just not who I am. I can't relate to what he is talking about."

John then engaged the teenagers in a dialogue drawing out their thoughts about Christianity and their feelings about their church. The conversation became so engaging that he invited them to meet again. The students were surprised at his interest. No one in the church had ever asked them these questions before.

Later that week, in squeaky vinyl booths at a twenty-four-hour restaurant, John paced with his new adolescent acquaintances. He discovered that their thoughts, feelings and lifestyles did not fit with the ministries the community's churches were offering. To his surprise, he learned that the students not only were *not* disinterested in spiritual matters but were deeply moved by their quest for a personal experience of God. One by one each student recounted how she or he had grown distant from the church. John had encountered through pacing a hidden world of spiritual searching and frustration never before expressed in the *telling* contexts of their churches.

Out of these relationships birthed over coffee and dessert in the diner, John began to move his relational investments outside the box of traditional church programming. Student ministry had been forever redefined for John because he had stopped to pace.

Steven and Carol are pacers. As parents of adolescents and lay youth leaders, they take seriously the ways students experience God in real life. Carol and Steven begin their weekly small group with a "check-in" time. Each student is asked to describe how he or she is presently feeling by choosing from one of the following emotions: *happy, sad, angry, scared, excited, tender.* The students offer to the group the feeling most descriptive of their present experience and explain what is causing those feelings. As each member takes a turn, the others listen to one another, pacing, and affirming.

At first students were hesitant and uncertain about discussing their emotions. In time, however, they began to value "check-in" as an important part of their lives. Now they would not dream of getting together without a "check-in" time. Pacing has created a safe environment for students to be who and where they are spiritually.

Steven and Carol do not have to compete for the attention of their small group members. The students want to listen to and be led by their spiritual caregivers, because they know that they have been heard.

To pace is to listen to and genuinely learn the thoughts, feelings and experiences of an adolescent. To lead is to speak truth meaningfully into that real-life context. To have paced and then led is to have loved well the adolescents to whom we give spiritual care. Just ask Carol and Steven's small group and the teenagers who live in their home.

Wanted: Outside-the-Box Spiritual Caregivers

"There's no way in. We've tried everything; the place is completely packed."

What good friends these four were. They had shared his life, they had shared his loss, and today they had been sharing his hope. Now, it seemed, they were to be yoked forever to the oppressive burden of his despair.

"We *haven't* tried everything. We haven't tried the roof," one of the five announced impulsively. Soon, in spite of the implausible outside-the-box plan, the five found themselves on the roof. Four worked, breaking through layers of dried mud and tile; digging then pulling, sweating and straining in a furious effort to create a sufficient opening. One, the motionless fifth friend, waited and wondered.

The four finally cleared the hole and lowered their friend toward a shocked and, for the most part, rather irritated crowd. With dust falling onto the squinting upward-turned faces, the four carefully maneuvered their broken friend down. If their friend were to ever feel again—the warmth of sand on his feet or the joy of hope in his heart—they knew that he must be taken into the healing presence of Jesus.

Jesus, as only Jesus could do, used the moment not only to give life to dead limbs but to present life to dead souls. His words drew a line of division between those who possessed genuine faith and those who were obsessed with fabricated religion. When it was all over, all five friends walked out of Peter's house; the Pharisees fumed at Jesus' words, as their religious categories deemed incompatible the Way, the Truth and the Life; and the crowd gave glory to God, exclaiming, "We have never seen anything like this!" (Mk 2:12).

Confined to the mat, the paralytic was ushered into Jesus' presence by friends. What a difference faith, love, persistence, creativity and boldness made in the life of a desperate man. Carried along by his friends' commitment, he was taken to the one place he had to go, a place he could not have reached on his own.

Alberto does not feel the desperation of the paralytic, but he shares the man's need for help in finding his way to Jesus' presence. On the surface all would seem to be well with this energetic, people-pleasing eighth-grader. He has survived the final cut of the junior-high varsity basketball team; last month his family moved into a beautiful new home financed by his dad's recent promotion; and his church youth leader has asked him to serve on a leadership team. Beneath the bright exterior, however, are unexpected emotions prompted by these changes. Fellow members of the basketball team mock Christ and ridicule Christians. Dad's promotion means more travel and less time to be with his son. Being a leader in youth group only heightens the sense of failure Alberto feels in his ongoing battle with lustful thoughts. Alberto is pressed upon by fear, loneliness and guilt. His young spiritual life is at a precarious place, a point in the journey that is unsafe for one so young if left to fend for himself.

Jonathan needs a helping hand of spiritual companionship as well. Last year, as a high-school freshman, he crossed over a threshold of innocence that dramatically altered the course of his life. He never saw it coming. He was self-assured in his ability to be friends with these guys, to spend recreational hours with them without participating in their drug use. Now he is paralyzed by dependence, trapped in the unrelenting grip of psychological dependence on the mood-altering effects of the drugs. And he is socially dependent on the only friends who seem to understand and accept him. Jonathan is broken and cannot find his way back to the comfort of his previous trust in Jesus. He needs help. He needs parents, adults and peers who can help him take steps scarier than he has ever imagined. He feels as if he will die if he changes his friends and habits. The truth is that he will die if he does not.

Rachel is lost, in every sense of the word. She is estranged from her parents, with whom she lives only when she is not sharing an apartment with her boyfriend. She is torn between her emotional dependence on his attention and the fear that he will once again hurt her in a drunken rage. She has tried church but deemed it unsafe for a person like her. The one Christian guy she knows is as much of an alcohol abuser as her boyfriend. Rachel is fifteen. She is skeptical, jaded at the notion of true love. She repels the idea that she can and should do better for herself in relationships. Rachel would like to know Jesus, but she cannot see a place for herself in what she knows of Christianity. Her parents are in no condition to offer help. She needs adults and peers who can patiently embrace her with the grace that is available in Jesus. She needs the Way, the Truth and the Life. And she needs him soon, for she has set herself on a self-deceiving course that is accelerating her toward internal and eternal destruction.

Talitha belongs to Jesus. She desperately lacks spiritual guidance, though, in making her way into his healing, hopeful presence. Talitha is nineteen, a Christian who wants to give her life to full-time ministry for her Lord. But she has lost her way. Somewhere along the path to her late adolescence she suffered a gradual paralysis of the soul. Trapped by sadness, unresolved anger and spiritual confusion, she has tried it all. She prays, she has devotional readings, she confesses her sins, and she serves in a ministry to young teenagers. Still she is alone within herself. The only one who reaches her is her boyfriend, whom she loves. But even that love is painful, as they too often turn to physical intimacy to compensate for an incapacity to share deep emotions. Talitha needs help. She needs spiritual caregivers to help move her beyond seemingly impenetrable walls of self-protection.

Carrying the Mats

Who will be the millennial generation's mat-carriers? In the midst of post-Christian and postmodern cultural shifts, who will dig holes in the roofs that hide Jesus from these students? Who will provide sufficient relational safety for their unveiling of broken selves and fractured relationships? Who will engage their spiritual journeys in order to usher them into the healing presence of Jesus? *Spiritual caregivers who have learned the love language of pacing, then leading.*

Like the first-century mat carriers, the relationships of these caregivers will be compassionate and faithful. Like the paralytic's friends, these twenty-first-century mat carriers will be characterized by faith, love, persistence, creativity and boldness. Their outside-the-box relationships will connect adolescent hearts to the heart of God. In that place of connection lies hope for the healing of a generation—the kind of healing that can prompt a hopeless world to cry with wonder, "We have never seen anything like this before!"

Reflecting on Your Journey

☐ How did you feel when you read Dana's and Melissa's stories? Do you remember ever feeling alone as an adolescent? Describe the thoughts and feelings you experienced when it seemed no one was there for you.

☐ Describe the characteristics that enable a person to be an effective pacer and leader.

☐ How would you describe your parents' effectiveness in pacing with you and leading you on your adolescent journey? Very effective, somewhat effective, marginally effective, very ineffective?

☐ If you had a spiritual caregiver on your adolescent spiritual journey, how would you describe his or her effectiveness as a pacer and leader? Very effective, somewhat effective, marginally effective, very ineffective?

☐ In terms of pacing, then leading, where do you see yourself mirroring the strengths of your parents and other spiritual caregivers? the weaknesses?

☐ Identify a specific time when you defaulted to a telling response with an adolescent. Why do you think you lived out the telling model? How could pacing, then leading have improved your relationship?

☐ What are the major internal obstacles you face as you pursue the pacing-then-leading approach? In what ways are these obstacles related to your adolescent experiences in your home or in relationship to significant adults and peers?

☐ How has God paced with you in your spiritual journey? What has his pacing and leading taught you about love?

☐ What would it look like for God to provide you with the pacing, then leading you need to grow as a spiritual caregiver who paces and then leads? Seek these gifts from your loving Father.

Pressing In

☐ Keep a journal of your relational conversations with adolescents in the coming week. Note the feelings and thoughts behind your words and actions. What happens within you as you pay attention to relating through pacing and then leading?

☐ Schedule "hang time" to listen intentionally to the thoughts, feelings and experiences of an adolescent in your world. Take them to a place that they would consider their turf. Have no other agenda than to listen, learn and love.

☐ Read the Gospel of Mark or John with a view toward observing Jesus as a pacer and leader.

☐ Write a letter expressing your gratitude to a parent or mentor who paced with and then led you through a difficult period in your life.

☐ Lead a "check-in" within your ministry team or small group. Have each person identify the one emotion (from page 22) most descriptive of how they are feeling. Listen to understand each person's emotion *and* its sources. Your "check-in" may seem artificial at first. With affirmation and a safe environment, however, check-ins can become a valuable discipline for pacing with one another.

This is not a generic generation. We are facing a new set of obstacles that have never been faced before. We are the first generation to grow up in a post-modern society, where right and wrong are dirty words and tolerance is considered the greatest virtue. We are the first generation to grow up in a post-Christian society. . . . We are more likely to get into trouble for praying in school than possessing drugs.
GOODNEWSMAG.ORG

Today's teenagers face a much riskier passage than previous generations at a time when adults are much less available to help them.
RICH GELMAN, *NEWSWEEK*, 1990

Drugs. Suicide. Death. Hopelessness. These words don't even begin to describe the battle your students are facing every day on their campuses and in their communities.
TAG LINE FOR "WHEN ALL HELL BREAKS LOOSE," A DARE 2 SHARE YOUTH CONFERENCE

We don't need a need another ministry model—we need a church that's rooted in loving God and others, in contemplation and action, in prayer and justice.
MARK YACONELLI, *GROUP MAGAZINE*

Now that same day two of them were going to a village called Emmaus, about seven miles from Jerusalem. They were talking with each other about everything that had happened. As they talked and discussed these things with each other, Jesus himself came up and walked along with them, but they were kept from recognizing him.

He asked them, "What are you discussing together as you walk along?"

They stood still, their faces downcast. One of them, named Cleopas, asked him, "Are you only a visitor to Jerusalem and do not know the things that have happened there in these days?"

"What things?" he asked.
LUKE 24:13-19

2

Postmodern Pilgrims
in Progress

Emmaus is less about where Cleopas and his companion are going and more about what each is leaving behind. Entombed in Jerusalem was the One to whom they had entrusted their faith, their hopes and their hearts. Now all that remained was doubt, fear and brokenness. Theirs had been the ultimate loss, the death of all they had come to believe as truth. The road to Emmaus was all that was left for them, a path of escape for two disillusioned, disoriented and disconnected souls.

Adolescents in the early twenty-first century travel their spiritual journeys along a path akin to the road to Emmaus. North American youth attempt to explore spiritual meaning in the midst of what has been termed a "postmodern" culture.[1] In this cultural climate, biblical teachings on God and Jesus, sin and salvation, heaven and hell are increasingly treated as naïve, antiquated theological ideas. Postmodern scholars and pop-culture trendsetters, seeking to embrace a global village full of diverse religions, reject the exclusive nature of Christian truth claims.[2] The triune God of Christianity, with his assertion of being the only Way to spiritual life, is deemed archaic and ill-suited to a pluralistic, fully inclusive understanding of human spirituality.[3] Furthermore, in a world plagued by civil wars,

AIDS, hunger and decaying morality, the Christian God is seen as a detached, impotent religious icon.[4]

Twenty-first-century postmodern spirituality is thus less about where this generation is going and more about what young people have left behind. The worldview and ethos of our Judeo-Christian heritage no longer exert a prevailing influence on the culture within which North American adolescents mature. The flow of postmodern adolescent spiritual traffic speeds down a road to Emmaus, reducing the life of Jesus to an image rapidly shrinking in the cultural rear-view mirror. Along the way, this generation finds itself increasingly disillusioned with the religious Christianity they have known, disoriented in a sea of youth culture and disconnected from spiritual caregivers whose pacing and leading could provide a conduit for encountering a resurrected Messiah. Like Cleopas and his companion, young people chart spiritual territory emptied of the gospel of hope. Disengaged from this hope, their hearts desperately await a burning recognition of the Way, the Truth and the Life. Pacing-then-leading spiritual caregivers are the living models and ministers of this hope. Without them, the postmodern version of the Emmaus Road is a lonely, frightening journey into despair.

Designer Gods

True postmodern seekers, in the spirit of the age, become collectors of religious ideas and experiences. Frank McCourt, nurtured in an Irish Catholic family, embodies the postmodern search for a God more satisfying than the God of his childhood religion:

> People ask me if I'm still Catholic. Well . . . in a way I am. I drop in to churches. I talk to Saint Francis of Assisi and Teresa of Avila, my favorites. I light candles for people's intentions. But I don't confine myself to the faith of my fathers anymore. All the religions are spread before me, a great spiritual smorgasbord, and I'll help myself, thank you.[5]

McCourt represents the soft side of postmodern spirituality. He pieces together his spiritual patchwork quilt from thoughtfully selected fabrics of several well-worn religious garments.

Marina Warner, in a commentary on the first of the Ten Commandments published in *Self,* takes a harder stance against the God of Judeo-Christian faith:

The phrase "no other gods before me" could be Yahweh promising, with monotheism, a pact so intimate, so tight, that his proteges will not need intermediate divinities to make contact. There will be no pagan confusion, as in Egypt, the country Moses and company have left behind: no younger godlings like Horus, no goddesses like Nut or Isis, no divine messengers like jackal-headed Anubis, ferryman of the dead. But the phrasing still reveals an intrinsic problem: The God of monotheism is talking of other gods as if they exist, and exist as a threat to him. . . .

Now that I have returned to the Decalogue for the first time since childhood, the voice of the deity strikes my ear as that of a petulant and charmless tyrant who is covering up his own ineffectual promises with bluster, the kind of humorless boss who is given to loud renditions of "My Way" at the annual office party.[6]

McCourt and Warner have rejected the God of Scripture. Whether seen as an inadequate god to be redefined or an oppressive god to be rejected, the true God is dismissed as inconsistent with spirituality that is mature, sophisticated and adaptable to contemporary social realities.

Rooted in postmodern spirituality is a philosophical contempt for all absolute propositions of truth.[7] Considered extremist and fundamentalist, those who hold to such propositions are denigrated by the brokers of popular intellectual thought. D. A. Carson, in his insightful *Gagging of God*, notes:

Recently at an East Coast university, the most frequent term chosen in a word association exercise by non-Christians to describe a Christian was "intolerant."

Doubtless some of this perception derives from insensitive Christians. But some of it derives from significant changes in what "open-minded" means. It no longer means that you may or may not have strong views yet remain committed to listening honestly to countervailing arguments. Rather, it means you are dogmatically committed to the view that all convictions that any view whatsoever is wrong are improper and narrow.[8]

Having disregarded the biblical God, the postmodern seeker opts for the more alluring creation of one's own Designer God.[9] God is sought for spiritual enrichment, personal fulfillment and an overall sense of connection with the transcendent. One woman, constructing her own spiritual patchwork quilt, describes her experiences of spirituality in these "what works for me" terms:

There is a Buddha in my backyard, a Mexican santo on my mantel and a yoga mat in my bedroom. But my heritage is definitely Protestant: My father's father was a Congregational minister, my great-grandfather on my mother's side a Presbyterian minister, and regular church attendance was a given in our household. I myself joined the church at 13 but became a skeptic in college and renounced organized religion as hypocritical. Yet I returned to the fold a few years later when I thought that I—and my two children—could use spiritual support. The community of my big-city church, the opportunity to interact with people from many walks of life and different races, nourished me immensely. Now I am churchless again. I grew tired of being preached to. Instead, I follow my own path—relying on messages from many traditions instead of the doctrine of any one religion. I practice yoga and look to its ethics for guidance, but I do not consider myself given over entirely to any one way. I believe I can grow in understanding—as long as my mind and heart are open.[10]

In the climate of "creating a god that works for you," church, traditional religions and the promise of heaven are out of style. Shared experiences, spirituality and the potential of humanity are definitely in. Absolute truth claims, whether moral or religious, are out. Personalized belief systems and pragmatic moral commitments are in. Discovering a transcendent God who seeks to communicate his will is out. Experiencing a domesticated God who wants persons to fulfill themselves is in. In short, Yahweh is no longer an acceptable God for our culture—he is being left behind in search of more favorable alternatives.

Chasing One's Theological Tail

In the 1990s Hollywood produced a plethora of story lines about human encounters with supernatural realities, particularly angels.[11] Representative of these spiritually minded productions was *City of Angels*. Nicolas Cage plays an angel who falls in love with a beautiful yet guilt-plagued physician, Maggie (Meg Ryan). As the plot develops, the angel contemplates "falling," a choice, we are informed, afforded to angels who desire to leave their eternal angelic status to experience all aspects of finite humanity, including death. Cage, overwhelmed with desire, chooses to fall and becomes a man named Seth. Seth then enters into a fully human, emotional and sexual relationship with Maggie. Tragically, just as their relationship is beginning, Maggie dies in an accident. The "fallen angel" loses the love he gave up heaven to hold.

Nathaniel, an angel and friend of the former angel, appears to Seth. He quietly inquires, "If you'd known this was going to happen, would you have done it?"

Seth replies, "I would rather have had one breath of her hair, one kiss of her mouth, one touch of her hand than eternity without it."

The subtle yet disturbing message of *City of Angels* elevates human experience to a place of religious reverence. Better to experience the embrace of a human lover for a day than spend eternity in heaven in the presence of God.[12] The most recognizable song from the film in fact states, "I would give up eternity to be with you." The fulfillment of emotional and sexual desires in an intimate relationship with his human lover represents Seth's highest aspirations. How, one is left to ponder, could God hope to compete with the ultimate fulfillment of passionate intimacy between two human lovers? God finishes a disappointing second to Meg Ryan.

As represented in this film, the anthropocentric universe of postmodern spirituality commonly bypasses organized religion in pursuit of relief from spiritual disillusionment. The loss of confidence in traditional sources of faith has not, however, led to a loss of fervor in the search for spiritual meaning. Kenda Creasy Dean and Ron Foster reflect on the inevitability of the human quest for connection to the transcendent:

> All of us long for a god, something trustworthy toward which we can direct our entire being. "To be a self," wrote H. Richard Niebuhr, "is to have a god"—although, admitted Niebuhr, sometimes we choose the God of Jesus Christ, and sometimes we choose the god of a job, family, or football instead. Choosing a god is fundamental to the process of identify formation, and we soon discover that not just any god will do. Power and status, money and education, drugs and alcohol, even friends and family are common gods toward which we direct our lives. Yet what human beings crave is an *un*common god. We hunger for a God who is bigger than the self. Choosing an inadequate god, a god too small to transcend our limitations and who therefore can neither save nor transform us, drives us to keep hunting.[13]

Martin Marty notes that assigning transcendent meaning to life's experience is an unavoidable reality of being human: "Humans cannot easily sustain a world that's entirely random and haphazard and plotless. . . . A French philosopher once said, 'We are condemned to meaning.' There's an almost universal impulse to endow our joys and our sorrows, and our failures and our successes, with meaning."[14]

Humans will not stay in a state of unbelief. As Ecclesiastes confirms, God has "set eternity" in our hearts (Eccles 3:11). Yet by casting aside the Way, the Truth and the Life, the postmodern spiritual road to Emmaus leads to a theological façade, an experience with a lesser god destined to fail the ultimate longing for love and meaning. Like a dog's chase of its own tail, the search is an exhausting exercise in futility.

Postmodernity's Impact

The pervasive cultural impact of this postmodern shift cannot be overstated. My first parental encounter with the challenges of postmodern philosophy occurred in 1996. Our then first-grader, Jessica, attended a school with a strict commitment to religious political correctness. The curriculum led the children through a series of studies that paralleled a university Comparative Religions course in its diversity and tenor. After discussing Native American, Jewish and Christian spirituality over a period of time, my six-year-old's question was "Dad, how do we [as Christians] know that we are right and everybody else is wrong?"

I found myself gasping for theological air as I attempted to articulate an apologetic for a Christian worldview—in a way that could be intellectually grasped by a first-grader.[15]

Cultural, philosophical and religious shifts pose a subtle challenge to the trusting faith of Christian children. For adolescents the subtlety is lost. Even convinced, committed Christian adolescents struggle with questions such as

☐ How can I believe that my Jewish friend is going to hell?

☐ How can I believe Jesus is the only way when there are so many other ways that people claim to have a spiritual relationship with God?

☐ How can I tell another person they are wrong about their beliefs when their spiritual experiences are so real to them?

☐ With so many testimonies of the power of spirituality outside the Christian faith—power to heal relationships or get off drugs or overcome depression—how am I supposed to share with another person that I believe they need Jesus Christ? What if my faith is simply a product of the family and culture I was brought up in? If I had grown up Muslim in an Arab country, wouldn't I reject Jesus too?

The contemporary syncretistic approach to spiritual belief creates a thoroughly confusing climate for adolescents seeking to move into adult spiritual maturity. In this complex spiritual climate of post-Christian North America, high-school students can embrace Jesus alongside Buddha and Native American spirituality. The college freshman can finish a prayerful meditation from Psalms, call the Psychic Hotline to get an update on what might be in her romantic future and then participate in an evening yoga class.[16] Never before in North American history has a generation of adolescents more desperately needed pacing-then-leading spiritual caregivers.

Beyond Disillusionment: Toward Genuine Christian Spirituality

In the midst of profound disillusionment with church and religion, adolescents are crying out for genuine spiritual experiences with a living God. If twenty-first-century adolescents do not engage the living Christ in authentic relationship, they are destined to commit idolatry with a succession of what Dean and Foster term "thin gods":

> We know how quickly teenagers rip through thin faith. Teenagers can find thin gods anywhere, and if the God of Jesus Christ isn't more awesome and substantial than the seething rush of the mosh pit, the ecstasy of LSD, the mystery of sexual intercourse, the security of cash, the affirmation of the A or the adulation of the cheering crowd in the gym—then why bother with Christianity at all? Thin gods are available by the dozen, and teenagers see right through them. If we are honest, so do we.[17]

With so many lesser, thin gods attractively packaged and readily available on the postmodern road to Emmaus, spiritual caregivers must offer adolescents nothing more or less than an authentic encounter with the real Jesus. Paul's words to the Corinthians, "I knew nothing among you but Jesus and him crucified" (see 1 Cor 2:1-5), provide a rallying cry for this generation of spiritual caregivers. Jimmy Long echoes the longing for authenticity among Generation X, the generation immediately preceding the millennial generation:

> The key question for Xers is "Is it real?" not "Is it true?" Their lives are more likely to be changed through the heart than through the mind. They need to see the incarnation of the gospel in people's lives more than to hear the proclamation of the gospel through our words. Do we have places where seekers can see the gospel in action? Do we invite them into our community? They need to experience the love of Jesus more than they need to be informed that Jesus is love.[18]

The "been there, done that" millennial generation even more intensely seeks authentic, personally meaningful relationships with God. Nothing less than a real Jesus for a real world will suffice. The theological mandate of pacing, then leading provides the only acceptable response to the current generation's intense thirst for genuine spiritual experiences with a living God. Postmodern adolescents want communion with a God who can do what they cannot do for themselves: provide ultimate love, hope and meaning in a world littered with the residue of religious disillusionment.

Chad, his wife Lisa and their team of spiritual caregivers have committed themselves to leading high school students beyond religion and into relationship with Jesus Christ.[19] I have the privilege of walking alongside Chad as he pastors our church's senior high students. If asked to describe their "Crossing" ministry strategy, Chad and his staff would unanimously respond with three words: *authenticity, relationships* and *risk.* Crossing students are challenged to drop false religious pretenses and come face to face with their real selves in relationship to a real God. That challenge is delivered primarily through relationships rather than programming. The pacing-then-leading spiritual caregivers and the students themselves are "the ministry." Programs simply facilitate deepening authentic encounters with God and each other.

The Crossing team knows from experience that on the road to Emmaus a real encounter with a living Jesus is the only means for restoring hope. Like the conversation on the road to Emmaus, their relational encounters with students connect the revealed Word in Scripture with the revealed Word Jesus. The spiritual caregivers embody his love, teach his truth and model his life in the midst of students' spiritually charged, confusing culture. Noting the congruence between the message (God's Word) and the medium (the spiritual caregiver's life with God), adolescents become desirous of rather than disillusioned by the promise of a spiritual encounter with the God of Christianity. They want to taste for themselves the sweetness of personally worshiping their God in spirit and truth.

Adolescent Spirituality: Disoriented in a Sea of Culture

Student ministry does not occur in a vacuum. Popular culture, expressed in music, movies, television shows, videos, clothing fads and teen product lines, has to be reckoned with as a dominant force in shaping the spiritual experiences of twenty-first-century adolescents. How potent is popular culture in a teenager's life? Quentin Schultze, a prominent authority on the role of the media in North American culture, argues:

> If youth workers could ever have ignored popular culture, they no longer
> have that luxury. Professional and lay youth leaders find themselves trying to
> communicate with people from an alien culture. Youth ministry has become
> a missionary activity to an adolescent subculture shaped by the media and
> other popular culture.[20]

Schultze explains the process by which a youth culture is formed:

> Popular culture includes not just the products themselves, but also the way
> the youth use them. It includes the dances created to go with certain styles of
> music as well as the clothing worn particular ways. These actions, together
> with the products, create powerful systems of meaning appropriately called
> subcultures. T. S. Eliot once defined *culture* as the "entire way of life of a
> people." Youth-oriented popular culture is nothing less than the way of life of
> youth—all of it increasingly organized around the industry of popular cul-
> ture.[21]

As adolescents look primarily to media for guidance in how to live out
the "youth way," they are shown products and experiences to consume with
their discretionary time and money. When adolescents buy the music of a
new artist, the record company learns what sells. By consuming this music
the adolescents are helping shape the record company's future strategies for
appealing to members of the youth culture. The record company creates
more of what will sell and spends millions of dollars marketing to the target
group's tastes while the adolescent gains a means for identifying his place
in the youth way. Youth culture thus mirrors the adolescent's experience of
his world while it also creates and defines that experience. Thus emerges
what has been termed a symbiotic relationship between youth and the media of youth culture.[22]

Postmodern culture provides the perfect environment for hearty growth
of the youth way. Contemporary postmodern culture has been described by
Roger Lundin as a *therapeutic* culture.[23] Rather than confronting and challenging an individual's beliefs, convictions or commitments, the culture assists individuals in making peace with whatever they choose as the path to
personal fulfillment. Popular culture, in the form of the youth way, acts like
a bad parent in the lives of adolescents.[24] Rather than asking, "Will this be
good for your health?" the youth culture asks, "How much more do you
want?"

Like listing ships drifting aimlessly on the ocean, adolescents ride youth culture, tossed about by the ebb and flow of what is hot and what is not. The widespread increases in sexual activity, substance abuse, violence and stress-related illnesses among adolescents are like flares filling the evening sky with signals that all is not well on board. The entire subculture faces a potentially *Titanic*-like spiritual disaster: millions lost to the cold, dark emptiness of the godless sea of therapeutic postmodern culture.[25]

The Impact of Youth Way Enculturation

The total effect of the youth way on the lives of adolescents cannot be fully measured. To suggest that youth culture in itself creates all the self-destructive behaviors found among adolescent peer groups would be naive. Individual adolescents certainly engaged in self-destructive and immoral lifestyles in every generation prior to the emergence of the electronic media. Neither is it productive to stereotype all adolescents as experiencing the same level of impact from exposure to and immersion in youth culture. Though there are too many horror stories, there are many stories of adolescent heroism. Even in the midst of tragedies such as the one at Columbine High School, many adolescents exhibit bravery and faith. Twenty-first-century teens can be found sacrificially serving the homeless, mentoring younger children in impoverished communities and creating environments where it is safe for their peers to hear of the love of Jesus.

Given these limitations, it is nevertheless possible to identify patterns that have emerged in contemporary adolescents' experience of a postmodern therapeutic culture. Christian spiritual caregivers seeking to pace with and then lead postmodern adolescents will find that youth culture is characterized by three disturbing and interrelated ways of experiencing life: (1) a sensate worldview, (2) pleasure pragmatism and (3) pseudo-attachment.

Experience Is Reality: A Sensate Worldview

In *The Sensate Culture*, Harold O. J. Brown explores the seminal cultural analysis of expatriate Russian scholar Pitirim A. Sorokin. Brown summarizes a major thesis of Sorokin regarding the process of cultural change:

> Sorokin identified three distinct phases through which cultures pass: *ideational, idealistic,* and *sensate.* . . . Every aspect of society reflects the phase

in which that society finds itself: Philosophy and religion, government and law, literature, music and the arts, family structures, and economic life are largely determined by the underlying principles of the mentality of that particular phase.[26]

Brown identifies phase one, the *ideational* stage, as a "mentality that sees spiritual truth and values as virtually the only truth and values worthy of the name. God and the divine world are the highest and truest realities; the good is what God wills."[27] As the culture continues over an indeterminate period of time, the culture gradually transitions into the *idealistic* phase, which, like the ideational phase, "rates spiritual truth and values above all others."[28] However, the idealistic phase "also appreciates the realities and values of the sensory world and does not treat them as meaningless or nonexistent."[29] The idealistic phase emphasizes the transcendent but also embraces the importance of the material world of the senses. By contrast,

the sensate mentality is the exact opposite of the ideational mentality. It is interested only in those things, usually material in nature, that appeal to or affect the senses. It seeks the imposing, the impressive, the voluptuous; it encourages self-indulgence. A huge oil canvas such as Rubens' "The Drunken Hercules" is a representative work of sensate art. Virtually all glossy magazine advertising is sensate. No apology is made for encouraging people to squander their resources on self-indulgence. Let us "eat, drink, and be merry," forgetting that "tomorrow we die." Sensate culture and sensate art go beyond simple materialism in that materialism merely defines matter as the only reality; the sensate mentality becomes enthusiastic about it.[30]

Gathering evidence of the sensate mentality among popular youth cultural artifacts (media, products, events) is about as challenging as using twenty-first-century technology to prove that the world is round. The sensate culture is evidenced everywhere. Music videos, soft-drink commercials, $100 million nonstop action movies, deafening concerts with laser lights, seductive dance numbers at professional (and even high-school) sporting events, computer games, *Seventeen* magazine, extreme sports, professional wrestling extravaganzas, home theater surround sound—the list could go on and on. The need for speed and volume and sensation increases with each new wave of youth-culture media.

The sensate worldview is a logical outcome of immersion in a sensate culture that has cut loose from its ideational roots. In postmodernity what one can experience *is* one's reality. The next concert, sporting event or party is one's avenue for reaching beyond the mundane world of homework, family life and work responsibilities. Adolescents naturally begin to gauge the value of their lives by the level of sensory payoff.

Pleasure as God: Pleasure Pragmatism

In a sensate culture, needs are met by consuming pleasurable experiences or products that promise pleasurable results. The sensate culture's youth way hawks its wares via glossy teen magazines, radios, T-shirts, websites and television commercials. The appeal is rarely the product itself; the lure is the pleasure that the adolescent associates with consumption of the product. By passively consuming the loudest and most scintillating of youth culture's offerings, adolescents unknowingly become consumers of a sensate worldview.

The sensate worldview leads to a "frenzied pursuit of pleasure" as the supreme goal of life.[31] Anticipation of pleasure rather than commitment to values becomes the criterion for discerning choice of vocation, sexual orientation, use of leisure time, management of financial resources and approach to ethics. Individuals sold out to the sensate view of life become "pleasure pragmatists." The sense of pleasure is their god.

The initial stage of pleasure pragmatism can be summarized by the saying "If it feels good, do it." In this stage, previously accepted moral boundaries no longer provide adequate restraint against personal impulses. Eventually moral boundaries no longer have to be considered: they have disappeared from the decision-maker's consciousness. In this latter stage the motto becomes "Do it—unless it starts to feel bad." One is no longer left with moral dilemmas; questions of personal well-being are the only issues to be addressed in any decision-making process.

The net effect on a society is the morphing of morality. As participants in North American postmodern culture shift in their experience and expression of what is "good" (in the case of pleasure pragmatism, "what brings me pleasure"), the moral conscience of the culture shifts accordingly. To remain consistent with a commitment to tolerance, moral consciousness must be morphed to encompass previously divergent moral values.[32] As the moral consciousness of the culture embraces more divergent moral perspectives, the definition of society's moral center changes. What was radical and extreme becomes commonplace and mainstream.

The morphing of morality can be observed in every corner of teen-oriented media. One can trace either the degenerative path of story lines and characters from the inception of *Beverly Hills 90210, Melrose Place* or *Dawson's Creek,* or the moral digression of animated series from *The Simpsons* to *Beavis and Butthead* to *South Park.* Moral guardrails are gradually moved to create a broader path to experiment with sexual content and deviant social behavior.

If moral guardrails have been adjusted by network and cable television, they have been virtually removed by Hollywood. Characters in the film *Cruel Intentions,* for example, are primarily adolescents. A review begins with a comment on three other movies about high school life showing in local theaters: "If such movies as 'She's All That,' 'Jawbreaker,' and 'Varsity Blues' are any indication, high school is getting fairly raunchy, not to mention dangerous." The reviewer observes that significant elements of the film seem to be aimed at very sophisticated adult audiences, yet this R-rated film about students on summer vacation is made to appeal to the fictional characters' peers. "A teenage twist on 'Dangerous Liaisons,' 'Cruel Intentions' is a classic tale dressed up—or would it be down?—with nubile young actors and lots of f-words. [The actors and actresses] and their sexy, revealing costumes make them tailor made for the *Seventeen* crowd."

Here is a summary of the plot:

> Step-siblings Kathryn Merteuil (Gellar) and Sebastian Valmont (Phillippe) lust after each other while voraciously stalking others to fulfill their sexual desires. Kathryn wants Sebastian to seduce the naïve Cecile Caldwell (Selma Blair), who has unwittingly stolen Kathryn's beau. But Sebastian is more interested in Annette Hargrove (Witherspoon), a virgin who has made public her intention to save herself for marriage.
>
> Kathryn and Sebastian make a bet. If he fails to bed Annette, Kathryn will win his classic car. If he succeeds, he'll get to bed Kathryn as well.[33]

As a parent and as a spiritual caregiver of adolescents, I am not sure whether to weep or to scream. *Cruel Intentions* represents the extent to which the North American youth culture has undergone a morphing of morality. What five years ago would have engendered moral concern, if not outrage, now passes for state of the art. More troublesome is the likelihood that in five more years *Cruel Intentions* will seem less "on the edge" and more in the center of the teen-oriented film genre. When a sensate world-view dominates the subculture, the acceptable moral edge must be constantly moved in order to appease pleasure pragmatists' demands for excess and scintillation.[34]

Meaning Is External: Pseudo-attachment

"Men have forgotten God," Aleksandr Solzhenitsyn observed in his critique of Western culture.[35] J. I. Packer extends this critique to its logical conclusion: "In the last generation we lost God. In this generation, we are losing man."[36] The loss of personal identity is bound to follow the loss of knowledge of and relationship with the Creator.

Postmodern culture, with its sensate worldview and pleasure pragmatism, provides little hope of meaningfully defining the value of personal identity. As a result, individuals look to a *pseudo-attachment* to bring meaning to their lives. Pseudo-attachment occurs when "something out there" provides my sense of belonging and meaning in life. I become attached to something—the Internet, a drug, a girlfriend, a job—in order to fulfill my drive for personal identity and value.

As a resident of the Chicago suburbs in the 1990s and an avid basketball fan, I lived in "hoops heaven" as Michael Jordan and the Bulls dominated National Basketball Association tournaments for a number of years. My most lingering memory of that dynasty, however, was a television interview with the Bulls' key players following their first NBA championship. The talk-show host expressed gratitude to Michael by saying, "Thank you for making all of us feel good about ourselves." That phrase rings in my ear as I watch twenty-first-century adolescents pursue dating relationships, material possessions, concert tickets, autographs from professional athletes, careers that will guarantee financial gain and, in some cases, even a relationship with a youth pastor.

"Please help me feel good about myself" is at the core of much adolescent behavior, whether moral or immoral, seemingly godly or ungodly. In a youth culture that markets enticing pseudo-attachments at the speed of light, feeling good is routinely confused with having achieved a good feeling about who I am. Adolescents often lack the personal maturity and life experience to distinguish between the two. Without genuine attachment with Christ and others (real relationships), pseudo-attachments become a way of life in the consuming ethos of North American culture.

Disconnected: On the Lonely Road to Emmaus

Walt Mueller's *Understanding Youth Culture* takes the reader on a comprehensive, sensitive and sometimes chilling journey into the precarious world of youth culture. Reflecting on how much life has changed from his era and that of the contemporary adolescents, Mueller laments:

> I've always wondered, if Norman Rockwell were alive and painting American experience today, what would his pictures look like? Maybe he would paint the family kitchen, with only half of the members sitting at the dinner table while the others were off doing other things. Or a picture of a third grader arriving home from school to an unsupervised house with several hours of unlimited TV viewing and Nintendo. Maybe it would be a picture of a tenth-grade girl walking to school with books under one arm, a diaper bag under the other, and her baby in a stroller.[37]

Placed alongside images of real life in the 1990s, paintings by Rockwell would appear to be from a totally different culture; and they were. Note what is absent from each of the three portraits Mueller imagines. The piece missing from each of these images represents the most profound problem facing twenty-first-century North American adolescents. Consider Sarah, a sixteen-year-old who is battling anorexia and bulimia. Sarah, who identifies her greatest pressures in life as "looks," "grades for getting into the right college," "drinking," "sex" and "popularity," adds to her list this letter:

> I come from an upper-middle-class home. I'm a straight-A student, class president, and an overachiever in every way. I don't really know why I am anorexic, but I think it's partly because I thought that if I got really sick, people would pay attention to me. The irony of it is that my father is a psychologist. He doesn't know.
>
> My mother always compares her life to mine, so much that sometimes I feel smothered by her. I cannot talk to my father at all about important things. I never could. My father is home every evening at 6 P.M., but my mother is never home. She recently opened a business so she has to work from 9 A.M. until midnight. Sometimes she comes home to see me in the afternoons, and sometimes she is around on weekends. Incidentally, my parents do not get along very well.
>
> My mom says that if I get therapy, it will go on my record and may keep me out of Princeton or Amherst, the colleges to which I am applying.
>
> I know my parents love me, but they think that I am so bright and capable that I don't need help or attention anymore. I just want people to realize that

I do not have a perfect life and that I am lonely. I want people at school to notice me more and like me. Actually, I'm not at all sure what I want.[38]

Sarah is alone. She has friends, boyfriends and social success. The adults in her world, however, are missing in action. Even if they were Christian parents, their lack of availability would render them unable to minister God's embrace of grace to their hurting daughter. Consequently Sarah chases "thin god" after "thin god," hoping to attach herself to something or someone that will make it all better.

Sarah has been relationally set up for spiritual failure in a postmodern sensate culture. In *that* sense she is not alone. Sarah represents millions of adolescents—the vast majority of North American adolescents—who lack a mature Christian spiritual caregiver to pace and lead out of the disillusionment and disorientation of the youth way. On her spiritual road to Emmaus, Sarah finds no companion to open her heart to the truth of the love of Jesus, who cares more about who he made her to be than what she can make of herself academically and socially.

Pacing, Then Leading on the Postmodern Path

Leading postmodern adolescents into growing, intimate relationships with Jesus Christ begins as spiritual caregivers start pacing with the adolescents in their homes, churches and communities. Only intentional pacing relationships will be adequate to build bridges across chasms of disconnection, disorientation and disillusionment. Of all the failings of twentieth-century Christian youth ministry, perhaps the greatest was using programs and techniques to shortcut that need for relational proximity. Hence this scathing analysis:

> The church youth movement reflects the second misguided solution to the youth problem: adults isolate youth from the adult community and virtually the entire adult world. Given the fact that generational discontinuity is a major part of the "youth problem," the creation of all kinds of youth-specific institutions cannot be seen as any solution. In fact, youth organizations, even those sponsored by churches, largely serve corporate North America by accentuating the various trends of the teen culture and thereby increasing market segmentation.
>
> How are youth going to mature except by contact with adults?[39]

Pacing and then leading has been exchanged for shortcut, sound-byte disciplemaking—at the expense of the spiritual well-being of the present generation.

Our churches are marked by a pervasive generational discontinuity that encourages adults and adolescents to live in distinct cultural enclaves.[40] The sociocultural magnetic pull to remain in generational groupings is so strong that only the most intentional efforts lead to authentic intergenerational relationships. Dramatic cultural shifts, as described throughout this chapter, accelerate the widening of the gap. Adults and adolescents not only have fewer shared experiences but also have fewer common categories for interpreting experiences. The millennial generation is more experiential, synthetic, syncretistic, visual, diverse and intercultural than its modern predecessors. Churches, homes and organizations that include adult spiritual caregivers and adolescents are truly bicultural contexts.

The spiritual caregiver and adolescent relationship should thus be considered an *intercultural* as well as intergenerational friendship. In previous generations, seeing life from the perspective of an adolescent was like learning a new dialect of the same language. In this generation caregivers encounter an entirely new language, spoken by postmodern sensate adolescents. Until one can hear and translate truth into this language, attempts to lead sadly serve only to widen the intercultural, intergenerational gap further. Pacing relationships are the primary access we spiritual caregivers have to the vocabulary and structure of the postmodern sensate life language.

Jesus paced and then led Cleopas and his companion's spiritual journey on the Emmaus road. When he led it was in concert with their thoughts and experiences—so much so that they kept asking for more. Their disillusionment, disorientation and disconnection were answered in an encounter with the Way, the Truth and the Life.

If the church prevails in twenty-first-century North American culture, it will be because spiritual caregivers have responded with that same commitment. Those who have answered God's call to walk with adolescent pilgrims in progress will find a lot of mud building up on their sandals on the way to connecting burning hearts to the resurrected Jesus.

Reflecting on Your Journey

☐ How would you characterize your response to the description of the postmodern sensate culture? Were you surprised, frustrated, scared, confused, motivated to make a difference?

☐ To what degree do you recognize these elements of youth culture in the lives of adolescents you know? How deeply affected are these adolescents by the ethos, images and experiences of youth culture?

☐ Where can you identify, in the lives of adolescents you know, the three aspects of the youth way (sensate culture, pleasure pragmatism, pseudo-attachment)?

☐ Compare and contrast your own adolescent cultural experiences with postmodern adolescents' experiences. Describe specific similarities and dissimilarities.

☐ What is God's heart for the adolescents in our homes, churches and communities who are left to travel the postmodern Emmaus Road without spiritual companionship? In what ways have you found yourself experiencing God's heart for these lonely souls?

☐ How do you feel in regard to your effectiveness as a guide for adolescents on the Emmaus road? Where have you observed your greatest sense of making a meaningful difference? Where have you experienced the strongest sense of failure?

Pressing In

☐ Read Walt Mueller's *Understanding Youth Culture* or Quentin P. Schultze et al., eds., *Dancing in the Dark*. For a more philosophical discussion of broader cultural issues, read Harold O. J. Brown's *The Sensate Culture*.

☐ Pick up an issue of a teen magazine popular among your adolescents and their peers. Read with a view toward identifying evidences of the postmodern sensate culture described in this chapter. Ask yourself, *How can I communicate genuine truth, life and love into the lives of adolescents bombarded by these messages?*

☐ With your peers and a set of mature late or middle adolescents, hold an open discussion on the topic of "being in the world, but not of it" in terms of the media choices (movies, concerts, music, Internet). Enter the conversation with a commitment to listen and learn, not tell.

☐ Journal for a month regarding your own lifestyle choices and attitudes. With a partner, begin to critique the impact of the sensate culture on your inner world.

We are not human beings having a spiritual experience; we are spiritual beings having a human experience.
PIERRE TEILHARD DE CHARDIN

Holy is our best word to describe that life—the human aliveness that comes from dealing with God—Alive. We're most human when we deal with God. Any other way of life leaves us less human, less ourselves.
EUGENE PETERSON, *LEAP OVER A WALL*

We reach for God in many ways. Through our sculptures and our scriptures. Through our pictures and our prayers. Through our writing and our worship. And through them He reaches for us. His search begins with something said. Ours begins with something heard. His begins with something shown. Ours, with something seen. Our search for God and His search for us meet at windows in our everyday experience. These are the windows of the soul.
KEN GIRE, *WINDOWS OF THE SOUL*

All the natural relationships of life—to family, classmates, co-workers, neighbors, and even to those in the political and artistic and intellectual realms—are very good in themselves, when taken rightly. They too are essential to life together in the kingdom. There is no human spirituality apart from those relationships. We must seek our spirituality in them.
DALLAS WILLARD, *THE DIVINE CONSPIRACY*

Desire cannot live without hope. Yet we can only hope for what we desire. There simply must be something more, something out there on the road ahead of us, that offers the life we prize. To sustain the life of the heart, the life of deep desire, we desperately need to possess a clearer picture of the life that lies before us.
JOHN ELDREDGE, *THE JOURNEY OF DESIRE*

That which was from the beginning, which we have heard, which we have seen with our eyes, which we have looked at and our hands have touched—this we proclaim concerning the Word of life. The life appeared, we have seen it and testify to it, and we proclaim to you the eternal life, which was with the Father and has appeared to us. We proclaim to you what we have seen and heard, so that you also may have fellowship with us. And our fellowship is with the Father and with his Son, Jesus Christ.
1 JOHN 1:1-3

3

A Theology for Pacing, Then Leading

*F*or more than an hour we had shouted anxious encouragement as Rachel and Kara faced the daunting challenges of "Jacob's Ladder." We had cheered loudly as the two petite sixteen-year-olds worked to climb a free swinging, seventy-foot vertical ladder made of telephone-pole-sized logs. On the lower end, the four-foot span between rungs had allowed them to climb independently. On the higher rungs, however, the six-foot spans they encountered required nothing less than absolute interdependence. Rachel and Kara had been forced to be greater than the sum of their parts in order to accomplish their goal: to stand together at the top of Jacob's Ladder, the most formidable element in this high ropes course. We had been there to inspire confidence in their ability to achieve the goal.

As the triumphant pair descended from their victory, those on the ground experienced excitement and relief. We had feared that ultimately Kara and Rachel would experience deep disappointment. The higher they climbed, the more they had hesitated, until it seemed on the final rungs that they were simply catching their breath before turning back. More than once the girls had stopped for at least ten minutes before attempting the next level. What great joy we shared, therefore, as we welcomed them from their seventy-foot free-fall descent off the top pole.

After receiving several hugs and congratulatory praises, the exhausted pair began to talk about their climb. We, the faithful cheering throng, were congratulating ourselves on our roles as encouragers. Our feeling of self-satisfaction was dampened, however, when Kara and Rachel informed us that they had not heard us when they were at the top. How could they have not heard us? Hadn't we been alongside them in spirit, emotionally engaged in their quest, vicariously experiencing their triumph?

During the final stages of their climb, they told us, they had cried together, sharing in physical, mental and emotional exhaustion. Each spoke of the fear they had encountered and how their long pauses were often times of prayer, seeking God's assurance and strength to overcome their weakness. They had relied on each other and God for the courage, stamina and hope necessary to advance to the next level. While they appreciated our efforts to inspire them, in reality we had been of little help at the most difficult points.

Rachel and Kara demonstrated an important life truth: when we face challenges and struggle bigger than we are, it matters less who is cheering for us in the distance and matters most who is alongside us in the midst of the battle.

Climbing Jacob's Ladder: The Practice of Spiritual Caregiving

Kara and Rachel were compelled toward their physical goal by a shared experience of being dependent on God and each other. Such relational experiences are the God-designed means for compelling adolescents toward the spiritual goal of Christlikeness. Authentic, real-life relationships with God and his people are means God uses to lead students to greater heights of spiritual maturity.

The pacing-then-leading model of nurturing adolescent spiritual maturity is grounded in the conviction that the adolescent's life itself is the context for spiritual growth. Given this conviction, it follows that to the degree a spiritual caregiver wants to affect the spirituality of an adolescent, to that degree the caregiver must become involved in the reality of the adolescent's life.

But what does it mean to be a spiritual caregiver "on the ladder" with a twenty-first-century adolescent? How does a caregiver enable teens to relate experiences in a deceitful, sensate "real world" of daily life to the God of all life? And what is the goal of adolescent spiritual maturity?

Of course life is a challenge far greater than Jacob's Ladder. Life's journey is scarier, more exhausting and filled with many more reasons to give up hope. Adolescence may be the scariest part of all. Going it alone is not an option. God, in his design of humanity, has given us a theological mandate for climbing the Jacob's Ladder of life with the teenagers in our homes, churches and communities. To fail to do so is to relegate our influence to anxious cheering and fretting in the distance—a place that is low in influence and high in irrelevance for adolescents who are spiritually hanging on for dear life.

Whole Person Transformation: The Purpose of Spiritual Caregiving

Today is going to hurt. This was my first waking thought every day for five months. A herniated disk had introduced such chaos into my sciatic nerve function that I could neither sit nor walk without debilitating pain. I knew I could turn to prescribed potent pain relievers for only a short period of time. Surgery was my only alternative. So after weeks of constant pain, I limped into the hospital hoping for a permanent cure.

As I awaited the arrival of the anesthesiologist, I asked my surgeon, "How did they treat a person with this condition a century ago?" The only "prescriptions" I could imagine would have been whiskey or a bullet.

"A century ago they would have simply cut off your leg. Lacking the knowledge that the root of the problem was in the lower back, they simply would have amputated your leg to eliminate the pain."

I winced and unconsciously began to rub my aching but suddenly appreciated right leg. A well-intentioned yet misguided nineteenth-century surgeon would have *removed my leg*. Intending to care for me, the physician would have in fact permanently disabled my body. I would have been left with a debilitated back *and* a missing limb!

True healing, not symptomatic relief. Anne, herself the mother of teenagers, recently reminded me of the potential harm of well-intentioned yet misguided spiritual caregivers. Anne told me that as a Christian teenager she

> was taught a lot about obeying God. The adults in my church always communicated to us why and how we should be living for God. We were taught the Bible and we were taught to feel guilty if we did not follow its commands. What we did not receive was a relationship with any of the adults who were teaching us. They expected us to do what was right though they never really

connected with us. What's more, we never saw them actually living out biblical truth in their own lives. . . . We always felt a sense of anger toward them and shame toward ourselves.

Spiritual growth for Anne's youth leaders was a matter of addition and subtraction. "Do these things for God and don't do these sinful things against God"—a mathematical formula for becoming a "good Christian." The application of the formula was simple: add reading the Bible, praying and witnessing to your life while subtracting sinful thoughts, words and actions. A religious answer was given in response to the perceived religious problem.

But spiritual growth is not a matter of addition and subtraction. It is a matter of *personal transformation.* That transformation process, God's redemptive work within us, has one goal: "to make us more and more like God, or more and more like Christ who is the perfect image of God."[1] Several passages reflect the singular focus of God's work of transforming his people into the image of Christ:

> For those God foreknew he also predestined to be conformed to the likeness of his Son, that he might be the firstborn among many. (Rom 8:29)

> And we, who with unveiled faces all reflect the Lord's glory, are being transformed into his likeness with an ever-increasing glory, which comes from the Lord, who is the Spirit. (2 Cor 3:18)

> Do not lie to one another, since you have taken off your old self with its practices and have put on the new self, which is being renewed in knowledge of its Creator. (Col 3:9-10)

Becoming a "good Christian" is not God's goal for our adolescents. His goal is nothing less than transforming each student into an increasingly accurate likeness of his Son.

The whole of the goal. Transformation into the likeness of Jesus is a whole-person process. One common misunderstanding concerning the nature of spiritual transformation is betrayed in the oft-repeated critique "I think her problem is really a spiritual issue." Parents and youth leaders, trying to find a way to describe what is happening in a teenager's life, often use something like this as a default response:

> I've been discipling Maria for a year now. She seems to take one step forward and two steps backward. One day she is boldly living her life for Christ,

the next day she is following the crowd. Every few months she experiences God in a powerful way, either at a retreat or during an emotional student ministries outreach. Then, less than a week later, she is blending back into the party scene with her school friends. She claims that she wants to change, but it never lasts. She really gets down on herself for her lack of willpower to resist her friends' social pressure. But you know what I think? *I think it's a spiritual problem.*

Is it accurate to define Maria's struggle with peer pressure as a spiritual problem? *Everything* is, at its root, a spiritual problem. In the Garden, prior to sin, Adam and Eve were secure in their identities, their relationships with one another and with the created world in which God had made them caretakers. All of this changed when sin entered the picture. Shame entered their sense of self (they were ashamed), blame entered their relationships ("the woman you gave me . . ."), and painful strife entered into their relationship to the created world.[2] The whole mess humanity finds itself in is, at its root, a spiritual problem.

Peer pressure *is* therefore a spiritual problem. The simplistic conclusion "I believe she has a spiritual problem" fails, however, in its attempt to describe the whole reality of Maria's life journey. This severely limited critique represents an extreme reaction I call *overspiritualization.* Overspiritualization is a reductionistic approach to problems that lumps everything into transcendent categories. An overspiritualized perspective on Maria's bout with peer pressure would conclude that her *real* problem is that she has (1) failed in her prayer and devotional life, (2) developed a rebellious, hardened heart or (3) fallen under attack by demonic forces. The prescription would be to have her pray and read the Bible more or have others pray over her more in order for her to be released from her spiritual bondage.

At the other extreme, adults often *underspiritualize* issues such as peer pressure. Underspiritualization would lead to the diagnosis that Maria's issues are exclusively about low self-esteem or perhaps a poor relationship with her parents. An underspiritualized approach concludes that all human experiences can be explained in purely physiological or psychological categories. The prescription of underspiritualization, in Maria's case, would be limited to instructions to see a counselor or to find an environment where her genuine self is accepted.

Spiritual caregivers who move to either extreme fail to address the whole of the goal of transformation. Underspiritualization, as illustrated above, neglects the reality of the presence of sin and the battles of spiritual warfare. Overspiritualization neglects the reality of human experience and the significance of psychological and emotional factors in an adolescent's life. The complexity of human personality and spirituality defies such simplistic categories. Robert Mulholland has observed Christians' frequent failure to understand whole-person spirituality: "We tend to be dualistic—spiritual life on one side and the rest of life on the other. We have not realized how deeply our spiritual life and growth into wholeness—genuine spirituality—is interwoven with the dynamics of our being and doing."[3]

Spiritual caregivers: conduits for life. An appropriate response to the problem of peer pressure thus takes into account the whole person engaged in the struggle. In Maria's case, her failure to live up to her convictions in the face of peer pressure is certain to be multifaceted. A spiritual caregiver would need to address myriad issues with Maria in the pacing process:

☐ How does she perceive God in her life?

☐ How is she experiencing God in her life?

☐ How is she responding to God's invitation to walk daily with him?

☐ How does she feel about herself?

☐ How secure is she in relationship with her parents?

☐ What needs are being met by gaining the acceptance of these peers?

☐ What skills does Maria lack when it comes to making good decisions or communicating those decisions to her friends?

☐ How does Maria deal with failure?

These questions suggest that there are many angles from which Maria's life can be intersected. Furthermore, many layers remain uncovered in the discernment of the root of Maria's poor decision-making. Failure to pace well with the fullness of an adolescent's whole-person spirituality will mean a caregiver will lead in incomplete, inadequate ways.

Teenagers are wholly, but not exclusively, spiritual beings. Maria needs spiritual care. True spiritual care, however, requires a holistic rather than dualistic approach. All the interwoven materials making up the fabric of her struggle with peer pressure need to be taken to God and engaged in relationship to his Spirit at work in Maria's life. Engaging a gracious, loving and powerful God at this point in her personal journey is the spiritual need. No part of her life is detached from her spiritual life with God. Therefore,

God should not be approached apart from the various dimensions of Maria's personhood.

Failure to connect with and speak into Maria's whole self leads to a failure to enter authentically into Maria's world. Pacing is the process of communicating an embrace of grace at the point of an adolescent's personal needs. Without the pacing any leading will be inadequate, any transformational healing experience incomplete. Without the holistic leading that comes from authentic pacing, Maria is left to "do the math" of spiritual addition and subtraction.

Redemptive Relationships: The Power of Spiritual Caregiving

Ultimately the spiritual caregiver cannot transform Maria; all she can do is pace with her and lead her to the Creator, Redeemer and Transformer of her entire being. The goal for Maria's spiritual caregiver is to lead her into a full experience of God's whole-person transformational work in the midst of real life.

How then should the spiritual caregiver view herself? How does God use her to make a difference in the adolescent's life?

Gilbert Bilezikian wisely couples the relationships of Christian community with the redemptive work of God:

> There is a lot more to the restoration of the image of God in human life than the cultivation of personal holiness as a private spiritual exercise. The nature of the Godhead as a plurality of interdependent persons provided the model for relationships among humans. It was not good for the man to be alone because his creation in God's image called for a union of oneness with someone like him. Soon after the creation of human oneness, this interrelational dimension of God's image became the first casualty of the Fall, with the destruction of community. And in God's program of redemption, it becomes the first focus of sanctification.[4]

Our call to "body life" is rooted in what it means to be image bearers of the One who created us and redeemed us for relationship. Therefore, Bilezikian writes:

> the making of community may not be regarded as an optional decision for Christians. It is a compelling and irrevocable necessity, a binding divine mandate for all believers at all times. It is possible for humans to reject or alter God's commission for them to build community and to be in commu-

nity. But this may happen only at the cost of forsaking the Creator of community and of betraying his image in us; this cost is enormous, since his image in us is the essential attribute that defines our own humanity.[5]

Human relationship is not a luxury option for either the adult or the adolescent spiritual journey. God's redemptive work in the midst of real life is mediated through the connecting of the spiritual caregiver's heart to the heart of the adolescent. Larry Crabb describes the awesome nature of this spiritual heart-to-heart connection:

> There is a power within the life of every Christian waiting to be released, a power that could lead to further and deeper change, a power within you that could help someone else connect more intimately to the heart of Christ. . . . Releasing the power of God through our lives into the hearts and souls of others requires that we both understand and enter into a kind of relating that only the gospel makes possible, a kind of relating I call connecting.[6]

Receiving and giving that connection represents a fundamental need imprinted in us by the Creator. In the absence of true Christian spiritual connection, each of us will find some alternative way to feel connected (negative or pseudo-attachments) in order to fill the God-created need for spiritual relationship.[7] Whether a seventh-grader walking into the cafeteria for her first junior-high lunch or a college freshman spending his first day on campus, no one can bear the journey of life alone. The most powerful echo of the Word that spoke the human image of God into being is the persistent longing for love. That echo can be heard in every song in the local music store and in every novel available in the online bookstore. It is the echo of the Creator's voice calling for life to be lived in relationship.

Here is the theological basis for pacing and then leading by means of personal relationships. Because of the Fall, in the absence of true relational connection with spiritual caregivers, the natural path of the adolescent spiritual journey is into the darkness of idolatry. Adolescents need spiritual caregivers who will (1) pray for God's Spirit to work in their lives, (2) pray for their spiritual battles in the midst of a perverse world, (3) guide them to a meaningful engagement of the truths of Scripture and (4) walk with them into a personal encounter with the living God. They require caregivers who also offer assistance with self-esteem, family conflicts and life skill development (decision-making, building friendships, working through failure). In sum, adolescents need to be paced with and then led by spiritual caregivers who are able to perceive and engage a whole-life spirituality.

Consequently the greatest resource spiritual caregivers offer adolescents is their own life of intimate connection with the heart of God. Like a conduit for life, the love of a spiritual caregiver links the adolescent with a real God whose real love is available in the midst of real life. It is for such a relationship with him and others that God created and now acts to redeem those made in his image. No one was meant to climb the ladder alone.

Balancing Life with God: The Process of Spiritual Caregiving

The pacing-then-leading spiritual caregiver becomes an active participant in God's redemptive work of restoring the fullness of his image in an adolescent's life. No one needs a graduate degree or a library of books to be qualified to be that spiritual life-giving connection. Having acknowledged that the model requires more love than information, we seek understanding of the nature and process of guiding real-life adolescent spirituality.

As spiritual caregivers walk into adolescent life spaces, they will find that often a connection is hindered or even missing between the hearts of adolescents and the heart of God. Restoring the flow of life-giving grace and truth into these areas of spiritual disconnection, not fixing their "spiritual problems," fulfills the true call of spiritual caregiving. To facilitate an understanding of that process, we need to explore two critical areas of balance in the spiritual journey. First, we examine the call to authentic, balancing spirituality in the adolescent's knowing, being, and doing in relationship with God and others. Second, we investigate the need for balancing responsibility-taking as adolescents move toward an adult ownership of their walk with God.[8]

Note that the emphasis is on *balancing,* not *balanced,* spirituality. Because all of life is dynamic, constantly in a state of flux, no one reaches the static state of a "balanced life." Spiritual vitality is to be found in the balancing, as the journey continues moment by moment in the presence of a living, loving God.

Knowing, being and doing. Adam and Eve experienced God without sin in all of their knowing, being and doing prior to the Fall. After the Fall, however, the balance of spiritual life was destroyed by the absence of God. Cain embodies the impact of the Fall on spiritual relationships. Religion, not murder, is the first sin described in Cain's life. He tried to approach God on his own terms, and when that failed he resorted to murdering his own brother in his anger toward God.

When an adolescent does not experience God at work in the whole of his life, he too becomes snared in being merely religious in his attempts to know, relate to and obey God. The contrast between the religious and the relational can be laid out as in figure 1.

RELIGIOUS FOCUS	APPROACHING GOD	RELATIONAL FOCUS
Intellectual knowledge about God	Knowing	True knowledge of God
Emotional life experiences	Being	Affection for God
Right behaviors	Doing	Loving obedience to God

Figure 1. False religion, true relationship

Two students in the same small group may exhibit the same level of biblical knowledge, overt participation in worship and disciplined service in the church. However, as the leader paces with the students, she may find that one is trapped in religious conformity without the vitality of a growing relationship with God. As she paces with the other, she finds a student who is aware of her need for grace and is opening her life to the authority of God's truth. Unless she has entered into involved relationships with the two, she may fail to see the points at which each student needs to be led in her spiritual journey.

What does it look like to pace and then lead in knowing, being and doing? How does one lead an adolescent out of the bondage of religious knowledge, experiences and actions into the righteous freedom of relational knowing, being and doing? Figure 2 represents a healthy, growing relationship with God.

The student learning to balance his or her whole self with God is increasingly able to submit thoughts, emotions and choices to the mind, heart and will of God. The desired outcome is a mind that is being transformed to think with a "God view," a heart being transformed in its capacity for sharing emotions and affections with God, and a will being transformed

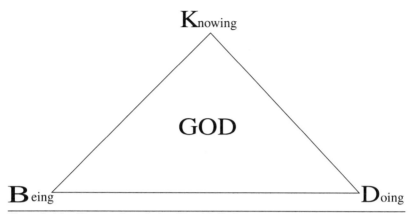

Figure 2. A healthy, growing relationship with God

into loving obedience to his leading. Learning to balance themselves in the love and power of God, adolescents relate to God in the midst of their personhood, not in addition to or in spite of their thoughts, feelings and choices.

Religious knowledge versus transforming knowing. Jesus prayed in John 17:17, "Sanctify them in the truth; your word is truth." Without knowledge of Scripture and theology, we are all prone to create conceptions of God based primarily on our private spiritual experiences. Yet biblical and theological knowledge is a means, not an end. The end goal is right understanding for the purpose of right relationship. The adolescent's growth in theological knowledge should look like figure 3.

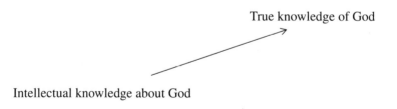

Figure 3. Appropriate adolescent growth in theological knowledge

Spiritual caregivers facilitate the movement from knowledge about God to knowledge of God by aiding the personal contextualization and experience of truth.[9] James Wilhoit, in *Christian Education and the Search for Meaning*, makes a distinction between learning content that is meaningful and experiencing meaningful learning.[10] For example, every page of the Bible is meaningful. The truth of the Scriptures and the essential doctrines of the faith are meaningful in themselves. However, there can be quite a gap between knowing a truth is meaningful and learning that truth meaningfully in one's own life.

I once walked into a room of eighty high school students who were being lectured on the meaning of the atonement. The truth being communicated was outstanding in its accuracy and substance—and it meant almost nothing to those seated in the room. The only thing the students seemed to be learning was that theology has nothing to do with real life. How unfortunate!

Contrast this to Alan's recent experience. As the junior-high youth pastor of our church, Alan uses small groups to help students personalize the meaning of what they are learning in church and student ministries. After discussing the role of the Holy Spirit in accurate and substantive terms, Alan sat down with a small group of eighth-grade boys to reflect on the importance of the Holy Spirit in their lives. The result? Meaningful learning. By the end of the meeting, the boys began to identify what it meant to have the Holy Spirit present and at work in their lives. The doctrine of the Holy Spirit had become a relational reality as Alan led the students from a base of knowledge to a place of relational understanding. Alan's personal relationship with the students provided a relational conduit as he paced with them and then led them to make meaning out of the truth of the Scriptures in the context of their own lives.

Adolescents' learning truth meaningfully in a real-life relationship to God is the spiritual caregiver's goal in communicating biblical-theological knowledge. Having new ideas about God without the transformation that comes from such personally meaningful learning leads to a dead orthodoxy that numbs the spiritual sensitivity of the adolescent heart.

Emotional sensation versus affectionate relationship. All humans are experiential: we all learn our world through the five senses. Contemporary adolescents do so with a vengeance. The twenty-first century thrusts students into a hyper-sensate environment. The road to adulthood for this generation passes through a bombardment of sights, sounds and sensations. In a previous era, one listened to music to experience its full effect. Today's adolescent enjoys a musical experience that is not simply heard. Music's power to affect the soul is exponentially amplified through video interpretation and a vibrating pulse of surround sound that can be felt in one's chest.

Today's youth ministry not only acknowledges but also often makes a high investment in responding to adolescents' enculturated desires for high sensory impact experiences. Christian concerts, warp-speed youth events and frenetic team competitions are staples in youth ministry programming. (Ten years ago the coveted buzzword for youth ministry events was *awesome*. In this era the adjective is *extreme*.) As means for pacing and then leading a large group of students into an experience with God, such high-energy experiences can be useful. However, when adolescents begin to substitute such sensational encounters for genuine affection for God or when emotional sensation becomes a substitute for depth of intimacy with God, the experience becomes religious rather than relational.

Concerts, ropes courses and dynamic retreats are avenues for reaching into the adolescent's inner being. Worship, drama and personal stories are means of communication that likewise engage students emotionally in response to the truth of God. All of these are powerful means of engaging a person's heart with the message of God's love. However, as ends in themselves they can move the student into a false sense of God that will crumble once the sensation has ceased. Intense emotional experiences—whether involving music, drama or emotional sharing of the heart—must be consistently fastened to the anchor of God's love for the adolescent, as figure 4 pictures.

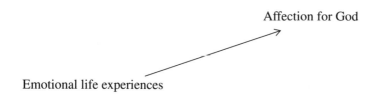

Affection for God

Emotional life experiences

Figure 4. From reacting to life experiences to responding to God's love

The very nature of the adolescent passage makes it challenging to guide adolescents into meaningful relational experiences with God. Carter and

Sydney were youth leaders who encountered students' tendency to focus on emotional sensation rather than affectionate relationship. As participants and later leaders in their church youth group, the couple watched a pattern develop over a period of three years. In the first year, on a summer missions trip, the students faced very painful interpersonal conflicts. By the last night, anger and resentment ran high. Around a campfire, worshiping and sharing thoughts, individuals finally began to be honest about their feelings. Tears of repentance and forgiveness began to flow. By the end of the evening, the group had never felt closer to God or each other. The next year, Carter and Sydney noticed, the same thing happened. Once again the final night's campfire produced a cleansing catharsis. By the third year, the students had begun to prime themselves for the last night. Expecting "God to work" again this year, the students seemed to set themselves up by harboring painful tensions. This time, however, the anger was not resolved well. The tears still flowed, but the damage was beginning to corrode the students' relationships.

As leaders, Carter and Sydney had to step in and confront the students' manufacturing of emotional spiritual experiences. The focus had to be shifted from "feeling" God at work to lovingly responding to a God who was at work in an emotionally charged environment. The caregiving couple paced by embracing meaningful emotional spiritual experiences in the adolescents' lives. They then led by helping the students move toward a loving response to God in the midst and aftermath of the rush of feelings. By leading the students to a place where they experienced their emotions *with God,* not just in a "spiritual context," the couple helped the group grow into a deeper affection for God rather than an increasing need for crisis emotional experiences.

Dutiful obligation versus loving obedience. No one was more dutiful than the Pharisees. No one received more scathing and consistent rebukes from Jesus than the Pharisees either. The Pharisees were able to get a lot of behaviors right, yet they forgot to love the Ruler more than the pride that comes from keeping the rules.

As evidenced by the Pharisees, religious behavior can be taught and managed. "Christian" behaviors such as witnessing to friends, keeping oneself sexually pure and reading the Word daily are elements of lifestyle that apart from a vital relationship with God can be mere dutiful choices. Students can be shamed into observing these behavioral guidelines even though they find no joy in pleasing God. The call of God is to obey lovingly. Leading adolescents toward loving obedience rather than dutiful obligation requires walking alongside their hearts rather than simply teaching them to manage their external behaviors.

Lamar may be able to curtail postgame drinking with his teammates because of pressure from his parents and his small group of peers at church. Though this simple response to pressure is immature, the end result still has some genuine merit. Certainly a dad would rather his son give in to pressure not to drink than pressure to drink. A long-term problem arises, however, in the source of motivation. Peer pressure, whether positive or negative, has power because of individuals' fear of rejection. When the environment changes, such as when Lamar attends a state school on an athletic scholarship, his behavior may shift too and conform to the new source of greatest pressure. The long-term maturation goal is to enable Lamar to obey out of love for God rather than out of a fear of rejection by a group of peers.[11]

How does one pace and then lead toward the long-term goal of a changed heart? Pacing involves seeking to understand the motivation for an adolescent's behavior. Leading implies challenging the student to respond to God's call for righteous acts from a righteous heart. Getting out of balance in either direction can be devastating to the adolescent's spiritual maturation. Pacing that does not include leading leaves a student with a sense of being cared for, yet without transformation. Leading without pacing leaves the student with a sense of responsibility yet without the support necessary to fulfill it. The former creates immaturity and a sense of spiritual impotence. The latter creates exhaustion and a sense of spiritual guilt.

When the two are held in balance, the spiritual caregiver provides a connection to the power of the Holy Spirit to work within God's people to accomplish spiritual transformation. The caregiver walks with Lamar as he examines his heart's willingness to obey the call of God in his life. Not only Lamar's decisions but the responsiveness of Lamar's heart becomes a part of the discipling journey.

The process of leading toward right action born from a right heart can be diagrammed as in figure 5.

Not all disobedience results from an unwilling heart. Whether in the area of sexual purity or abstinence from substance use, I have discovered that many students fail to succeed because they have failed to prepare for

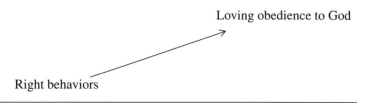

Figure 5. From behaving to obeying God

success. In fact, often an adolescent simply lacks sufficient skills for fulfilling genuine commitments to follow God's will. Spiritual caregivers are important teachers of the life skills necessary for building healthy relationships with the opposite sex or navigating the social jungle of a university campus. Many Christian students fail morally because of a lack of "how to" rather than a lack of "want to." Thus skill development is an important component in the spiritual maturation of an adolescent seeking to lovingly obey God. (Chapter seven addresses these issues in more detail.)

Relating life to God: the balancing middle. Ultimately spiritual caregivers are called to walk students into a deeper awareness that the Christian life is not simply the sum total of one's biblical knowledge, worshipful feelings and obedient actions. The Christian life is rather the relationship of one's whole being to a God intimately at work in one's real life. The spiritual caregiver therefore leads the adolescent to discover that every thought, emotion, and action is a place to meet and join God in his miraculous work of redemption. The spiritual caregiver focuses on *pacing and then leading adolescents into fully experiencing their thoughts, feelings and choices in relationship with the living God.*

The image of the balancing triangle can help us assess the degree to which pacing and leading has been holistic. Each of us is prone to gravitate toward one corner or another of the triangle. Having spent more than a decade teaching in undergraduate and graduate theological institutions, I am in my comfort zone in the "knowledge corner." So sometimes I find myself out of balance in my mentoring. I can become quite satisfied with pacing and leading the adolescent's *thinking* but fail to enter into the emotions and choices that accompany the change in thinking. As a spiritual caregiver, however, I am called to be attentive to the whole person: knowing, being and doing. To emphasize one aspect at the expense of another is to create an imbalance that is inconsistent with God's creative and redemptive work.

Whose life is it? The most significant difference between the life of a child and the life of an adult is the different amount of responsibility each carries for life direction. Pacing and then leading adolescents into a whole-person experience of God requires caregivers to challenge them toward taking increasing responsibility for their own spiritual lives. What is the teen's responsibility in spiritual growth?

I once sat on a panel of professors and campus leaders whose task was to field Christian college students' questions about living a life of faith. Cindy, a quiet yet brave first-year student, asked the question that surely was on everyone's mind. "You just said, 'Rely on God's strength to help you.' How do you do that? I try to obey God and live the way I know he wants me to. But then I fail. What am I doing wrong? Everybody says that you should rely on God, but I don't know how to do it."

Because I had given a lengthy response to the previous question, I felt it appropriate to defer to my colleagues on this vital question. So I waited. We all waited. Finally another member of the panel spoke up: "The best I can tell you to do is pray. Whenever I face a difficult decision or problem in my life, I pray and trust God to help me."

Sadly, several persons simply nodded their affirmation and we moved on to the next question. (Until I could stand it no longer, and then I brought us back to Cindy's question.)

What *does* it mean to rely on God? How can adolescents understand what it means to have the Holy Spirit at work in their lives? Responding in theologically meaningful terms to these questions moves caregivers beyond the level of Christian cliché to a place of spiritual nurture. Philippians 2:12-13 provides an important framework for pacing and leading adolescent journeys: "Therefore, my dear friends, as you have always obeyed—not only in my presence, but now much more in my absence—continue to work out your salvation with fear and trembling, for it is God who works in you to will and to act according to his good purpose."

Note the emphasis on both divine and human responsibility. God is at work to redeem—work only God can do.[12] The human recipient of divine grace responds cooperatively—work each of us has been redeemed to do.[13] If we deemphasize human responsibility, the adolescent is left with an expectation of "microwave sanctification." Having this perception of God's work, Cindy would seek an experience with God that would instantaneously deliver her from all of her struggles with sin and disappointment. On the other hand, a failure to emphasize God's transforming work would place on Cindy the ominous burden of having to make herself more spiritual.[14]

Teens, particularly in late adolescence, desperately need guidance in how to begin to take own their knowing, being and doing in relationship to God. Consider Jordan, a seventeen-year-old who confessed to his small group leader that he had lost control in his battle with Internet pornography. Jordan added, "I have prayed and asked God to help me stop—but it doesn't help." He is in a spiritual double bind. He is experiencing God as either unwilling or unable to help. He is also experiencing himself as a failure in fulfilling what he knows to be God's will.

Whose life is it? Who is going to take responsibility for rescuing this young man out of the depths of his internal imprisonment?

Toward responsive responsibility. The spiritual caregiver's goal is to lead Jordan to a place where he neither passively waits for God to take his addiction away *nor* expects that he must somehow rid himself of the urge to experience lust. Pacing with Jordan would include listening to Jordan's understanding of his problem (knowing), his feelings about himself and God in the midst of his self-control failures (being), and how he has attempted in the past to rid himself of his destructive habit (doing). Leading Jordan would begin with prayer responding to God as Father. Jordan's concept of God has to be nurtured into a right understanding of who God is and how he works (knowing). Engaging Jordan's view of God with the revelation of Scripture is essential.

Focusing on God as Father rather than God as antidote, Jordan can move into the strong, loving presence of the Father with honesty about how he feels about himself and God (being). Jordan's responsiveness will connect his heart to God's affection for him, thereby opening the floodgates of his hurt. By walking with God's love into his hurt, Jordan is walking himself into the healing power of that love. From this place of relationship, the problem with Internet pornography can be seen within the context of Jordan's ongoing spiritual journey with God. Jordan is being encouraged to seek a healing from God that is less about stopping a habit and more about purifying a heart.

Jordan may find that increased intimacy with God is itself the full experience of healing that enables him to walk away from the pit of pornography. He may find that God chooses to remove his addiction miraculously and instantaneously. Or he may not. Often God embarks on a deep spiritual work that leads a person into the hidden layers of the heart that are the source of addictions. In either case, Jordan will need to discipline his time more effectively, invite others into his life to help him with his new commitments, change his computer habits and develop ways of meeting his God-given intimacy needs in healthy nonsexual relationships with peers of the same and opposite sex (doing).

The spiritual caregiver cannot rescue Jordan from his struggle with pornography. He can, however, lead Jordan to a place of responsiveness where he is participating in God's redemptive work of spiritually maturing him. He can also pace with Jordan as he experiences "spiritual walk rehab," learning to walk in the will of God rather than the lust of the flesh. Thus Jordan will be delivered from the graceless demand of "straightening out his life" in the hope that he will stop experiencing God as distant. Alongside Jordan in the walk of life, the spiritual caregiver will find himself balancing pacing and leading, supporting and challenging. At times the caregiver will comfort, at other times he will confront; at all times he will love.

The synergistic nature of human beings' cooperation with God is learned only in the living of life. Without wise counsel from a consistent source of spiritual caregiving, adolescents are likely to move toward either abdicating their call to be responsive or missing their call to be dependent. Pacing and then leading enables a student like Jordan to understand that God is always fulfilling his responsibility to be at work *and* that Jordan is always responsible for working it out responsively. Pacing and then leading enables an adolescent to experience the synergistic sanctifying work sought by Cindy, the freshman who loved God but was totally confused about her role in relationship to his gift of the Holy Spirit.

"Live Spirituality": The Perspective of a Spiritual Caregiver

Like Kara and Rachel's interdependent journey up Jacob's ladder, the spiritual caregiver chooses to become a personal participant in the real world that is the context of an adolescent's spiritual journey. As in my walk with the four-year-old Zachary, the pacing caregiver learns to linger in the midst of daily experiences of "live spirituality." Involvement births influence, and influence is the very definition of leading.[15]

The leading, however, is not toward some external standard or coveted religious experience. Leading guides the adolescent toward relating her daily thoughts, emotions and choices to the God who is at work to transform her entire self into the image of Jesus. Leading, like pacing, is a part of the journey itself. Far from being dualistic, our focus must be on whole lives wholly in relationship with a real God in a real world.

Reflecting on Your Journey

☐ Would you say you have encountered more *underspiritualization* or *overspiritualization* among Christians you have known? Which tendency do you see most active in yourself in the present?

☐ Describe a time when you found yourself working in partnership with God to make a redemptive impact on a person's life. Specifically, what behaviors, words or attitudes seemed to make the greatest difference for that person? What does this tell you about the key components of connected redemptive relationships?

☐ Would you describe yourself as more of a "knower," a "be-er" or a "doer"? In what area have you seen yourself grow the most in the last year? Where do you still need to grow in order to be more balanced?

☐ Given your responses to the above questions, reflect on the emerging themes. What is your spiritual relational profile? In other words, what relational styles and spiritual emphases are most comfortable for you? least comfortable?

☐ What do these insights suggest in terms of your strengths in redemptive relational connecting with adolescents? Where are your most obvious growth horizons? What would it look like to grow in grace in these areas?

Pressing In

☐ Read Ken Gire's *Windows to the Soul* or Robert Mulholland's *Invitation to a Journey* to explore how to cultivate an authentic, "real-time" spirituality.

☐ Go to a trusted friend who has been a consistent companion to your soul. Ask them to join you on an intentional journey toward a more holistic spiritual life. If you do not have such a friend, begin praying with God for the gift of authentic redemptive connection. Be prepared to give as well as receive in the relationship.

☐ Read Eugene Peterson's *Leap over a Wall*. Journal your insights into the life of David as he dealt with God in the midst of his tragic yet triumphant life.

☐ As you reflect on where you learned your relational style, ask God to reveal and redeem places of selfishness and self-protection. Invite spiritual life companions to pray for healing of old wounds that cause you to enter relationships fearfully rather than faithfully.

Section 2

Sacred Practices
of Loving Well

Preparing for Your Journey

As you prepare to read chapters four through eight, take a few moments to ask God to move the learning through your mind and heart into the very depths of your soul. Pray that God will speak truth and grace into your life concerning the following questions:

☐ How effective am I as an empathic listener? In what key areas do my skills need development? Where may my heart need to be changed?

☐ How does God want to shape or perhaps reshape my prayer life as a pacing-then-leading spiritual caregiver?

☐ How effective am I as one who leads with the truth? In what key areas do my skills need development? Where may my heart need to be changed?

☐ How effective am I when I am called upon to confront or to resolve conflict? In what key areas do my skills need development? Where may my heart need to be changed?

☐ How will I become different if I yield more fully to God's process of transforming me into a pacing-then-leading spiritual caregiver?

☐ How do I equip adolescents to live with moral purpose and purity in the midst of a sensate culture? What does pacing and then leading look like in relationship to the moral selves of postmodern adolescents?

☐ How do I provide an environment for the nurture of adolescent spiritual maturation in the midst of a sensate culture? What will have to change for me to provide spiritual caregiving in view of the adolescents' generation rather than my own?

The road to the heart is the ear.
VOLTAIRE, *PARROT 30*

If you want an adolescent to listen to your facts, you must first listen to her feelings.
UNKNOWN

Knowing how to listen is probably the most important communication tool there is.
WILLIAM J. ROWLEY, *HOW TO LIVE WITH YOUR TEENAGER*

To be an agent of transformation, dialogue needs to become a lifestyle. It begins as a mechanism for verbal communication, but if practiced daily, it can become an orientation or an attitude towards life. It is an attitude characterized by real understanding and empathy for life experiences or points of view different from one's own. It is characterized by patience, nonjudgment, and moderation. It is a way of being in which we make the intentional response instead of the instinctive one.
HARVILLE HENDRIX & HELEN HUNT, *GIVING THE LOVE THAT HEALS*

Nature practices entrainment so gracefully we barely notice. Crickets in a field chirp in one chorus. Clocks ticking on a wall find the same rhythm. Communication scholars point out that we subconsciously adopt each other's body positions when we face each other in conversation. Women will tell you that living with female roommates means everybody inevitably winds up on the same menstrual cycle. People sleeping within an earshot of one another naturally adjust their breathing to that of the person beside them—which is why snoring annoys us. Snoring impedes our ability to adopt another's rhythms.

Entrainment is also an apt metaphor for the spiritual life. When we draw ourselves alongside God, when we stop and listen to the breath of the Holy Spirit—God breathing in us—our rhythms align with God's. The Hebrew word for "spirit" (ruach) means "breath," the life force God breathed into Adam at creation. We listen to God breathing in us so that our spirit becomes completely entrained to God's.
KENDA CREASY DEAN & RON FOSTER
THE GODBEARING LIFE

4

How to Listen Before You Lead

Kayla's parents love her deeply. They have consistently provided all she has needed to achieve her dreams. During Kayla's grade-school years, Mom planned her life around Kayla's swim lessons, ballet lessons and piano lessons. Dad, a highly successful sales representative, adjusted his demanding travel schedule to accommodate swim meets and a multitude of recitals. Transfers were accepted and houses bought with Kayla and her brother's needs in mind. Kayla cannot recall a time when her parents failed to provide their loving support. Moreover, that support was always given with an extra dose of encouragement to "just do your best."

Kayla's church cares for her as well. In spite of limited resources, the small church has committed itself to providing for the spiritual needs of its children and adolescents. Kayla has been one of the beneficiaries of that commitment. The lay leadership team worked hard to help Kayla feel included when her family moved to the community in the middle of her seventh-grade year. One leader took a personal interest in Kayla. Gayle, a young mom with rambunctious twin toddlers, took time to share her world with Kayla. Tammy, wife of the part-time high school youth pastor, has recently taken a special interest in Kayla as well as her best friend, Kelsey. Tammy has provided encouragement, often sending the girls notes or inviting them to go for ice cream at the mall. Tammy also began a Bible study that meets twice a month with Kayla, Kelsey and two other girls.

Kayla receives love from her parents. At church she has been given spiritual care and encouragement through Gayle and Tammy. However, no one knows. No one knows the Kayla who quietly cries herself to sleep. No one knows the fear, shame and sadness that creep up within her soul. Kayla reconciles her hidden experience of herself and the obvious love of her spiritual caregivers with the thought *I would love me too if I believed what they see was the real me.* The genuine love she experiences from her caregivers penetrates only to the shallow levels of Kayla's façade. In spite of external evidence to the contrary, she is not experiencing being loved well.

No one really knows what is going on in fifteen-year-old Kayla's inner world. No one really knows her feelings of disgust about her body—feelings intensified by humiliating, guilt-laden experiences of sexual experimentation with a ninth-grade boyfriend. No one suspects that she has begun obsessing about her weight and is choosing baggy clothing because it minimizes her feminine appearance. No one knows that in Kayla's mind God has become a source of shame more than salvation. In silence and secrecy Kayla has learned to avoid God lest he confirm her worst fear—that at the core of her being she is undesirable and unlovable.

Listening Well, Loving Well

To some degree we all feel like Kayla. Only God knows the complete picture of our inner self. For Kayla, however, the distance between what she knows about herself and what others know about her is excruciating. If her heart is never "seen" and embraced by grace, Kayla will continue to live in parallel relational universes. In the surface world she is competent, engaged in a full range of social and family relationships. In her concealed self, however, she is insecure and isolated, longing for release from her self-protective imprisonment.[1]

How will the guilt and fear buried in her heart be exposed to and embraced by God's grace? If you are Tammy, where do you start? How do you pace with Kayla in order to lead her into the embrace of God's grace?

Listening well: the pacing process. In chapter one I defined *pacing* as listening to the thoughts, feelings and experiences of an adolescent. In the language of relationships, especially between adults and adolescents, the thought *No one understands the real me* translates into *No one loves the real me.* Adolescents who live as internal islands thus fail to experience the reality of a spiritual caregiver's love for them. Conversely, those who feel *heard* do feel *loved.* For Kayla's spiritual caregivers, then, as well as the rest of us, the challenge is to listen well, to the heart of Kayla and to the heart of God for Kayla. To be sure, listening well begins at the surface. Listening well, however, must have as its goal to fathom the deeper, hidden layers of her unseen self.[2]

Pacing by listening well is composed of two sacred relational acts: *pacing empathy* and *pacing prayer.* Pacing empathy moves caregivers, like spiritual miners, more deeply into the hidden regions of an adolescent's self, building on the principles of any empathic listening. Pacing prayer moves caregivers on a worshipful journey into the unseen depths of the heavenly Father's heart for this adolescent. Pacing prayer is therefore listening prayer.[3] We listen to adolescents through pacing empathy and to God through pacing prayer in order to be agents of his relational healing.[4]

Larry Crabb identifies two characteristics of healing communities that parallel pacing empathy and pacing prayer, respectively. Crabb describes *friendship* as "the art of caring engagement" and *spiritual direction* as "the art of discerning the deepest recesses of the soul with a sensitivity to what the Spirit is doing accompanied by offering one's presence to another."[5] Practicing pacing empathy and pacing prayer with reverence and authenticity creates an environment of relational healing. Like one of the paralytic's four friends, the spiritual caregiver offers himself as an interpersonal link to the Wonderful Counselor, Mighty God, Everlasting Father, Prince of Peace (Is 9:6).

The Art of Pacing Empathy

Pacing empathy is like interpersonal virtual reality. In pacing empathy I am entering into the way the world looks and feels from another person's point of view. Consider the contrast between the following conversations. The first conversation represents listening that seeks to identify from an external, surface point of view what is going on in an adolescent's world. The second conversation demonstrates listening that seeks a "virtual reality" experience of an adolescent's world.

Conversation 1

YOUTH PASTOR: Matt, you haven't been yourself lately. What's going on with you?

MATT: I don't know. Just stuff, I guess.

YOUTH PASTOR: What kind of stuff? Are things tough at home?

MATT: Not really.

YOUTH PASTOR: What about school?

MATT: It's okay—it's always boring, but I just expect that.

YOUTH PASTOR: How about your spiritual life? Are you getting good time with God?

MATT: I read my Bible most every day, if that's what you mean.

YOUTH PASTOR: Are you growing closer to God?

MATT: Yeah, pretty much. I know he's there for me, which is better than last year.

YOUTH PASTOR: Is your small group helping you grow closer to God too?

MATT: Yeah, you were right about getting in a small group—it really helps.

YOUTH PASTOR: Then what do you think has gotten you so down?

MATT: I don't think I'm really down . . . just maybe tired, I don't know.

YOUTH PASTOR: Well, you seem down to me. I think we should pray and ask God to give you strength, You know he promises that if those who wait upon him will renew their strength, they will mount up with wings like eagles, they will run and not be weary. I think you could use that strength. You seem pretty weary.

MATT: Yeah, I guess I am.

YOUTH PASTOR: Well, I've been through the same thing myself lately. Maybe we are experiencing the end of a long year or maybe it's spiritual warfare to keep both of us from seeing all the great things God wants to do in our lives. Let's pray for you and me both to ask God to give us his strength.

Conversation 2

YOUTH PASTOR: Matt, you seem like you've been feeling a little down lately.

MATT: No . . . I'm not feeling down. I just . . . I don't know. I've just got a lot going on, I guess.

YOUTH PASTOR: You sound like a guy who is pretty overwhelmed.

MATT: Yeah, wouldn't you be?

YOUTH PASTOR: Maybe I would. I could answer your question better if I knew more about what's gotten you so overwhelmed.

MATT: I don't know, just stuff.

YOUTH PASTOR: Stuff at school, at home, with your friends?

MATT: Yeah, all of it.

YOUTH PASTOR: So, you're overwhelmed by all the people and things in your life.

MATT: I'm just tired of having to make everybody else happy.

YOUTH PASTOR: Matt, I get the picture that you feel a lot of pressure to please everybody else, but you don't feel the freedom to please yourself.

MATT: No kidding. It's like my dad thinks I'm lazy because I don't improve my math grade—you know, I'm not like him, I'm not that good at math. My mom is constantly on me about the way my room looks or how I dress. Give me a break, you know I've got too much going on in my life to have to listen every day to her complaints about my room and clothes.

YOUTH PASTOR: That's the second time you've mentioned "a lot going on." You seem to have a lot of other demands in your life besides home.

MATT: Too much, man. Look at my life. I have to make honor roll to keep my driving privileges, so I have to make at least a 90 on my algebra test on Wednesday. I have to work ten hours at the hardware store this week because I took off last weekend for the youth leadership retreat. Our concert band has a competition on Saturday night, so we have extra practices all week. I still haven't started raising money for the mission trip to Mexico, and you just said tonight that if we are serious about going on the trip we should already be raising our support now. And here I am trying out for the city's traveling swim team—I have to swim my best times this week or there's no way I will make the cut. I don't even feel like swimming tomorrow, I might as well just give up.

YOUTH PASTOR: You do have a whole lot going on in your life, especially this week. It sounds like you're afraid you're going to fail at something that really matters to you.

MATT: I don't think I'm afraid, but I do think I'll probably spend all week studying and practicing and still blow the algebra test and the swim team—no matter how hard I try. Then I'll still be behind on the Mexico trip when you ask how we are doing next week. And my mom will still be nagging me about how messed up my room is, and my dad will be giving me a lecture on "applying myself" just before he grounds me from driving.

YOUTH PASTOR: Matt, I hear you saying you feel trapped because you feel like you are facing an impossible set of demands this week.

MATT: This week and the next and the next. It's like being on the *Titanic*—you're just watching it all go down and there is nothing you can do. It's like I'm drowning and there's nobody there to help.

YOUTH PASTOR: So, you're trapped in this impossible set of demands and you feel like there is nobody there for you.

MATT: Yeah, that's it. All anybody ever does is want more from me.

YOUTH PASTOR: That must feel pretty lonely.

MATT: Yeah, well, what are you going to do? That's just the way it is, I guess. I just gotta do what I gotta do.

YOUTH PASTOR: And you have to do it alone.

MATT: That's the way it's always been.

Both youth pastors are concerned about Matt. Both ask questions that attempt to discern what is happening in Matt's life. In the end, both have a sense of Matt's being overwhelmed by his life. The first youth pastor, however, comes away with the sense that Matt is just tired and needs God to (a) encourage him and (b) provide him with more strength. So he leads Matt to that place. By contrast, the second youth pastor understands that Matt is struggling *because* he feels trapped and alone as he faces what he sees as impossible demands. He is glimpsing the enormous pressure Matt feels in all areas of his life. If he is listening closely, he will recognize that Matt is even beginning to see the youth pastor through this same lens of "you must perform to my standards in order to be valued." Through a brief, three-dimensional "virtual reality" look from within Matt's world, this youth pastor can begin to sense how to pray for and introduce God's embrace of grace into Matt's life. He knows Matt needs God (a) to assure him that he is loved unconditionally with no performance stipulations attached, (b) to enable him to overcome the sense that he must make his life all by himself and (c) to give him wisdom for investing his time and energy given the multitude of demands he faces this week.

The pacing youth pastor has now shared in a significant part of Matt's internal experience of his world. With such insights, he is better prepared to lead Matt to places where he can receive the gifts he needs most.

Practicing Pacing Empathy

Pacing empathy cannot be reduced to a set of skills. As in all empathic listening, the techniques are "just the tip of the iceberg. The great mass of the iceberg is a deep and sincere desire to truly understand."[6] Pacing empathy does, however, include a set of relational behaviors that can be described, practiced and evaluated. These behaviors are *affirming, reflecting, clarifying, pausing* and *emptying oneself while respecting the process.* Each of them can be illustrated from the conversation between Matt and the second youth pastor.

Affirming. Opening our thoughts, feelings and experiences to another person is scary. The deeper we go, the scarier the process becomes. The spiritual caregiver must therefore proactively affirm the adolescent both for the choice to open up and for the content that is voiced. The most obvious way to do this, of course, is through direct statements: "I appreciate your being willing to be so honest with me," or "What you are saying really makes sense," or "It's OK to feel that way." Each of these statements affirms the individual by validating his communication.[7] When a spiritual caregiver senses significant uncertainty or uneasiness within the adolescent, such direct messages are critical.

The dialogue between Matt and the second youth pastor represents less direct approaches to affirming. First, the pastor affirms Matt by simply initiating the conversation. He lets Matt know that he has taken the time to notice him. His concern is stated in a nonthreatening statement of what he has observed: "Matt, you seem like you've been feeling a little down lately."

Second, he affirms Matt by respecting his question—"Yeah, wouldn't you be?" He could either dismiss Matt's question or become diverted by talking about himself. Instead he takes the question seriously and asks for Matt's help to understand Matt's world.

Third, he affirms the reality of the demands in Matt's world, "You do have a lot going on in your life, especially this week." Matt knows that his feeling overwhelmed by demands is understood and accepted. He feels affirmed for having verbalized what seems to him to be the source of his problem.

The choice to listen may be the most affirming aspect of the youth pastor's conversation with Matt. In the first scenario the youth pastor may report that he has listened to Matt and "ministered to him" in prayer. Matt would certainly feel that the youth pastor is concerned about him. However, he would not feel listened to or affirmed in what he is feeling. In fact, the implication is that he now needs to add something new to his list: he has to learn to trust God more! From what the second conversation revealed, we surmise that he will take this upon himself and try do it alone. Without consciously doing so, this youth pastor has set Matt up for a greater sense of inadequacy than he had before. He has also established personal distance between himself and Matt.

To listen well spiritual caregivers must *listen well!* Nothing affirms an adolescent like an adult who persists in listening to understand. Listening for understanding is infinitely more important than getting it right in terms of the techniques of pacing empathy.

Reflecting. Les Parrot III defines empathic reflection as "responding sensitively to the emotional rather than the semantic meaning of a person's expression."[8] Spiritual caregivers enable the adolescent to identify thoughts, feelings and experiences as they reflect back what they are hearing.

The youth pastor in conversation 2 uses several reflecting statements:

☐ "You sound like a guy who is pretty overwhelmed."

☐ "Matt, I get the picture that you feel a lot of pressure to please everybody else, but you don't feel the freeedom to please yourself."

☐ "So, you're trapped in this impossible set of demands and you feel like there is nobody there for you."

Contrast these reflections of what is being heard with the first youth pastor's approach:

- ☐ Is your small group helping you grow closer to God too?"
- ☐ "Then what do you think has gotten you so down?"
- ☐ "Well, you seem down to me" (in response to Matt's "I don't think I'm really down").
- ☐ "Well, I've been through the same thing myself lately."

Pacing empathy proceeds as the spiritual caregiver attempts to match what she is hearing with what is being said. Notice how some of Matt's responses in the second conversation confirm a communication match:

- ☐ "No kidding."
- ☐ "Yeah, that's it."
- ☐ "That's the way it's always been."

Each of these statements in the context of the conversation tells the youth pastor that Matt is experiencing being understood. What the pastor is saying back is what Matt is wanting to communicate. Matt grows in his confidence that the youth pastor has not only heard but has listened well.

Also note that when the youth pastor misses the match, he respects Matt's response and attempts to understand more clearly. When Matt tells him he is not afraid, the pastor listens for another feeling that would more accurately describe Matt's inner world. "Trapped" and "alone" prove better matches than "afraid." Contrast this to the first youth pastor, who invalidates Matt's "I'm not really down" with "Well, you seem down to me." This fails to affirm Matt; furthermore, refusing to accept the adolescent's perspective on a mismatch communicates "I am not really listening to you."

Reflecting has been accomplished when the adolescent can look into the words of the spiritual caregiver and see a mirror image of what he wants to communicate.[9] Reflecting requires discipline and patience on the part of the spiritual caregiver. No shortcut can circumvent the reflecting process— nor should anyone try. Pacing takes root in the process of reflecting.

Clarifying. "I thought you said you were going to . . ." These are words we don't want to hear often. Hearing them can lead to mild frustration, as when a husband and wife discuss who was supposed to pick up the dry cleaning this afternoon. Or it can lead to full-scale panic, such as when a husband and wife realize that no one picked up their eight-year-old after her soccer practice. Whatever the topic, communication is rarely complete without clarification.

Because all communication passes through the sending filter of one person and the receiving filter of another, spiritual caregivers seeking understanding will have to pursue multiple clarifications. Fostering pacing empathy in a relationship with an adolescent, given generational and cultural gaps, particularly demands effective use of clarification questions and statements. The first youth pastor uses clarification questions to probe ineffectively for all the things he thinks may be going wrong in Matt's life. He uses his categories to interrogate Matt, and when none of Matt's responses match his categories, he decides to impose his own conclusion. The second youth pastor, however, uses clarification to increase understanding of Matt's interpretation of and inner responses to his world:

☐ "That's the second time you've mentioned 'a lot going on.' You seem to have a lot of other demands in your life besides home."

☐ "And you have to do it alone."

The first clarification statement is designed to clarify Matt's perception of what is going on in his world. The pastor is certain he has not heard all of the pressures that feel like a snowball chasing Matt down the side of a mountain. The second statement seeks to evoke a clarification of feeling. He is not making a value statement but checking out Matt's sense of reality. The youth pastor thinks he has uncovered a critical feeling of loneliness in Matt. Rather than ask directly for a yes or no response, he offers Matt a chance to comment on the statement. Matt's response, "That's the way it's always been," clues the pastor in on where to enter into Matt's heart.

Reflecting and clarifying often go hand in hand. Consider how the following "empathy formulas" seek both to reflect and to clarify:

☐ "You feel _____ because (or when) _____."

☐ "It sounds like you are feeling _____, but I'm not sure what is making you feel that way."

☐ "On the one hand you feel _____ because _____, and on the other hand you feel _____ because _____."

In the midst of reflecting and clarifying, the bridge of communication can be washed out. There are several potential hazards to avoid during this phase of communication:

1. interpreting why an adolescent is feeling a certain way rather than enabling his exploration of his feelings' sources ("Matt, I think you are just tired because it's the end of a busy school year," or "God must be saying

something to you about how you spend your time")

2. pretending to understand when you really do not ("Wow, Matt, I see what you are saying")

3. parroting back phrases rather than using similar words and phrases in order to reflect and clarify (in response to "I don't even feel like swimming tomorrow, I might as well just give up," you say, "You don't feel like swimming tomorrow. You just want to give up, don't you?")

4. offering spiritual truth in the form of a cliché ("Matt, when I am in a situation like this, I just try to remember 'all things work together for good for those who love God,' " or "What would Jesus do, Matt?")

5. giving advice on how to change circumstances or feelings ("Matt, the first thing you need to do is pray that God will remind you that you are not alone," or "If you could just channel all that worrying into acing that algebra test and swimming those laps, I believe you could pull it off," or "I think you should consider giving up the swim team so that you can fulfill your other responsibilities")

6. sympathizing with feelings rather than pacing empathically ("Matt, I am so sorry to hear all of this. I had no idea that you had so many incredible demands on your life," or "Oh, Matt, that is so hard! How in the world are you making it with all of that pressure on you? No wonder you are so tired!")

Each of these responses fails to communicate "I am understanding you and I want to keep listening so that I can understand more clearly."

Pausing. Silence can be deafening, especially when you have the perspective *I am supposed to know what to say next.* A tearful eighth-grader who believes I have words to make her feel better can lead me to inflict a lot of pressure on myself. Maturing the discipline of the silent pause has, for me, been one of the most difficult challenges of learning to listen well.

We typically substitute default responses for silent pauses. The above six hindrances to reflecting and clarifying are examples of default responses. Because silence can feel relationally deafening, we default to saying something. Anxiously we think, *I am supposed to know what to say next.*

When words cease to flow, I remind myself that the goal of pacing is not to say the right thing. I focus my efforts on hearing the adolescent's true heart. I concern myself with what he needs to clarify regarding his thoughts and feelings. Silence provides time for reflecting on words already spoken, choosing new ways of communicating what we are sensing internally, and listening for God at work in the conversation.

The youth pastors' conversations with Matt do not afford specific examples of pause. However, no one is capable of effective, extended pacing empathy without strategic pauses. The responses in the second conversation could not emerge from rapid-fire dialogue. The wise spiritual caregiver therefore heeds the words of James, "be quick to listen, slow to speak" (Jas 1:19).

Emptying oneself while respecting the process. In *Giving the Love That Heals* Harville Hendrix and Helen Hunt offer this account of a son's experience with his stepfather:

> My stepfather's style almost never varied. First a slow and elaborate introduction to the subject at large, and finally, at the right moment, a sudden reduction to the essential. It was simple and remarkably successful—after the bewildering opening verbiage, he would turn eagerly, his eyes sparkling and his head thrown forward in a parody of anticipation to see the effect of his logic. It was always a difficult moment. He wanted more than a sign of recognition, a sign you had understood; he wanted you to *become him*, to discard immediately all ideas of your own and totally accept the closed frame of reference in which he saw whatever problem it was you were discussing.[10]

The son, Frank Conroy, experienced the polar opposite of pacing empathy. Young Frank was not important to the relational equation of his stepfather. The stepfather sought compliance, total conformity. The stepfather powered Frank with the intent of making Frank into a pseudo-clone of his unseen world. In the words of Hendrix and Hunt, "Frank has to act, think, talk, and feel just like him. He is there to be an actor in his stepfather's drama, to meet his stepfather's needs for affirmation and even affection."[11] Hendrix and Hunt refer to such an unhealthy relationship as *symbiotic*.[12] The relationship, and therefore the communication, is about the stepfather meeting his needs through Frank.

Unknowingly the youth pastor in the first dialogue is practicing symbiotic communication. He needs to know and fix whatever Matt is experiencing. He uses his categories, assumptions and expectations to frame the conversation. When Matt's self-disclosure fails to confirm any of what he was expecting, he chooses an interpretation that fits his agenda. He knows how to pray for Matt and give him scriptural counsel, so that must be the need. The first pastor, as I often do, fails to listen for the purpose of pacing empathically. He listens with the unconscious purpose of identifying a solution he can fix because *he is more focused on the goal of finding a solution than on the goal of pacing empathy.*

The second pastor does not attempt to bypass pacing in order to discover a solution. He does not *need* to fix Matt. Therefore he does not need Matt to fit into his categories, assumptions and expectations. He simply looks to Matt to guide him into understanding Matt's unseen real world. Matt is a complex set of thoughts, feelings and experiences to be engaged, understood and loved. Ultimately the youth pastor's "virtual reality" experience of Matt's world must be enabled by Matt. That was the Creator's design— for communication to be our window into each other's world.

Listening has to be learned. Creating a relational environment of genuine understanding is costly. Affirming, reflecting, clarifying, pausing and respecting the process require spiritual caregivers to empty themselves. We must empty ourselves of the need to be right, to feel in control, to demand internal conformity, to be successful at fixing adolescents and their problems, to elevate our own categories and assumptions, and to stay comfortable by using default responses as substitutes for listening well. Moreover, spiritual caregivers are asked to embrace the process as God's, not their own. We are never called to do God's work. We are rather privileged to be called to join God's work. In our lives and in the adolescents we love, we are always joining a work in progress.

The Art of Pacing Prayer

Spiritual caregivers who pace with adolescents are partners rather than pioneers. They are not charting new territory as they come alongside an adolescent's thoughts, feelings and life experiences. They are following after God as the One who precedes them in his redemptive work.[13] To follow in partnership with God's work includes a commitment to pacing prayer, the power that joins pacing empathy in supporting spiritually engaging relationships.

David affirms his experience of an unseen God at work in his unknown self in Psalm 51. Here David aches with repentance for the sin that had spewed forth from dark layers of his inner man. He prays, "Behold, you desire truth in the inward parts, and in the hidden part you will make me to know wisdom" (v. 8).

If David could experience an intimate, searching God within his inner self, then certainly those of us who stand this side of Pentecost can anticipate the depths of God's pacing and leading. Those who truly call him "Father" have received an indwelling of the personal, intimate presence of his Spirit (Rom 8:14-27). In the New Testament we find the Spirit confirming our relationship with the Father (vv. 15-16), interceding for us (vv. 26-27), guiding us into truth (Jn 14:5-7), comforting us (vv. 25-27), enabling us (2 Tim 1:7), empowering us (Acts 1:8), renewing us (2 Cor 3:18-21) and reproducing Christ within us (Gal 5:16-25)—and that's just a part of the picture! The Spirit acts as the Christian's personal guide into who God is, who we truly are and the formation of our relationship with him.

What then is the spiritual caregiver's role in partnership with God's Spirit in Kayla's or Matt's life? Ultimately the caregiver hopes to guide adolescents into experiencing their own personal, internal pacing and leading of the Spirit. Caregivers should not wait, however, for an adolescent's readiness to join the Spirit at work. Kayla, for instance, is not presently compelled to connect with God on an intimate level. When confronted with spiritual defensiveness, caregivers should not attempt to force readiness; spiritual pressure would be the antithesis of pacing. Instead Kayla's spiritual caregivers must begin by engaging God in pacing prayers on her behalf.

The pacing prayers of spiritual caregivers. Adult prayers for adolescents generally center on specific requests for God to make something happen. "Dear God, please help John be a strong witness on his soccer team." "Dear God, please protect Mary from the ridicule of the popular crowd in her homeroom." "Dear God, please give Hank a stronger sense of your love for him." Each of these prayers is outstanding. Asking God for strength, protection and confirmation should be an essential component of prayer times for all of our adolescents. In calling for pacing prayer I do not suggest we stop praying for God's provision and protection in adolescents' lives. However, these are not pacing prayers. Pacing prayer can be exemplified as follows:

> Dear Father, you know Matt so much better than I ever will. You also love him more than I ever could. I want to join you in your relationship with him. I want to be your partner in affirming truth and ministering grace to his life. God, help me pace with your work in him. Through your Word, your Spirit, your ordering of his circumstances, the lifestyle he is living and the godly

people you have placed in his life, open my eyes to see you at work in him. Help me find your fingerprints on his life. Help me see more clearly where he needs you most today. Confirm through your Spirit in me those places where my loving words and actions can point him to your loving words and actions. Give me a listening heart that can hear between the lines of his life, to see his need and your response. Guide me into a true vision of how I can enter into what lies below the surface of Matt.

Pacing prayer focuses on pacing with God's Spirit at work within the unseen person. To fail to enter into dialogue with the Spirit at work in an adolescent's life would be like a dad and mom trying to parent their child without ever discussing the child with each other. Rather than beginning with "What do I need to do *for* God in Matt's life?" the caregiver begins with "What do I need to do *with* God in Matt's life?"

Each of my three children is unique. Each builds relationships very differently, each receives affirmation in a particular way, and each approaches relationship with God very differently. After two decades of youth ministry, I have likewise found that adolescents are personally, and therefore spiritually, like snowflakes—no two are exactly the same.

As a parent I often come to places where I do not understand how to reach into my daughter's or sons' inner worlds. As a pastor I get confused as to how I can touch the unseen rivers running deep below the surface of an adolescent who seems stuck in his spiritual walk. Trying harder will not help. Reading more books will not help. Pulling back would be the worst response of all. I have but one place to turn: pacing with the God who creates and sees our unseen worlds.

Listening for the leading. Pacing prayer is incomplete until the heart of the one praying listens for an answer. Such listening cannot be confined to a time frame. There is no prayer formula such as "talk for five minutes, listen for ten." Neither can the response to listening be controlled by the one praying. Pacing prayer can only be described as a posture of listening prayer.

A call to listen to God must acknowledge that rarely does he speak to the physical ear. I have never personally experienced an audible voice from God, though I would not preclude the possibility. However, on a number of occasions I have "heard" God clearly. Sometimes it was through the Word of God, as I read through Scripture seeking to learn more about him. At other times I "heard" him through the wise counsel of a friend. "Hearing" God simply amounts to having his Spirit confirm within us that there is truth in what we are sensing as we listen for his shepherding voice. As a father and a shepherd, I want to be leading adolescents toward God's voice. To teach them to be followers of his voice, I must learn to follow him myself.

How do I practice pacing prayer? First, I engage God in dialogue concerning what the Word teaches me about being a parent and mentor. I listen for his guidance as I meditate on the significance of his truth for my current spiritual caregiving relationships.

Second, in my daily spiritual caregiving I listen *with* him as I reflect on adolescent behaviors that indicate a "God-need" or God at work. I am quick to label actions "selfish," "immature" or "rebellious." I need God's guidance for seeing the need behind the behavior. What is the adolescent seeking through this behavior? How can that need for love or esteem be met in a way that leads to a deeper sense of God's love for and value of him? What can I do—even when I apply discipline to correct behavior—to enable God's "I love you" to be heard more clearly?

Third, I ask the Father to open my eyes in my pacing empathy. I want to "see" with discernment greater than my natural ability. Just a few hours ago, on a break from writing, I became angry and raised my voice at one of my children. As I reflected on my child's response, I sensed that I had wounded him with my abruptness. I became convicted that my anger was more about me than about the child's behavior. I was further convicted that raising my voice had been inappropriate.

As I prayed for insight, I asked him to help me understand what it felt like to be my son in that situation. I wanted to reach back into that place and touch the wound with healing love. Then as I sat down to grab a snack and zone out in front of the television for half an hour, I caught the beginning of a *Dateline* story on anger in the home. For twenty minutes I listened as parents and children discussed how it feels when someone yells at you, why raising your voice is a poor way of resolving problems, and how saying "I'm sorry" is an important part of healing the wounds inflicted by angry voices. All I could think of was my son's face when I had spoken harshly to him.

God had answered my prayer for him to speak to me—through a television show! Now I knew what my son was feeling, and I knew I had to find him, ask his forgiveness and pray for God to complete the healing.

Fourth, I ask God to speak to me through wise friends and mentors. I look to my own "pacers" to guide me into a greater understanding of his will for the inner lives of Jessica, Zachary, Benjamin and those who look to me for spiritual care. I do not want to parent or pastor alone. I trust God to use wise friends to teach me what I could never know on my own. I am convinced that those who refuse to find relational support in their own lives will never be effective relational supports in the lives of others.

Finally, I listen to God at work in my inner being, learning to be a child who connects with the Father who loves me unconditionally and faithfully. I have always been better at being an adult than being a child. As an only child of teenage parents, I grew up in a young adult world. I was socially twenty before I reached the age of twelve. Every day I am learning more of what it means to be a child. I am learning to listen, to trust, to follow. As I experience being God's child, I ask him to teach me how to share that experience in ways that are meaningful for those to whom I give spiritual care. Honestly, I would rather be the leader first. I am called, however, to be the child as my primary role. I want to lead, but first I must listen with pacing prayer.

Potential Pitfalls of Pacing Prayer

I am relatively new at pacing prayer. The methodology I am describing has grown out of repeatedly trying to pace *for* God rather than *with* God in my spiritual caregiving relationships. Even in this novice state, however, I have encountered two pitfalls that can subtly disrupt the pacing process.

The first pitfall has already been foreshadowed: *focusing on fixing rather than pacing*. I am often impatient with pacing prayer, particularly for my children. Soon after I enter a listening posture with God, my mind begins racing toward ideas and action plans that can be implemented. I am looking for solutions. I fall into the attitude that I have gone "online" with God to get new information to instruct my course of action.

Genuine pacing prayer does not dwell on asking God to reveal new caregiving assignments. Pacing prayer is like an ultrasound, searching with the Spirit for what cannot be seen on the surface. Later, in the leading process, we will need to act. If we jump too quickly to the prescription, however, we are likely to be responding to an incomplete diagnosis.

The second danger of pacing prayer is *imposing my will on the adolescent's life*. A common faulty logic for all types of listening prayer goes like this: *God speaks to me not through words but through strong feelings and impressions. Therefore the stronger the feeling or impression, the more likely that God has truly spoken to me.* If only life were so simple. At best I can say only, "I believe God is teaching me . . ." or "I sense God saying to me . . ." My subjective apprehensions of God's heart cannot be translated as authoritative revelation for my life. More important, they cannot become authoritative messages for those whom I love.

I have seen children, youth and adults deeply wounded by "I believe God is saying to you . . ." or "God is telling me that the issue you are facing is really . . ." The purpose of seeking to understand God's work in adolescents' lives is not to enable us to tell them our version of God's perspectives. The potential for interjection of our personal agenda is enormous. We must resist the urge to use God as a basis for saying what we want adolescents to hear.

Therefore when we believe God is giving us insight into the inner world of an adolescent, our posture should continue to be listening, pacing empathy. We pray pacing prayers so that we can see how to build more meaningful pacing relationships, not to act as God's authoritative messenger for an adolescent's life.[14]

As a corollary I have also seen the weakness of *substituting pacing prayer for pacing empathy.* In spiritual caregiving God never calls us to replace deep interpersonal relationships with relationship to him. Praying to God *about* an adolescent can feel much safer than listening well to an adolescent's inner world. We feel much more in control without the variable of the adolescent in the equation. Pacing empathy without pacing prayer fails to shepherd well the lives of those we are leading.

There are times, of course, when an adolescent is unwilling to open herself to be known and understood. Parents and pastors should not feel guilty because they cannot find a way to get through. Sometimes adolescents, out of anger or fear, block all entry points. Then pacing prayer becomes our only means for seeking to understand. However, falling back on prayer because it is easier rather initiating a listening relationship with the adolescent is not acceptable. God designed adolescents with a genuine *need* for pacing empathy from their spiritual caregivers.

A God Who Paces with Spiritual Caregivers

On my wife's most recent birthday, I bought a nice gift bag and filled it with several items I thought she would like. I also brought home a small bouquet of flowers. To my amazement, my birthday surprises did not place me in the winner's circle as this year's Outstanding Birthday Husband. In fact, I found myself in the loser's bracket. Each of the gifts was *similar to* something she had asked for in previous weeks. None of the gifts was what she truly wanted.

For instance, days before she had commented, "If you get me flowers for my birthday, please remember that I would love some fresh tulips." I nodded cheerfully. On her birthday, however, I proceeded to select a spring bouquet that included no tulips. Rather than giving my wife a reminder of my love, I presented her with several concrete examples of my lack of pacing as a husband.

I am certain my children too often experience the same lack of pacing with their dad. I am also certain that the adolescents *and* adults in my life have often felt misunderstood by me. I am comforted, however, by the realization that spiritual caregiving is not about getting it all right. Spiritual caregiving is about growing a right relationship. I need to be embraced by the same grace that I hope to share with others. I have to experience God's embrace of grace if I am to pace with and lead others to that place of rest.

What astounds me is the degree to which God paces with me as the perfect spiritual caregiver.

> Therefore, since we have a great high priest who has gone through the heavens, Jesus the Son of God, let us hold firmly to the faith that we profess. For we do not have a high priest who is unable to sympathize with our weaknesses, but we have one who has been tempted in every way, just as we are—yet was without sin. Let us then approach the throne of grace with confidence, so that we may receive mercy and find grace to help us in our time of need. (Heb 4:14-16)

In pacing empathy Jesus hears my weaknesses and sins, then responds with mercy and grace. He has gone before me so that I may follow him to the Father's embrace of grace (Heb 6:19, 20).

My highest challenge as a spiritual caregiver is not leading. Leading connects me with answers that never change. Pacing connects me to ever-changing questions. Pacing is thus my greatest challenge—I am left to pace with God at work in me as well as God at work in the unpredictable worlds of adolescents' lives. I have to learn to walk in rhythm with God *and* with the rhythm of an adolescent's life. In doing so I recognize that I am both subject and object in the incredible mystery of God's redemptive work in those to whom I provide spiritual care.

Reflecting on Your Journey

☐ In terms of pacing empathy, I would have to say that I am a (circle one) novice, experienced beginner, intermediate-level practitioner, seasoned veteran, expert.

☐ When I read the two youth pastors' conversations with Matt, I recognized myself when one of them said, _____
_____.

☐ My biggest hindrances to pacing empathy are_____
_____.

☐ The one skill I could develop that would bring immediate improvement in my pacing empathy is_____
_____.

☐ When I read the section on pacing prayer, my initial response was to (choose one) strongly agree, agree, disagree, strongly disagree. The development of the concept of pacing prayer left me with the following questions:

_____

_____

☐ How do you feel when you read of God's pacing with you as his child? Do you commonly recognize God's pacing with you, or does this seem to be distant from your daily experiences? What hindrances do you want to see removed from your life so that you can more thoroughly enjoy God's companionship?

Pressing In

☐ Read the empathic listening sections of Harville Hendrix and Helen Hunt's *Giving the Love That Heals* and Stephen Covey's *The Seven Habits of Highly Effective Families*. What do you learn from these authors who are not in the Christian faith? How does your faith reframe or enrich their understandings of intimate human communication?

☐ Invite close friends to critique you as a listener. How do they experience you when a feeling is expressed? when a misunderstanding occurs in communication? Do they feel confident that you not only *want* to hear them but *are working* to hear them? Where would they suggest improvement?

☐ Ask an adolescent you know to respond to the same questions of critique.

☐ Choose a partner with whom you can practice empathic listening skills.

Though the practice may seem stilted at first, as you push through the experience you will find yourself becoming a more disciplined, self-aware listener.

☐ Read Leanne Payne's *Listening Prayer.* Pray with God and explore his Word in a journey toward owning a more personally meaningful understanding of pacing prayer.

☐ Set aside time weekly for pacing prayer with God in relationship to the adolescents in your life.

☐ Search the Scriptures to read the prayers of the patriarchs, prophets, psalmists, apostles and Jesus himself. How do these prayers reflect the principles of being paced with by God and pacing with God as one partners in ministry with his Spirit?

The most important thing about any of us is the image of God we carry in our hearts.
SCOTTY SMITH & MICHAEL CARD, *UNVEILED HOPE*

No one can love God and not be a theologian. No one can follow Christ and not be committed to taking truth seriously.
OS GUINNESS AND JOHN SEEL, *NO GOD BUT GOD*

To teach is to create a space in which obedience to truth is practiced.
PARKER PALMER, *TO KNOW AS WE ARE KNOWN*

Do not let any unwholesome talk come out of your mouths, but only what is helpful for building others up according to their needs, that it may benefit those who listen.
EPHESIANS 4:29

Like apples of gold in settings of silver is a word spoken in right circumstances.
PROVERBS 25:11

Sanctify them in the truth.
JOHN 17:17

Go, sell your possessions and give to the poor, and you will have treasure in heaven. Then come, follow me.
MATTHEW 19:21, SPOKEN TO THE RICH YOUNG MAN

I tell you the truth, the tax collectors and the prostitutes are entering the kingdom of God ahead of you.
MATTHEW 21:31, SPOKEN TO THE CHIEF PRIESTS AND ELDERS IN JERUSALEM

You have a fine way of setting aside the commands of God in order to observe your own traditions!
MARK 7:9, SPOKEN TO THE PHARISEES AND TEACHERS OF THE LAW

5

How to Speak the Truth in Love

*J*esus not only spoke and taught truth, he identified himself as "the way and the truth and the life" (Jn 14:6). Because of who he was and the truth he taught, he left no option concerning a disciple's responsibility to heed his commands and corrections. To recently converted Jews he said, "If you hold to my teaching, you are really my disciples. Then you will know the truth, and the truth will set you free" (Jn 8:31-32). To the Twelve he revealed, "If you love me, you will obey what I command" (Jn 14:15). To encounter Jesus relationally was to encounter Truth that demands an obedient response.

Pacing opens windows into previously uncovered regions of adolescents' minds and hearts. To shepherd well spiritual caregivers must couple pacing prayer and pacing empathy with speaking the truth into those newly discovered regions. The expression of truth will be in response to the need revealed in the student's heart.

In some places we will find evidence of God at work revealing himself and transforming his child into the glorious image of his Son. We will catch glimpses of love, joy, peace and all the fruits of the Spirit in those whom he indwells. In these places of redemptive health, the truth serves as a rudder to point the soul toward its desired destination: God's will.

Pacing well with an adolescent will ultimately lead to the discovery of hidden sinful attitudes, selfish desires and lack of faith in who God is. Idolatry is in our sinful DNA, and only the final resurrection will complete our transformation into perfect worshipers of the one true God. All believers still cling to remnants of the myth that we can be our own gods. In these self-centered places, the truth acts as a light to expose a soul in need of repentance.

Finally, pacing will lead spiritual caregivers into recesses in adolescents' inner lives that are in need of affirmation more than direction or confrontation. Adolescents will need the encouragement that truth brings concerning their identity, their call to make an impact for Christ in their world and the rewards that await those who choose obedience over immediate gratification. In these maturing places, the truth acts as a source of nourishment to bring the soul to life.

When and how, then, do spiritual caregivers transition from listening well to "speaking the truth in love" (Eph 4:15-16)? How do you speak truth without shutting down the pacing process? How do caring adults speak the truth in love even when they sense indifference, resistance or rebellion in the heart of an adolescent? How can a spiritual caregiver be confident that speaking the truth is appropriate even though he knows the adolescent may respond negatively, perhaps with shame or anger? When does a spiritual caregiver risk the relationship itself because the truth must be spoken?

To equip spiritual caregivers to become increasingly wise and loving truth-sayers, two sets of principles are developed respectively in chapters five and six. In this present chapter we examine *principles for speaking the truth in love*. In the following chapter we explore *principles for confronting and resolving conflict*.

How important should these principles be considered in the relationships between spiritual caregivers and their students? *The Gift of the Blessing* provides a powerful illustration of the significance of our spoken words:

> With words, we can express acceptance and love, both vital to emotional health and well-being, or we can express rejection and degradation.
>
> As an example, Denise grew up in a home where her father saw to it that she received every element of the blessing. He encouraged her, went to her sports activities and school open houses, and supported her every way he could.
>
> One of the most supportive memories for Denise was his pet name for her:

Angel Darling. He even made up a little song that used her pet name and told of his love. The last time she heard the song was just before her father died. He asked her to sit on the edge of his bed, gave her a hug, and sang the Angel Darling song to his "little girl."

Denise said, "It was hurtful and healing at the same time. I hurt because I knew it was the last time I'd ever hear him sing my song, but it meant so much to me. It was Dad's way of saying, 'You're special and I've always loved you.' "

Donna grew up in the opposite kind of home. Donna's father provided one of the most degrading homes imaginable. Donna was tall and slender, stunningly attractive, but when I met her she refused to dress in any color but black. In part, her color choice came from the darkness she carried inside from hearing the nickname her father called her each day, *Demon Daughter.* Donna lived a miserable life until she met Christ and he freed her from the title her father had bestowed.[1]

Spoken truth has the potential to encourage, enable and empower a person to live a life of freedom. Even truth that is initially painful leads us to that place of freedom. Consider our own hearing of the gospel. In the midst of the truth that we are all condemned to death in our sinfulness (Rom 3:23; 6:23) lies the rest of the story: we are set free from sin and death by the loving, atoning sacrifice of our Lord Jesus Christ (7:24; 8:2). Spoken truth must therefore always represent the fullness of who God is; the God who at once seals our fate in his holiness and rescues us from that fate in his grace. Such words contain the "power of God unto salvation" (1:16 KJV).

Principles for Leading with the Truth

Jesus spoke truth in perfect pace with a person's unseen self. Ours is an ongoing learning process enabled by pacing empathy, pacing prayer and the disciplined practice of exercising our responsibility to lead with the truth in love. Each of the following nine principles reflects the commitment to speak the truth in love in pace with God at work in the adolescent's life. Each principle assists the spiritual caregiver in creating an environment that will foster loving truth-saying.

Principle 1: Reflective Self-Awareness

A spiritual caregiver's self-awareness must be fostered through reflection on the feelings, pressures and internal struggles that may be inappropri-

ately shaping the communication of truth to an adolescent.

Without thoughtful reflection on the *why* behind the *what* of our communication, we all find ourselves manifesting reactive styles of speaking the truth.[2] Kevin Huggins contextualizes Ephesians 4:29 as "Do not let any response motivated by personal need come out of your mouths, but only such a response that is directed at the strengthening of your adolescent according to his need at the moment, that it may be beneficial for his relationship with Christ."[3] Elsewhere Huggins writes to parents of adolescents, "Operating nonreflectively as parents, with little or no awareness of the motivational forces within, is the single most important obstacle to being effective parents."[4] Certainly the same can be said of all spiritual caregivers. Speaking the truth in love, whether for direction, confrontation or affirmation requires consistent self-reflection on the part of the parent, pastor or mentor. Without an informed self-awareness, we run the risk of communicating truth to the adolescent for *our* benefit, another symbiotic form of communication.[5]

Principle 2: A Right Goal and Right Expectations

A spiritual caregiver's goal must be simply to speak the truth in love; the only expectation should be faithfulness.

☐ Jeremy's frustration with Tommy had reached his limit. He knew something had to change. He simply could not handle any more of Tommy's attitude in their small group. Tommy was like rotten fruit spreading decay among the once-healthy group members. Jeremy finally decided to "straighten out" Tommy. He called him aside after the youth meeting to confront Tommy's behavior.

☐ Janice knew her daughter, Allison, did not feel good about herself. Allison's constant attempts to draw attention to herself were embarrassing to Janice and the rest of the family. Janice decided to begin affirming Allison so that she would no longer have to beg for attention. She gave Allison a list of Scriptures to memorize concerning her identity in Christ and daily reminded her that the acceptance she really needed was from God.

Both Jeremy and Janice choose wisely to respond to the need for truth to be spoken into an adolescent's life. Their responses both have merit as well. However, from the beginning the goal is flawed. Each is responding reactively rather than proactively loving well. Jeremy and Janice both have goals for changing behaviors. Jeremy needs Tommy to change the way he is affecting the group. Janice needs Allison to stop embarrassing the family. Because the truth is being directed at external behavior changes, they are failing to speak the truth primarily on behalf of Tommy and Allison. Their goals relate to their own needs for behavioral changes more than the adolescents' needs for hearing the truth in love.

Adolescents are like drug-sniffing police dogs when it comes to hidden agendas. They can smell a symbiotic message a relational mile away. Jeremy needs to confront Tommy, and Janice needs to affirm Allison. But they need to change their goal from what they cannot control to what they can.[6] Their expectations for causing immediate, visible change should be altered as well. While words are powerful, they often need time to take root. You do not water a garden with a fire hydrant. The best watering is with a soaker hose. A steady, consistent stream of truth always has a greater impact than a sudden full-force blast.

When spiritual caregivers expect immediate results they set up themselves and their adolescent friends for relational frustration. I have learned that God's processes usually fail to submit to the demands of my expectations. The fruit is in God's hands—it may or may not be what we had hoped.

Principle 3: Sufficient Trust
Spiritual caregivers must earn the right for their truth to be heard.

One of the most significant factors for receiving spoken truth well is the level of relationship between spiritual caregiver and adolescent. All communication theorists affirm that relational context plays an important role in what is heard and how it is interpreted. The right to be heard can only be earned through trust building. Trust can be built only by effective pacing over an extended period. To rush into confronting or directing with the truth before trust has been deposited in the "relational bank" feels threatening to the adolescent.[7]

Principle 4: Accurate Timing
Spiritual caregivers should listen for what is presently being experienced before choosing to speak the truth into an adolescent's life.

My wife, a therapist, intervened on a number of potentially life-threatening personal crises while counseling at a college. One of her key principles in working with suicidal students was "Do not try to reason theologically with a person who is overcome with anger and despair." The person has to be heard, to be paced with, before she or he is prepared to pace with God's revelation of himself in Scripture.

The same principle applies to less intense situations in spiritual caregiving. The truth is like a surgeon's tool, not a club. The correct entry point is critical to effective use of the truth. Using the truth to try to correct what a person is feeling without having heard those feelings is unwise. It's important to wait for emotional fog to begin to clear around the unseen self before asking a person to see the truth clearly.

That fog may involve anger at parents or a sense of guilt over sin. Leading with the truth is critical. Waiting for the appropriate time to speak is just as critical. Rebuking an attitude or affirming God's grace *before* understanding what an adolescent is presently thinking or feeling can foster a shallow reception of and response to the spoken truth.

Principle 5: Accurate Pacing Empathy
Spiritual caregivers' level of boldness in leading with the truth should directly correlate to their level of confidence in the accuracy of their empathic pacing.

Related to the need for proper timing is the need for accurate pacing empathy. Recently I pointed out a truth of Scripture that challenged an aspect of a friend's family relationships. The "what are you talking about?" look I received indicated that I had aimed my leading at the wrong target.

We need to take special care in the clarification process of pacing empathy. Trust is gained when an adolescent experiences congruence between how you see her and her own experience of her life. Even if the caregiver is wrong, if the concern is plausible the adolescent usually feels personally valued. If, however, the caregiver has totally missed, the adolescent feels more misunderstood than before.

Principle 6: Respect the Adolescent
Spiritual caregivers should, whenever possible, act as facilitators and guides as they lead with the truth.

Unintentionally, spiritual caregivers often communicate to adolescents, "I don't think you are capable of knowing yourself and taking responsibility for your self-care in relationship with God." We do this when we take too much ownership in the adolescent's process of maturity. We begin to feel overly responsible to help them solve their problems or fix their lives.

Or we shortcut their discovery of the truth by providing lots of right answers rather than asking meaningful questions.

Some issues call for being direct, even blunt, in speaking the truth. In most cases, however, speaking the truth should be more like giving a person his own flashlight than shining our own light onto the path that lies ahead of him.

Principle 7: Relational Follow-Through
Spiritual caregivers must make a commitment to follow through relationally once the truth has been communicated.

Truth-speaking must be not only preceded by and presented with love but followed by love. A parent, pastor or mentor who seeks to lead with the truth must be committed to leading with truth *and* love. Failure to provide supportive shepherding to help an adolescent walk out truth is like demonstrating to a nonswimmer the front crawl and then throwing her into the middle of a lake with a hearty "You can do it!" The truth is she *can* learn to swim, but she needs coaching in a safer environment before she will be successful on her own. Applying this principle in combination with respect for adolescents' personal relationship with God creates a safe, effective environment for their growth in grace.

Principle 8: Clear Communication
Spiritual caregivers should communicate truth in a manner that fosters clear understanding.

"But I don't want to hurt her." I hear this often from spiritual caregivers. A small group leader's love for the student makes him hesitant to say things that may be painful to hear. Or a parent fears that being truly honest will cause the adolescent to alienate herself. Such hesitance can lead adults to speak truth so vaguely that it has no impact on the adolescent other than to confuse her.

It is not sufficient to have said something truthfully; it needs to be able to be *understood* truthfully. Spiritual caregivers therefore ought to (a) think carefully and prayerfully about how they will speak truth that feels uncomfortable, (b) pace, using clarification questions, with the adolescent's understanding of the truth and (c) avoid indirect forms of communication such as hints or broad theological ideas that do not connect clearly with the adolescent's world.

Principle 9: Authentic Representation of God and Scripture

Spiritual caregivers need to communicate God and his truth in a way that is consistent with who he has revealed himself to be.

Spiritual caregivers must reckon with this awesome truth: we are often adolescents' most authoritative sources for understanding who God is. We should not take lightly our role in leading with his truth. Whenever we share Scripture, speak of our experiences with God or offer our perspective on how God views what the adolescent is telling us, we must reflectively ask ourselves, *Is this consistent with who God reveals himself to be?*

None of us has an absolutely correct concept of God. Thus none of us could ever paint a comprehensively accurate portrait of God. This does not, however, relieve us of the call to communicate God as accurately as possible. Particularly when introducing Scripture or own experiences with God, we should ask ourselves, *How is the adolescent seeing God as a result of this communication?*

It is possible to say true things about God, even to read from Scripture, in a way that leads to an unhealthy interpretation. For instance, reading Jesus' teachings on forgiveness to an adolescent who has been deeply wounded without providing a larger context for understanding what forgiveness means could cause the adolescent to feel that God is emotionally abusive.

Life is louder than words. For communicating an accurate picture of God, the caregiver's life will be as important as the content she speaks.

Pacing and Leading with Love: Melanie's Story

Melanie presented one of my greatest challenges for pacing and leading in love. She was a vibrant college student who had a true gift for ministry. At her request, we met to discuss an issue that she described as "confusing to me." I anticipated a theological discussion, perhaps about knowing God's will for her life. I was therefore a bit stunned when Melanie asked for insight concerning her lesbian relationship with a Christian friend.

When Melanie chose to move in with Charlotte, the arrangement seemed ideal. Both were struggling to get through school on limited budgets, each was seeking a deeper intimacy with God, and they had both felt isolated from the support of Christian friends over the past year. Soon after they began rooming together they began a weekly Bible study, which in turn spawned a commitment to pray together daily. Somewhere in the middle of all this, Melanie reported, they began to mix spiritual sharing with increasingly intimate physical touch. The relationship had progressed into a sexual one, which was especially confusing because of its connection to their Bible studies and prayer. Charlotte assured Melanie that God had blessed their relationship. Melanie, on the other hand, sensed that something was not right. What she could not sort out was whether her guilt was a genuine conviction of the Holy Spirit or a false guilt based on inaccurate church teachings. Melanie had agonized over all of this alone for too long. So she came to me for counsel.

I was startled. I had no category in my mind that would have placed Melanie in this situation. Prior to this relationship, neither had Melanie. After she told her story, she asked, "Does God think it is a sin for me to have this kind of a relationship with Charlotte?"

I immediately felt the need to say "Yes!" I knew several Scriptures that could be used to point Melanie toward God's teachings regarding homosexuality. Yet in my heart I knew that the question she was asking was not an accurate representation of her unseen self.

Melanie knew my answer to that question before she posed it—she knew her own answer too. She needed more than a predictable theological interpretation of Scripture.

My response to her was "Melanie, I will tell you what I believe. But first I want to know more about what is going on with you. How do *you* think God sees this relationship?"

For a long while Melanie spoke of her anger and confusion over God's apparent conflicting leading in her life. She wondered why God would answer her prayers for a close Christian friend, knowing that it would lead to sexual relationship, and then condemn her for that relationship. She questioned why God would ask her to give up the best friendship she had ever had over something that had felt so right until recently. Melanie felt betrayed by God. She did not like where she was, but she had no idea where to go now. Melanie felt trapped: neither way out seemed to promise anything but pain and grief. God seemed less like a resource to help and more like the source of the problem.

After an hour, I spoke truth into Melanie's life. First, I assured her that God had created her for intimacy, with him and others. God had no intention of condemning her to a life without the intimate relationships for which she had prayed. From pacing with Melanie I was certain that this was the heart of the matter for her. I had no doubt that she wanted out of the lesbian relationship. However, she greatly feared losing the most important relationship in her life.

Second, I told Melanie that her choice at this point was not God or Charlotte. Her choice was simply "Am I willing to trust God with my life, no matter what I may discover his will to be?" Melanie assured me that she did want only to do God's will but God's apparent betrayal left her feeling mistrustful of him. I reflected to Melanie my understanding of how she arrived at those feelings. This led to another opportunity to speak the truth in love. I challenged her not to make this simply an issue of God's will for her sexual preference. I confronted Melanie about how she was approaching God as her judge rather than as her Father and Redeemer. I encouraged her to open all of her fears, hurts and needs to God; to tell him that although she loved him, she did not trust him very much right now. I then talked with her about how to invite God into her process rather than keeping her distance for fear of condemnation.

When I was certain that she had understood my words about her relationship with God, I spoke about her relationship with Charlotte. I voiced my conviction that Scripture clearly identifies homosexuality as a sin. I asked her, during this period when she would be trying to decide for herself, to abstain from a sexual relationship with Charlotte. She agreed to do so.

After our next meeting she also agreed to accept my referral to a Christian therapist who I believed could do a better long-term job of helping her work through the intimacy issues that had set her up for crossing a moral boundary with Charlotte.

My leading with truth did not provide any immediate answers for solving Melanie's relational confusion. She did not leave with all the answers she had asked for when she asked to meet with me. In fact, she had a whole new set of questions to work with now. In the pacing and leading, however, she had walked with me into a new place in her relationship with God. Melanie discovered how to open her core thoughts and feelings to her Father rather than try to "correct" them before a Judge.

Had I simply given all the answers, they would have been digested within the same relational framework with God; he would have remained as distant as ever. Had I only paced with no clear speaking of the truth, God would also have remained distant. Pacing combined with speaking the truth in love, however, enabled Melanie to tell God, "I will obey you, but please help me learn to trust you again too. I want to love you and be loved by you—but I cannot do that without you." In so doing she learned that God wanted more than just to get her to choose sexual purity; he wanted her to experience being chosen by him.

Reflections on Speaking the Truth in Love

Melanie's struggle with homosexuality provides a complex example of how one must lead simply with the truth. There is no magic formula, no perfect phrase, no expert advice to be discovered. Just listening, learning, loving and leading in harmony with the grace and truth of Jesus. Fortunately, most of our truth-encounters with adolescents are much less complicated than this one, though no less significant. Leading adolescents will require us routinely to speak hope into shattered dreams, healing into broken families, acceptance into dark corners of self-rejection and forgiveness into shame-based condemnation.

When I think of my role as a spiritual caregiver, I envision myself being called to connect an adolescent's places of hurt, shame, fear, doubt and loneliness with the healing touch of Jesus. Through empathic and accurate words of truth, through time spent working that truth into personal reality and through prayerfully partnering with a loving Father at work in an adolescent's life, I become a part of God's language of love. I know that I can give students no greater gift than experiencing the truth of his love for themselves.

Reflecting on Your Journey

☐ Describe a time when you led poorly with the truth. What principles were violated or omitted? What was the impact of your words?

☐ What would have been your most natural response to Melanie? What internal obstacles would you have faced as you attempted to lead lovingly with the truth?

☐ Can you identify a person whom you would describe as an effective communicator of "truth in love"? What characteristics of his or her personhood or communication style create this effectiveness?

☐ Tell of a time when you were hurt by someone else's leading poorly with the truth. What principles were violated or omitted? How has that experience made an impact on you? on your communication of the truth to others?

☐ Which of the nine principles, if applied immediately, would bring the greatest improvement in your speaking the truth in love to adolescents? What resources or relationships will you need for that principle to become reality in your communication with the adolescents you love?

☐ Which of the nine principles are strengths for you? How were those strengths nurtured? What does this suggest for your role as a spiritual caregiver seeking to nurture loving truth-speaking in the lives of adolescents?

Pressing In

☐ What is your image of God as a communicator of truth? Do you see him as loving? as direct? How do the principles in this chapter resonate with your concept of God? Reflect on how your concept of God has affected your communication patterns, with him and others.

☐ How do past hurts continue to disable you emotionally when you attempt to speak the truth in love? Articulate these hurts in pacing prayer with God and a friend. Ask for healing, transformation and courage. Continue to be honest with God when those feelings surface in the midst of your efforts to live truthfully.

☐ Are there persons in your life to whom you need to go to ask forgiveness for truth spoken harshly without love? for truth not spoken due to fear? If so, covenant with God to approach those persons immediately to repair the brokenness in the relationship.

☐ Using a concordance, explore Jesus' emphasis on the truth. Read 1-3 John. Why is truth so important? What about truth most threatens you when it comes time to speak it into others' lives? If God were to write you a letter addressing your practice of speaking the truth in love, what would he say? Write out that letter and listen as he speaks the truth in love into your world.

☐ Speaking the truth in love includes cultivating a life of encouragement. Who needs a specific, personal and accurate word of encouragement from you today? Write them a note, send an e-mail, make a call or, best of all, go see them to deliver in person the renewal that comes from true encouragement.

☐ Read Gary Smalley and John Trent's *The Blessing* to deepen your understanding and hone your skills of encouraging with the truth.

*I just wished my dad had said no one time. Then I would have known
that he really loved me. . . . As it is, I don't think he even cared.*
JOSHUA, COLLEGE SOPHOMORE

*How thankful I am that over the years some godly people have dared to
speak truth to me. Time and again their words have altered the course of
my life. When I was a kid I went to a Christian camp where some
courageous counselors discerned that though I was religious, I didn't
have a clue what it meant to have a personal relationship with God.
They asked me if I really knew what it meant to be a Christian. . . . Those
young counselors risked embarrassment and rejection by probing into
the life of a fairly cocky, self-assured little boy, but as a result of their
questions I became a Christian. Where would I be spiritually if those
camp counselors had been more devoted to peacekeeping than to truth
telling?*
BILL HYBELS, *MAKING LIFE WORK*

*Conflict is natural, normal, neutral, and sometimes even delightful. It
can turn into painful or disastrous ends but it doesn't need to. Conflict is
neither good nor bad, right nor wrong. Conflict simply is. How we view,
approach and work through our differences does to a large extent
determine our whole life pattern.*
DAVID AUGSBURGER, *CARING ENOUGH TO CONFRONT*

*Then the LORD said to Cain, "Why are you angry? Why is your face
downcast? If you do what is right, will you not be accepted? But if you
do not do what is right, sin is crouching at your door; it desires to have
you, but you must master it." . . . And while they were in the field, Cain
attacked his brother Abel and killed him.*
GENESIS 4:6-8

*Then Joseph said to his brothers, " . . . do not be distressed and do not
be angry with yourselves for selling me here, because it was to save lives
that God sent me ahead of you."*
GENESIS 45:4-5

6

How to Confront & Resolve Conflict

e is the Lord of the universe. He is the Creator of all that is. He is holy, omnipotent and omniscient. He is, simply, God. Yet when the image-bearing couple chooses to exalt themselves as gods, their sovereign Father initiates with "Where are you?"

I know what would have been going through my mind if I had created Adam and Eve. *Who do you think you are—don't you know who is God around here? How could you do this to me, after all I have created for you? Do you realize what a mess you have made? Do you have any idea what this is going to cost me to fix?*

The Creator Father, however, asks a series of questions.

To Adam: "Where are you?"

To Adam: "Who told you that you were naked? Have you eaten from the tree that I commanded you not to eat from?"

To Eve: "What is this you have done?"

God then communicates the natural consequences of their scandalous behavior. The results of their choices are catastrophic, for them and all of their descendants. He has created the world consistent with his character. Sin therefore changes everything about how they will encounter him in that world. A holy God cannot ignore sin and remain true to himself. Neither can a loving God.

Consistent with God's loving character, he provides for them even in their rebellious state. For their vulnerable physical selves he makes garments from slaughtered animals. Death has entered Adam and Eve's world: the physical death of animals and the spiritual death of human souls created for intimacy with God. God's incarnate entry into the world will be required to restore intimacy and fight back the stinging power of death. This he also promises to provide, saying to the serpent, "I will put enmity between you and the woman, and between your offspring and hers; he will crush your head, and you will strike his heel" (Gen 3:15). God will meet the first humans where they are. For that reason he begins with "Where are you?"

God's engagement of Adam and Eve offers insight into the nature of redemptive confrontation. A fourfold pattern emerges from this portrait of a brokenhearted holy, loving Father.

First, *God engages them personally.* God's initial agenda is not the offense but the distance. The sin must be dealt with, yet it is the relational tear that he addresses first. God's question calls to Adam and Eve across the great interpersonal chasm that now divides them. He certainly knows where they are. But they do not. They have never before known fear, loneliness, guilt and sorrow.

Second, *God enables them to confront their sinfulness.* His questions point them toward taking responsibility for the choices they have made. They are not intended to condemn. They are rather designed to confront. Adam and Eve are the root of their own condemnation.[1] Here God deals with the sin for what it truly is: an offense against him personally (Psalm 51:6).

Third, *God applies discipline consistent with the offense.* Had God wanted to punish, hurt and shame these rebellious children, it was certainly within his power. In three of the most haunting verses of Scripture, God demonstrates the necessity of redemptive consequences.

> "[Adam] must not be allowed to reach out his hand and take also from the tree of life and eat, and live forever." So the LORD God banished him from the Garden of Eden to work the ground from which he had been taken. After he drove the man out, he placed on the east side of the Garden of Eden cherubim and a flaming sword flashing back and forth to guard the way to the tree of life. (Gen 3:22-24)

God protected Adam and Eve from a choice that would have condemned them to eternal life in their fallen state. The consequences were necessary to preserve his character and their hope.

Fourth, *God provides a way for redemptive restoration.* The Word will become incarnate; the Son will become the Lamb who takes away the sin of the world.[2] Hope for deliverance from sin and restoration of intimacy can be found in the salvation plan of God. Humanity will face the consequences of our choices and who we have become. We will also come face to face with God's perfect provision to address our sin.

God confronts Adam and Eve while simultaneously providing them with the resources they will need for moving toward healing. In Hebrews we discover that all of God's discipline in his children's lives is directed toward the same purpose: "God disciplines us for our good, that we may share in his holiness" (Heb 12:10). Can we do any less with the adolescents in our worlds?

Perspectives on Confrontation and Conflict

To give the fullness of the gift of truth, I have to be willing to move into the hard places where the truth may lead me. As a spiritual caregiver, I must be prepared to step into confrontation. *Confrontation occurs when I speak truth into an adolescent's life in order to challenge an attitude, thought pattern or behavior that is inconsistent with God's will.*

Conflict resolution is often a corollary to confrontation. Adolescents, like the rest of us, often respond negatively to being confronted, even by someone who cares for them deeply. On the other hand, when the confrontation paces well with the adolescent's inner world, the truth may even be welcomed. Given our natural tendency to defend ourselves, a realistic approach to confrontation acknowledges that conflict resolution may be necessary in the healing process.

If caregivers were asked, "What do you enjoy most about nurturing spiritual growth in a teenager's life?" none would respond, "I really appreciate the times when I have to confront students and we get into a conflict." Yet if we were to ask adolescents what characteristics they most desire in a parent or mentor, the response would almost certainly be "I want someone who loves me enough to accept me for who I am but too much to let me stay that way." How does an adolescent come to believe this about a spiritual caregiver? Confrontation and conflict are like Good Housekeeping test laboratories. You discover what a relationship is really made of when the stress of discord puts commitment to the test.

We should therefore lean into rather than turn away from potentially challenging aspects of our relationships with adolescents. The following perspectives provide more personal motivation for addressing potentially conflictual issues in our spiritual caregiving relationships.

1. Security in a relationship grows as an adolescent experiences a spiritual caregiver's commitment to work through relational difficulties and disconnections.

2. The goal of imparting Jesus through our lives as spiritual caregivers requires that we cooperate with the Holy Spirit's work in adolescents' lives. The Spirit's conviction and transforming work includes confronting sinful attitudes, thoughts and actions.

3. Confrontation and conflicts in relationships with spiritual caregivers cause an adolescent to encounter the significance of his or her need for God.

4. Confrontation and conflicts in relationships with adolescents cause a spiritual caregiver to encounter the significance of his or her own need for God.

5. Speaking the truth is often confrontational and conflictual. Leading with the truth therefore compels us toward places of conflict. When addressed in true love, in pace with God and the adolescent, such conflicts produce more growth than any of the more "fun" parts of being a parent, pastor or mentor.

When the process is approached as a normal component of growing, healthy relationships, both spiritual caregivers and adolescents can begin to value it. In fact, deep relational intimacy most often is birthed through the labor pains of resolving interpersonal tensions.

Conflict is not inherently wrong. Due to our natural selfishness, however, conflict does provide the perfect environment for relationally wounding one another. After the Fall, Eve blamed the serpent, Adam blamed Eve and God, Adam and Eve hid from God, and in the next generation conflict led to murder. Given our the inheritance of both a sin nature and sinful relational patterns from our ancestors near and far, we and the adolescents we love cannot afford to allow conflict to go unresolved. Leaning into rather than away from conflict is thus always the right choice.

Principles for Confrontation and Conflict Resolution

We have all experienced times when there is a "relational elephant" in the room. We sit in silence, an adolescent avoiding our eye contact at the family dining table or on the couch in the church youth room. When dialogue does occur, we can expect little more than controlled exchanges of information. If we venture to identify the elephant we are likely to hear "Everything's fine" or "Nothing."

At some point, if the relationship is to continue and order to be restored, the spiritual caregiver will have to find a way to name the elephant. The following principles provide guidelines for naming and then escorting the elephant out of the relationship.

Principle 1: Pace and Lead

Apply the principles of pacing empathy, pacing prayer and leading with truth. Effective communication varies little, whether in the midst of harmony or in conflict. Pacing with listening hearts and leading with loving truth remain the most essential aspects of walking through relationally difficult places. In imitation of God's personal engagement with Adam and Eve, we lead with the heart.

Principle 2: Pursue Relationships

Never withdraw relationship from an adolescent because of interpersonal conflict.[3] Spiritual caregivers communicate "I am distancing myself from you" when they choose either of two damaging responses to conflict. The first is retreat. In our anger or fear we go inward, moving away from connecting with the adolescent. The second negative response is revenge. We blame the person, either in silence or out loud, using a relational sword to back them away. In either case we can do incredible damage to the adolescent's sense of security in relationships. Spiritual caregivers must love enough to move toward the adolescent with the desire for authentic communication and reconciliation.

Principle 3: Be Self-Aware

Acknowledge and embrace your own feelings of relational hurt. Anger is not bad. Confronting a student in order to work out your anger is sinful. Feeling hurt is a normal part of loving and being loved. Dumping that hurt onto an adolescent in the midst of working through a conflict is sinful. "Adolescents should never be the persons spiritual caregivers use to work through our deeply felt emotions."[4] We adults need to go to God—usually with the help of a trusted peer or mentor—in order to have our relational wounds comforted.

Principle 4: Speak for Yourself

Use "I" statements to express honestly your thoughts and feelings. "I" statements discipline our conversation, causing us to own what we experience without blame or projection. "I" statements are necessary for the appropriate expression of our perspectives and emotions. "Expressing honestly" may at first glance appear to be a contradiction to checking our emotions at the throne of grace. Being honest in one's expression does not, however, require a complete, totally vulnerable self-disclosure. If a spiritual caregiver has experienced anger or hurt, it is appropriate to express that honestly. What is not appropriate is using the context to work through the depths of those emotions when they could be damaging to or manipulative of the adolescent.

Teaching an adolescent to use "I" statements in honest self-expression is a valuable byproduct of modeling this principle well. Adolescents who learn to apply this principle effectively will find greater confidence in dealing with the intense emotions that so often affect their daily lives.

Principle 5: Confront with Care

Communicate compassion without compromise when dealing with sin. When an adolescent has clearly chosen to be hurtful or rebellious, the temptation to "show them what they have done" is powerful. God, however, does not call us to add shame or condemnation to the offense. When I am confronting what I perceive to be sinful choices in an adolescent's life, my goal for him is to experience conviction without condemnation. The best way for me to enable that process is to communicate compassion without compromise. My compassion is best demonstrated in my willingness to pace with the process that led them to their choices. My commitment to avoid compromise is best demonstrated in my willingness to pace with God's Word as I lead them to the standards of his truth.

Principle 6: Be Specific

Thou shalt define problems clearly. When we enter into a conflict situation, there is always a "presenting problem," a catalyst for the conflict. Typically, however, as we pace with adolescents more deeply into a conflict situation, we discover that the root of the problem lies elsewhere. As we pace and lead into root issues, it is important to identify the exact nature of what needs to be addressed in order to bring resolution. In the case of confrontation, the need for definition is even greater. Leaving an adolescent with, "I want you to be more respectful of me and others" does not give her much to work with in terms of adjusting her attitude and behaviors. Providing specific examples of responses that would demonstrate progress in solving the problem is infinitely more helpful.

Principle 7: Work in Partnership

Build toward mutual understanding and consensus. The "win" we seek in confrontation and conflict resolution is a shared pacing that will lead us into a deeper pacing with God. The more adolescents have ownership in the process of defining the problem and posing solutions, the more effective the process. Patience is required to ask adolescents what they are observing, feeling and perceiving as a possible solution as the dialogue progresses. Pacing should occur not only on the front end but throughout the confrontation and resolution process.

To facilitate that win, an "affirm-disagree-affirm sandwich" can be helpful in fostering pacing. The formula for this technique looks like this: "Yes, I agree with you that _____, but no, I do not agree that _____. I do, however, understand that you feel _____ because of your point of view."[5]

Principle 8: Be the Adult

Respect your own authority. As adult spiritual caregivers, we stand in a place of gatekeeping. We determine what is allowed into the conversation and what is not. We are looked to for direction, control and guidance of the conflict resolution process. Taking that role seriously means not allowing adolescents to manipulate, monopolize or divert the conversation.

However, the role also requires discipline. We must not abuse our authority by manipulating, monopolizing or diverting the process to fulfill our personal agenda. Because this is so important, it is always wise to seek godly counsel and feedback from an honest peer or mentor before initiating a difficult confrontation. The authority of an adult spiritual caregiver should be invested in teaching and empowering adolescents in the ways of relational healing. We are not merely facilitators, we are shepherding leaders seeking to listen to and speak with the voice of the Good Shepherd.

Principle 9: Respect Individuality

Do not demand that a resistant adolescent respond in the way that meets your expectations. Spiritual caregivers can require that they and others be treated respectfully. However, it is inappropriate for a spiritual caregiver to attempt to "break" the resistance within the heart of a relationally disengaged adolescent. Kevin Huggins's words to parents are applicable to all spiritual caregivers who encounter the resistant adolescent: "Ultimately, parents must remember what their adolescent longs for more than anything else: a relationship that will not fail him. When they offer him unconditional involvement at even the most superficial levels, it's very likely he'll eventually soften toward them and want more."[6] Grace, truth, and time are the best allies on the side of the loving spiritual caregiver.[7]

Principle 10: Examine Yourself Continually

Be willing to be confronted, corrected and disciplined by God in the midst of confronting and resolving conflict with adolescents. A humble, teachable spirit smooths the jagged, self-protective edges adolescents may be carrying into conflict. When an adolescent senses that you are more committed to what is right than to being right, she is usually disarmed by the authenticity. She is more prone to invite you into her experiences of the issue at hand because she senses that you are there for her benefit, not merely to champion your own cause.

A Conflict Resolved

On a road trip our youth group took, the predictable pattern of "missions trip romances" had begun to emerge. I had concluded by this point in my youth ministry career that vans and buses must be laced with pheromones that cause high school students suddenly to be attracted to members of the opposite sex they have ignored all year. (Of course I am certain there are other, more plausible explanations.) This trip was complicated by a number of factors. First, it was my last trip with the group before I left the church to pursue my next calling. Emotions were running pretty high for all of us. Second, the trip was two weeks long—lots of time for all types of relational dynamics to develop. Third, the couples being drawn together like bugs to a zapper were guys and girls who had known each other for years. These students had wrestled with each other like brothers and sisters in grade school. I had never thought twice about their staying out late at night to talk or leaning on each other as they snoozed on a bus ride home. Now I was wishing that I could stop thinking about the sticky situations we might encounter!

The trouble started when I made a new rule about sitting up on the bus. No more lying down together in the seats. "It's just not a good idea," I told them. (Note that I had already failed on several fronts with just that one statement!) I was prepared for the "Awww, man! What's the problem?" and the rolling of the eyes—a skill that seems genetically tied to the adolescent period of life. What I was not prepared for was the near mutiny of my crew. By the next day I had the whole group angry at me, with emotional frustration spilling all over the place.

My first response was a mature "What's their problem?" Fortunately the leadership team moved beyond my limited perspective. We decided to call a meeting of the whole group and allow everyone to air what they were feeling. I dreaded having to explain the new bus-etiquette policies I had abruptly instituted. Most young youth pastors (I was twenty-five at the time) avoid like the plague statements that will sound to students like their mother is talking to them. (By the time you turn thirty-five you realize there is good reason to say some things their mothers say to them!)

We began by asking the students what they were feeling toward the leadership team and me. The first words were "You don't trust us," followed by "You treat us like we were little kids."

Soon my defensiveness melted away. I realized that I had failed miserably in confronting my concerns about their emerging physical relationships. First, I saw clearly that I had failed by not initiating dialogue with any of them. Second, I had avoided dealing with the true emotions I was feeling in the midst of this conflict. As a result, I had caused the whole group to distance themselves from me. Ten days into the trip, exhausted emotionally and knowing that this would be our last ministry experience together, they were deeply offended by how I had dealt with them—and they were right. For two hours we all talked, though by the end we were mostly crying. Finally we closed with prayer and singing.

I had never felt more loved by those students than when I saw that working through this conflict meant so much to them. Moreover, once they felt heard and then listened to my concerns, they were very responsive to our new rules. While they would not have agreed with their necessity, they were willing to accept my reasoning. God used that confrontation and conflict resolution to deepen trust that I believe they had been struggling with ever since I announced that I would be leaving that summer. I learned in that cabin in the Rockies how important it is for spiritual caregivers to confront and resolve conflict well. (By the way, in spite of my oppressive restrictions, one of the mission-trip couples remains happily married to this day.)

When to Initiate Confrontation and Conflict Resolution
Should I say something or just let this go? We have all felt this tension. On the one hand there is that relational elephant in the room. On the other hand we wonder if we are making a bigger deal of out of the issue than we should.

For years I tended to play it safe and confront only what seemed absolutely necessary. Now I know that was part of my personal dysfunction. I encourage spiritual caregivers (a) to follow the above principles for loving confrontation and (b) to expose relational elephants. Relationships with adolescents are too precious to play it safe and skim the surface. If listening, learning and loving have preceded leading with the truth, the relationship will grow only if confrontation and conflict are handled well.

Following is a comprehensive but by no means exhaustive set of issues that should always be confronted by a spiritual caregiver:
☐ clear acts of disobedience to God, parents, or adult authorities (whether they be willful or careless acts of disobedience)
☐ destructive patterns of behavior (either to self or to others)
☐ evidence of underlying attitudes or beliefs that are contrary to the truth
☐ failure to live consistently with stated beliefs or commitments
☐ immoral lifestyle choices
☐ inappropriate responses to people and circumstances (issues of maturity, values, character)
While discernment and judicious timing need to be applied, true love does not look the other way when issues such as these are at stake.

I can recall a handful of times when I hesitated to do the hard work of confrontation, either by procrastinating or by never doing it at all. I cannot think of a single incident when that hesitation led to a positive result. On the other hand, when I have confronted in a manner consistent with God's pattern, I have seen amazing changes in students' lives. Even when my confrontation or I myself was rejected, I have never regretted communicating what I believed to be true. I have learned that speaking the truth in love is always the right thing to do, even when it is the last thing I want to do.

Reflecting on Your Journey

☐ When I find myself in the midst of relational conflict, I most naturally (circle one) withdraw from the relationship, comply to avoid further conflict, lean into the process of resolution, go on the attack to prove I am in the right.

☐ In the midst of conflict I usually feel (circle one) confused, scared, angry, guilty, excited, sad, calm, other _____.

☐ Delineate the basic anatomy of a conflict/confrontation situation where you experienced a healthy resolution. Contrast this with a similar situation that ended in relational unhealthiness and hurt. What were the important differences between the two situations?

☐ What particular aspects of being an adolescent's spiritual caregiver either intensify or lessen the challenges you face in conflict/confrontation situations with him or her? Why does your relationship with the adolescent(s) have this impact on you?

☐ Of all the perspectives and principles presented in the chapter, which one made the strongest impression? Why was it most significant to you?

☐ If you could choose one place for improvement in your conflict resolution with adolescents, what would it be? To experience this improvement, what emotions will you have to work through? What skills will need to be developed? Who will be the key support persons/partners who will have to work through this with you?

Pressing In

☐ Commit yourself to pressing into this place of improvement. Count the cost and gather the resources you will require on the journey.

☐ Reflect on the big story of God's redemptive work by surveying the major characters and historical events of Genesis to Revelation. What additional insights do you gather as you follow God at work in reconciling individuals to himself? How does confrontation play a key role in the salvation story?

☐ With whom do you have an outstanding conflict? Resolve to do your part to initiate and complete the resolution process.

☐ What areas of adolescents' lives are you currently sensing the need to confront? Commit yourself to specific action steps, working through the content of chapters five and six. Ask God to share with you his heart for relational reconciliation and purity. Pray pacing prayers and practice pacing empathy so that your confrontation does not become about your agenda for "fixing" the adolescent.

*Every day [in America], according to the Children's Defense Fund,
2,795 teenage girls become pregnant, 848 undersized children are born,
27 children die of poverty, 10 die from gunshots and 30 are wounded, 3
children die of abuse, 211 children are arrested for drug offenses, 1,512
drop out of school, 1,849 are abused or neglected, and 3,288 run away
from home.*
FOSTER W. CLINE, *CONSCIENCELESS ACTS,
SOCIETAL MAYHEM*

*I decided to move back with my dad in San Francisco. I had had enough.
I was sick of being bullied, so I became a bully. I was tired of not being
popular—so I became popular. This was all accomplished over time—
through the right friends, drugs, alcohol and playing around with sex.
My brother stayed back in Michigan so there was no one to tattle-tell on
me. My dad was never around and my sister gave me drugs and
cigarettes. I was in the shade and had it all worked out until one day
Mom called. Three days later I was on a plane back to Michigan.*

*It was worse than the first time. I had no friends, popularity, drugs,
alcohol, girlfriends, etc. . . . I thought of myself as worthless and used.
Nobody cared (or so I thought) or loved me. I was suicidal on many oc-
casions and I dabbled in the occult. . . . I had the self-image of dirt on spit.*
A STUDENT RECALLING HIS MIDDLE SCHOOL
EXPERIENCES

*To cheat and lie is to be alone; to knock oneself out with drugs is to be
alone; to sleep with men because they want to knock you up, you and a
million others on a sexual assembly line that passes for a life, is to be
alone, even as to behave like that to women is to be alone; and finally, to
shoot to kill in order to survive and prevail (just barely, and so often only
for a short time) is to be murderously alone.*
ROBERT COLES, *THE MORAL INTELLIGENCE OF CHILDREN*

*Sin is the word we use to designate the perverseness of will by which we
attempt being our own gods, or making for ourselves other gods. Sin
isn't essentially a moral term, designating items of wrongdoing; it's a
spiritual term, designating our God-avoidance and our God-
pretensions.*
EUGENE W. PETERSON, *LEAP OVER A WALL*

Neither do I condemn you. Go and sin no more.
JESUS, TO A WOMAN CAUGHT IN ADULTERY

7

How to Nurture the
Adolescent Moral Self

*T*he Reverend Wallace approached me in tears. His son, he told me, had followed all the paths his father could have hoped for. James had been an active, responsive member of each church his father had pastored. When James reached adolescence, he became a true servant leader within his youth group. As an older adolescent James had even been a catalyst for promoting a Christian sexual abstinence program for his church and community. Twice, publicly with his peers and privately with his parents, he had announced his commitment to Christ to be sexually pure. Now, on the eve of his high-school graduation, he had confessed to his father that his girlfriend was pregnant.

Broken commitments, broken dreams, broken hearts. The pastor longed for me to tell him what had gone wrong. If I had an answer, he reasoned, perhaps he could fix the problem or at least make sense of it.

But I had no "right answer" for him. The intimate inner formation of a person's moral self can never be fully known.

To be authentic, spiritual caregivers must begin by acknowledging that there is no fail-proof method for *making* an adolescent develop the moral self we desire. Spiritual caregivers, if they are honest with themselves, realize this foundational truth: *adults are not ultimately in control of the process of an adolescent's moral development.*[1] In the end, as in all of life, we are left with mystery and faith.[2]

In spite of this lack of ultimate control, *spiritual caregivers can and do make a significant impact on adolescent moral formation.* Reflecting from the social science perspective, Robert Coles champions the adult's role:

> What ought to be done, might be done on their behalf? I'm all in favor of trying to be of emotional help, cognitive help: let us try to help those children who have been psychologically wounded in one or another way to be healed. But after the courses are over, and the therapeutic sessions end, there are those endless hours that await our children—and their questions ought to be ours: Where are the grown-ups in our life upon whom we can really rely, whom we can trust, whose values are believable, desirable, because they have been given us out of the shared experience, moment to moment, of a life together? Where is a moral companionship that has been experienced—a daily context for the expressed shoulds and should-nots, the injunctions that have been pressed on?[3]

Coles challenges adults to provide "moral companionship" (pacing) as the environment for "the expressed shoulds and should-nots" (leading with the truth). His call to make an impact reminds us that pacing-then-leading relationships do make an incredible difference.

The Three Rs of Moral Development

To develop a mature moral self that both seeks and fulfills God's will, adolescents like James need growth in three essential areas: *relationship, reasoning* and *responsibility taking.* In each of these arenas spiritual caregivers can take responsibility for (1) discerning deficits that disable the adolescent's moral maturity, (2) partnering with God in praying with and nurturing those areas of need and (3) creating environments that will foster maturity of the adolescent's moral self.

Relationship: the tractor-beam of attachment. Don Postema recalls this encounter in a home for the aged: "I wanted to present something comforting to the aging patients. So I began by saying, 'You belong.' I was about to continue when a ninety-year-old woman sitting near me in a wheelchair startled me by shouting in her high wheezy voice with both distress and longing, 'TO WHOM?' "[4]

In her loneliness the woman asked the fundamental question of humanity, "To whom do I belong?" From birth to death the most driving force in our lives is the need to find *attachment*.[5] For adolescents, the need to experience a sense of belonging is like the tractor-beam on the old Star Trek series. Teenagers who do not feel attached to spiritual caregivers find themselves drawn with a sense of urgency, almost helplessness, toward whatever environment offers the most acceptance. The resulting pseudo-attachments (see Lamar's story in chapter three) hinder spiritual intimacy and disable moral maturity.

Monica's experience profoundly illustrates the need for attachment. While working in a rehab center for behavior-disordered adolescents Monica found herself connecting with the extremely emotionally troubled David. For a long while her main contact with the boy involved restraint. She would immobilize David by wrapping him up in a full embrace, to prevent him from hurting himself and others. As the relationship developed, the fits of rage decreased; there was more dialogue and less physical restraint.

One evening, however, David lashed out at Monica. Stunned and frightened by his unexpected rage, she called for help. In the moments that followed she discovered the reason for the extreme behavior. Tearfully he told her that he had just wanted her to hold him. David had attacked her with the hope that she would restrain him with one of her embracing hugs!

David provides an image for understanding the motivation of much of the immoral behavior we encounter among adolescents. Whether in sexual experimentation or violent acts to gain gang membership, moral failure often indicates an internal plea for someone to respond with an embrace that communicates, "I care."

The deeper the sense of attachment with parents, spiritual caregivers, peers and God, the stronger the core of the adolescent moral self. Conversely, the greater the attachment deficit from childhood or adolescent relational experiences, the more vulnerable the adolescent is to moral failure. Moral failure frequently results from attempts to answer or medicate the painful question "To whom do I belong?"

All persons will find ways to attach themselves to others—even if it requires violating a previously held moral conviction. Once an adolescent chooses compromise, a negative cycle of moral disintegration is set in motion. Over time, the compromising behaviors have a way of reshaping beliefs; the inconsistency between conviction and behavior often leads to a rationalized change in conviction. The results can be tragic: substance abuse, internal tearing apart after broken sexual relationships, loss of self-worth, shame and guilt, pregnancy, abortion, lost friendships, the reinforcement of addictive tendencies through Internet pornography, the development of deceptive lifestyles—the list can go on and on. So much of life's long-term "baggage" and scars are rooted in adolescent moral faltering.

The spiritual caregiver's touch of the adolescent's inner self with the real love of Jesus provides a starting point for prevention and intervention in the moral lives of adolescents. Authentic spiritual attachment with God and his people, in fact, is the only love that can overcome the powerful enticement of postmodern pseudo-attachments.

Reasoning: the why behind the boundaries. My neighbor has an invisible fence. His dog, Barney, has learned the boundaries of that electronic barrier. Cars, people, even other dogs pass by, yet that huge chocolate Lab simply stands and barks. For Barney, the pain of being shocked is not worth the payoff of extending his freedom. Barney does not ponder why the fence is there. Nor does he complain, "Why do all of the other dogs get to run around the neighborhood? It's not fair." Barney accepts the boundary for what it is: a painful obstacle that cannot be overcome.

The invisible electronic fence works for my neighbor because dogs are great responders to behavioral modification. (Though I seemed to have found an exception in my own dog, Jake.) Adolescents, however, do ask, "why?" about boundaries. Adolescents do claim that the boundaries are not fair. They push back, often with very complex arguments to support their claims. And so they should—with respect and willful obedience.[6] Adolescents need to wrestle emotionally and cognitively with the principles behind the rules. The path from childhood to adulthood was designed by God to include the asking of these types of questions.

Jeff VanVonderen, in *Families Where Grace Is in Place*, offers an excellent treatment of the establishment of boundaries for children in the home. He begins by demonstrating the impact of boundaries in the toddler's world:

> When two-year-olds say no, they are finding out that they are separate human beings from their parents, with separate wills and separate opinions. Though most Christian parents have been trained to balk at this concept, it is our job to help them [the children] to develop a strong *no*. They are going to need a strong *no* when they are fourteen years old and someone wants to be sexually intimate with them or shoves a bottle of alcohol in their hand. Our job is to

recognize opportunities for them to exercise their *no*—not to strip them of their will in the name of maintaining authority as a parent.[7]

VanVonderen then develops a healthy view of the testing of boundaries as a child approaches and enters adolescence:

> When our eleven-year-old daughter questions the rules, and even breaks them, she is doing her job. She is conducting research to find out if there are things in the world that are dependable, laws on which she can count. Our job is to show her, through our structure and how we respond to her choices, that there are indeed firm rules. It is not our job to try to control her testing. In our family, she can count on being held responsible for her choices. She can count on experiencing consequences to help her learn about life. And she can count on being loved and accepted as a person, even if we may hate her behavior.[8]

Families and ministry environments that clearly establish boundaries in connection with attachment create the best possible environment for the formation of a mature moral self.

The greater the boundary deficit in an adolescent's life, the greater the need for consistent guidance and feedback from a spiritual caregiver. Many adolescents did not have the benefit of a home like VanVonderen's when they were young. They may have experienced boundaries as inconsistent, meaningless, arbitrary or abusive. Their homes may have been so devoid of clear boundaries and consequences that they do not know how to relate to the expectations of adults and God. In such cases, the adolescent simply does not grasp the love of God behind the moral boundaries God has created. In fact, he may never have observed or experienced the true benefits of staying within those moral boundaries. For their moral selves to mature, they will require spiritual caregivers who love them, embracing them unconditionally with grace while keeping them accountable for their failed commitments.

The spiritual caregiver, whether as parent or mentor, provides an accessible model of moral maturation in progress. Morality is always more "caught" than taught.[9] If parents have provided secure attachment, consistent and appropriate boundary setting, and an environment that fostered growth through success as well as failure, then the raw materials of adolescent moral maturity are abundant. If not, the battle can be fierce. Parents exert an unparalleled influence on the inner contours of an adolescent's world, particularly on convictions and commitments.[10] When walking with students from morally shallow homes, spiritual caregivers are therefore called to stand in the gap. They become living portraits of a God full of love and truth, grace and holiness.

Whether from morally rich or morally bankrupt homes, adolescents will ask "why?" when confronted with moral boundaries. By God's design their reasoning shifts from "What am I supposed to do?" to "Why am I supposed to do that?" Parents particularly often perceive such a dramatic change as a threat. Parents tire of responses like "But everyone else . . ." or "But you don't trust me." All spiritual caregivers should, however, seize opportunities to explore the whys. Clear boundaries become more meaningful when the why is understood. Gray-area boundaries—moral standards based more on principle than on direct biblical command or legal restraint—also provide a context for strengthening moral reasoning as "why" is discussed. Life is filled with such moral arenas; becoming an adult ensures that they must be confronted.

Adolescence is the greenhouse for the growth of healthy moral minds capable of withstanding the harsh elements of a sensate culture. Spiritual caregivers who demand compliance but deprive adolescents of the moral reasoning process prepare students for failure rather than success.

Responsibility-taking: rooted in personal value and efficacy. I remember the first day my youngest son accomplished the ultimate in potty-training performance—Benjamin did a "number two" like a "big boy." Soon the family was all gathered around joining Benjamin in his admiration of what he had done. There the five of us stood, celebrating his victory. (Unfortunately, Benjamin's joy turned to sorrow as his request to keep his trophy was denied. Tears washed down his face as the *whooosh!* of the toilet carried away the evidence of his newfound mastery.)

God made us with the need to feel a sense of accomplishment, to find joy in what we have done and to see those who love us celebrating those accomplishments—even as toddlers in potty training boot camp. Fortunately for all of us—especially parents—the potty-training stage passes rather quickly. The need for affirmation, however, does not. Soon, children are on swings yelling, "Daddy, look at me!" Later they begin telling parents, grandparents, friends and teachers what they have recently accomplished in math, gymnastics or baseball. As adolescence emerges, the need does not change, though it is less often voiced.

With identity formation in high gear, the need to feel successful, to enjoy achievements and to be celebrated takes on epic proportions. Failure to experience a sense of accomplishment can have a devastating impact. A learning disability can create a sense of "feeling stupid" that severely distorts a young man's sense of his personal competency. Failure to be chosen for a team or to be elected to a leadership position can cause a young woman to doubt her worth to others. Perceived relational failures cut even deeper. Rejection by a boyfriend or girlfriend may distort self-image into a negative caricature of the real self God has made. Being short on life experience, high in need for acceptance and focused on discovering his place in the world, the adolescent feels there is something wrong with him—a deficit in his sense of personal value. A long-term continuation of this deficit will cause him to experience a generalized sense of deficit in personal efficacy. If that perception persists, he will feel worthless and powerless to live according to his moral standards.

Students who fail to gain an emerging sense of value and efficacy thus have the double damnation of not being able to accept themselves and not being hopeful that they can choose to be anyone different. Such an adolescent struggles to believe that she has power to choose who she becomes. She feels more a victim than a victor. She may withdraw from tasks or people in order to minimize the risk of being hurt. Or she may feign lack of interest to avoid disappointment. Ultimately, the adolescent becomes unwilling or unable to take responsibility for life choices, including the important moral ones. Morality becomes more reactive than proactive, more a matter of conforming to the nearest environment than of forming internal convictions, and more likely to be overcome by peer pressure. In such cases, the potential for moral failure in the postmodern culture is great. Sadly, such failures seem to be more normative than exceptional as adolescents are plunged headlong and alone into a youth culture permeated with a sensate worldview.

Reacting in fear, caregivers are tempted to respond to internal deficits with external solutions. Parents and teachers look for "something she will be good at" as the ultimate solution. Having a place to feel accomplishment and affirmation is in fact one critical component of the nurture of a moral self. However, even when these adolescents find energy in a new relationship or discover a hidden ability to succeed, they may remain fearful. Lacking an internal sense of value and efficacy, they become frighteningly dependent on their new circumstances for their well-being. Though the external self may seem calm, deeply troubled waters can still lie just below the surface. Knowing this, the adolescent chooses to wear the mask of "I'm fine," despite being anything but fine.

Responsibility-taking thus represents a vital yet incomplete-within-itself component of nurturing the moral self. To foster the most complete maturity, the three *R*s need to intersect one another in the context of the pacing-then-leading love of the spiritual caregiver.

The Intersection of the Three Rs

In a "telling" model, the spiritual caregiver identifies the behavior that is to be chosen. The caregiver then explains to the adolescent why that behavior is the correct one according to God's Word. Finally, some tips on the best way to ensure that correct behavior are presented. The premise is *If you know what you should do, then you should be able to do it.*

In a pacing-then-leading model, spiritual caregivers seek to develop moral maturity through nurturing relationships, reasoning and responsibility-taking. The caregiver paces with the heart motivation behind the behavior. She listens to discover how the adolescent is thinking through her moral decisions. The caregiver guides the adolescent through the process of exploring the why behind God's boundaries and the corresponding rules that have been established in the home or group. She then seeks to empower the adolescent to develop the interpersonal and internal resources required not only to choose the correct behavior but to become a stronger moral person through walking with the Holy Spirit.

The security of attachment, the wisdom of moral goodness and the strong twin towers of personal value and efficacy are found in relationship with God and his people. Along the journey toward the maturity of those relationships, the Spirit of God is not there simply to give enough strength to do the right thing. The Spirit is there to transform the heart (being), the reasoning (knowing) and the responsibility-taking (doing). The student requires discipling in how to engage moral decision-making in the Spirit and truth of Jesus. Merely telling her what she ought to do will not suffice. She needs spiritual caregiving to walk out the transformation of growth toward moral wholeness.

Effective spiritual caregivers pace with various internal weaknesses that threaten to thwart mature moral decision-making and action. Only God can heal the weak areas, but the spiritual caregiver can nurture and create space for God to work in them. Knowing the right behavior is just the beginning of moral nurture in the pacing-then-leading vision. Much listening, guidance, confrontation and shared prayer are still to come on the journey toward a mature adult moral self. In partnership with God, that journey will bring moral transformation rather than mere moral conformity.

From Moral Belief to Moral Action

The formation of the internal moral self occurs in the context of real-life moral choices. What does the process of pacing with and leading the moral self look like? How are we to assist adolescents in connecting moral beliefs and moral actions?

Sarah was a seventeen-year-old high-school senior, the daughter of strict yet caring Christian parents. During her junior year she met Travis, an eighteen-year-old senior, at a coffeehouse sponsored by his church. Travis had become a Christian that same year and had led two of his friends to the Lord almost immediately. Sarah was attracted to him both physically and spiritually; his personality instantly made her feel at ease.

Sarah and Travis dated casually at first but quickly became exclusive in their relationship. By the end of the year they were convinced that they were truly in love. Travis had been recruited by a number of excellent small colleges to play basketball, but he decided to enroll at a local junior college with an above-average basketball program. His parents were disappointed, but they liked Sarah and were thankful for the change his newfound relationship with the Lord had brought.

During the summer following Travis's graduation, he and Sarah had lots of time together. They spent every possible waking moment talking, being with friends and dreaming of a future together. The closer they felt, the more physical their relationship became. By fall they had begun having sexual intercourse.

Both felt guilty at first. Sarah even broke up with Travis at Thanksgiving, burdened by her failure to keep her vow of sexual purity. She loved Travis, however, and they committed themselves to postpone sexual activity until they were married. That commitment was broken within four weeks. They prayed, read the Bible and even fasted. Nothing seemed to help them overcome sexual temptation—in fact, it seemed to be getting worse.

Sarah and Travis prayed together one night for more than an hour and concluded God knew that they were not strong enough to avoid temptation completely. They would try to limit their sexual activity, both to relieve the pressure of guilt and to lessen the chances of an unplanned pregnancy. With the anticipation of engagement and marriage, they no longer felt they were sinning against God. Deep inside they knew it would be better if they did not have sex. But they had mostly stopped thinking of it in terms of morality and sin.

But Sarah and Travis's relationship did not make it to engagement. As early as January, both sensed that things were not going well. Travis was getting significant offers from excellent out-of-state basketball programs. His excitement about those offers made him realize that he was not prepared for marriage and a family. Sarah knew this was true for her too. She wanted to be like the rest of her friends, experiencing college life, learning more about the world than she could learn in her hometown.

She couldn't make sense of their sexual relationship, though, unless they were expecting to be married. She wondered how she would ever recover from this relationship. What would her next relationship be like? What difference would it make that she was not a virgin?

Travis was deeply wounded as well. He was beginning to see that they had fooled themselves into believing there was some special exception for them. He blamed the moral failure on himself. After his salvation experience he had vowed to be sexually pure. He could not believe that he had let God, himself and Sarah down. A part of him believed he ought to go ahead and marry Sarah to make this right. Deep in his heart, however, he knew he did not love her the way a husband should love his wife. He suspected her love for him was similarly flawed.

The process of actualizing convictions. There are four steps in moving from moral conviction to moral action.[11]

Step 1. What do I believe? A sense of moral conviction is involved: *it would be wrong to keep money that was not mine.*

Step 2. Am I responsible for acting on that belief in this situation? Here there is a sense of moral responsibility: *I should give back the hundred dollars I found in this lost wallet.*

Step 3. What will I choose to do based upon my belief? An ideological moral commitment provides guidance: *Tomorrow I am going to turn in the wallet and the money to the police.*

Step 4. What do I do at the moment when a behavioral response is required? A behavioral moral choice is made: *When I hand the wallet to the police I include the hundred dollars.*

Turning in the money to the police is based on responses to the key questions of steps one through three. Note, however, that a *conviction* that one should turn in lost money does not ensure that the money will be given to the police. One could decide in step two that this particular situation does not warrant turning in the money. Rightly or wrongly, one could decide that there is no inherent moral responsibility given the unique situation. One could also accept moral responsibility yet decide in step three not to turn in the money. Perhaps because of financial pressure or a sense of antagonism toward the wealth of the true owner, the person may decide, *I know the right thing to do is to turn in the wallet, but I need the money more than he does. I am going to keep it.* Finally, a person could go through all three steps, walk up to the front desk at the police station and, in the end, not find the moral strength to part with the cash. Moral beliefs, moral choices and moral actions are dynamically interwoven in the fabric of one's moral life.

Walking through the four-step process in reference to Sarah and Travis's relationship provides a helpful picture of the moral nurture process. As a case study, their scenario displays the patterns that lie beneath the surface of students' public lives and highlights the potential for spiritual caregivers to nurture adolescents' moral selves.

The young couple begins with a conviction of clear moral boundaries in their sexual relationship. In step one they believe that God's will calls for abstinence from sexual intercourse while they are unmarried. In step two they are initially convinced that they are responsible before God to maintain sexual purity. In fact, they hold this belief long after they have become sexually active. However, after repeated failures and a breakup, they adjust their sense of moral obligation in light of their lack of self-control and their commitment to be married. They conclude that while it would be better if they were not sexually active, given the circumstances God does not see their sexual relationship as truly sinful.

The reframing of their moral obligation does not come quickly. For months the two make the commitment not to have sexual intercourse and yet find themselves unable to follow through on the choice. The inconsistency of their behavior highlights the challenge that occurs between step three (ideological moral commitment) and step four (behavioral moral choice). Travis and Sarah have made the commitment to follow through on the moral convictions of steps one and two. Yet they fail to actualize that commitment in their behavior. The Thanksgiving breakup and the subsequent impassioned, renewed commitment to overcome temptation result from the dissonance between steps one to three and step four.

In the end, Sarah and Travis do what many of us do. They restructure their responses to steps one and two in order to experience efficacy in steps three and four. After repeated failed attempts to change their behavior, they change their beliefs. This is a pattern common in all persons; adolescents are particularly vulnerable to such rationalization because of their in-process identity and character formation.

Ultimately internal dissonance and the guilt of moral compromise take their toll on their relationship with God and each other. The couple initially made the right moral commitment. Their hearts demonstrated a desire to follow God. As time passed, however, they could not keep those commitments. They failed morally—not because they were perverted or ill-intended. Travis and Sarah simply were spiritually, emotionally and socially unprepared for the relationship that emerged. The immaturity beneath the surface of this apparently successful Christian couple became evident. Now each is left with a tearing like a divorce. They cannot simply walk away—they have committed themselves to an interpersonal intimacy that was beyond God's boundaries for them.

For two decades I have walked through the tangled jungles of internal pain left behind by the moral immaturity of the Travises and Sarahs of our campuses, churches and homes. I have journeyed through the sorrow and relational dysfunction that emerges from moral failure in sexual relationships. Often I have heard couples recount how they tried to be more disciplined and how they prayed for God to help them. While discipline and prayer are essential, another essential ingredient is often absent: the active presence of a spiritual caregiver.

Exploring critical questions. Sarah and Travis needed help. They needed an effective pacing-then-leading spiritual caregiver to guide them through their relationship. Early on someone could have helped them sort out what was happening. Potentially dangerous issues could have been explored more authentically with God and one another had they been assisted by a spiritual caregiver—issues like the following.

☐ Were they substituting sex for the intimacy both longed for? Sarah had never experienced emotional embrace in her strict home. Travis had concerned but distant parents who did not accept the reality of his faith. Much of adolescent sexual behavior is pseudo-sexual; sexual acting out, whether intercourse or masturbation, is often rooted in the need to medicate or escape feelings of loneliness, fear or worthlessness.[12]

☐ Were Sarah and Travis simply immature in their understanding of what it means to build an intimate friendship? Adolescents, lacking models and skills for friendship building, can readily substitute romance for relationship. Physical intimacy becomes a fast-track substitute for feelings of personal intimacy. The law of diminishing returns sets the couple on the course of moral failure. As more physical contact is needed to bolster the insecurity of shallow friendship, increasing sexual pleasure becomes necessary to avoid the weaknesses of the relationship, thus creating a cycle of enhancing physical intimacy at the expense of true relational intimacy. In the end, the relationship is doomed to implode on its immaturity.

☐ Were Sarah and Travis either unwilling or unable to find the help they needed beyond themselves? Adolescent Christian couples can approach God with "Show what I need to do to get you to take away my overwhelming sexual desire so I won't sin anymore." A lack of understanding of their created sexual selves and an immaturity in approaching God's redemptive work in their lives prevents them from engaging God at their point of need. Internal self-condemnation and the fear of others' condemnation can also repel a young couple away from potentially healing relationships with others. Fearing *What would they say?* or thinking *I could never disappoint them with this,* couples foolishly choose to isolate themselves from the very help they need.

The potential for prevention of moral failure is greater when spiritual caregivers are meaningfully present. So also is the potential for redemptive intervention after moral failure. A long-standing, trusting relationship with a spiritual caregiver provides the best environment for seeking help when the bridge from moral conviction to moral action is being washed away.

Pacing through each step. A spiritual caregiver at step one could have helped Travis and Sarah begin to mature in understanding of God's creation of human intimacy and friendship. Rather than merely committing themselves to sexual abstinence, they could have grown in understanding God's call to relational wholeness. The best preparation for keeping a commitment to sexual purity would have been a growth in true relational intimacy apart from the physical.

At step two their moral reasoning could have been discerned and, if necessary, challenged. Early adolescence signals a shift from making moral choices based on receiving rewards and avoiding punishment to making moral choices in response to a sense of what one considers authoritatively right and wrong. For the Christian adolescent, this means learning to choose what is right and good because God has established his will for the good of his children. As adolescence progresses, the late teenager or early twentysomething becomes capable of internalizing God's moral standard as intrinsically valuable.[13] The choice of moral purity thus needs to begin moving from "God said that we should not have sex, so we have to resist our desires" to "we cannot have sex and realize the fullness of God's goodness for our relationship, so we need to find godly ways of expressing the desires we feel." The obligation moves from "playing by the rules" to "experiencing all God has provided." A spiritual caregiver or caregiving couple could have assisted Travis and Sarah in honestly reflecting on the self-deception that began to emerge as their sexual relationship progressed.

Ideally, a spiritual caregiver could have provided support and guidance to the young couple before they began to experience discontinuity between their moral commitments and moral choices. They lacked affirmation to strengthen their resistance to temptation and counsel on developing strategies for success in their moral purity. Christians in moral failure fail largely because they do not know how to guard their hearts, minds and bodies against that which they cannot withstand. Sarah and Travis suffered from a lack of wisdom throughout their relationship.

As the sexual relationship took control of their lives, Sarah and Travis, like King David, needed a Nathan (2 Sam 12) to speak into the incongruence. They needed confrontation that did not involve the shaming of "And you call yourself a Christian? No true Christian would act that way." Rather, a pacing-then-leading intervention would have begun with "How are you dealing with the gap between what you are saying about your convictions and what you are actually doing?" Leading would have included insight into both the struggles of the Christian faith and the call to victory over temptation. Truth and grace would be essential to draw them out of their self-deception.

Sarah and Travis required assistance for critically reflecting on what was happening in their minds and hearts. What was so strong within them that motivated them to cross over important boundaries against the will of the God they love? How were they perpetuating the split between what they knew to be true and how they were living? What damage was being done to their emotional selves as they rationalized behavior to self-protection like Adam and Eve hiding behind the bushes? Without spiritual caregiving, the couple would have had to journey into these scary places of reflection alone—something they, like the rest of us, were unlikely to do.

By the end of the relationship, it had become a desert; both Travis and Sarah thirsted for spiritual healing for their emotions and minds. Counseling, support and mentoring would surely be necessary for a whole-person healing process. Whatever the particular needs are, they include spiritual healing for the sins the two have committed against God, each other and their own selves. Repentance and renewal become absolutely necessary. Healing will never be complete until Sarah and Travis confront their desperate need for the Father's embrace, the Son's truth and forgiveness, and the Holy Spirit's comfort and power for transformation. The words of David, following his conviction over his sins with Bathsheba, reflect what Sarah and Travis need to experience to make their way out of their sinful trap.

> Have mercy on me, O God,
>   according to your unfailing love;
> according to your great compassion
>   blot out my transgressions.
> Wash away all my iniquity
>   and cleanse me from my sin.
>
> For I know my transgressions,
>   and my sin is always before me.
> Against you, you only, have I sinned
>   and done what is evil in your sight,
> so that you are proved right when you speak
>   and justified when you judge.
> Surely I was sinful at birth,
>   sinful from the time my mother conceived me.
> Surely you desire truth in the inner parts;
>   you teach me wisdom in the inmost place.
>
> Cleanse me with hyssop, and I will be clean;
>   wash me, and I will be whiter than snow.

Let me hear joy and gladness;
    let the bones you have crushed rejoice.
Hide your face from my sins
    and blot out all my iniquity.

Create in me a pure heart, O God,
    and renew a steadfast spirit within me.
Do not cast me from your presence
    or take your Holy Spirit from me.
Restore to me the joy of your salvation
    and grant me a willing spirit, to sustain me. (Ps 51:1-12)

Remember, even David needed Nathan in order to go to this place of truth.

Two additional important areas of lack should be addressed along the way to the restoration of this daughter and son of God. First, spiritual caregivers should pay attention to the relational deficits the young couple will carry out of their relationship. Trust, sexual identity, confidence in their interpersonal efficacy and hope for their future walk with God are among the issues they will face as they walk out this pain. Caregivers need to pace with these places of weakness in order to connect them to God's healing grace.

Second, spiritual caregivers should invest in the development of *executive skills* that may need to be strengthened.[14] Several executive skills (competencies required to turn moral commitments into moral choices) significant in the lives of adolescents' moral selves are reflected in figure 6.[15]

Interpersonal communication	Delayed gratification	Goal setting
Time management	Spiritual disciplines	Social skills
Friendship building	Self-care	Managing emotions
Planning for success	Critical reflection	Interdependence

Figure 6. Some executive skills for adolescent moral development

Lacking intervention, Sarah and Travis are more likely to repeat this moral failure than not. At best, they will avoid sexual sin yet unconsciously self-protect against true intimacy. Even years later, married to Christian spouses and walking with Christ, they may find themselves blindsided by the emotional and spiritual carnage of their sexual past. The work of spiritual caregiving is far from over in the couple's journey toward moral wholeness.

Adolescent maturation is typically an intense process of searching, one that calls into question the answers that appear on the surface of life. Adolescents challenge spiritual caregivers and Christian communities to reframe their understanding of what it means to be God's child in a fallen world. Pacing and then leading alongside the students in our churches or neighborhoods draws us out of the safety of our defense fortresses of theological cliché and onto the risky relational streets of the adolescent experience.

When I involve myself meaningfully in an adolescent's life, inviting him into the reality of my own very human journey with God, choosing to be affected by his experiences simply because I love him, I will not remain the same person. No longer insulated, my inner self is touched by the warm and cold fronts that gust into his postmodern relational environment. When life is shared in this connection, the adolescent is not left alone to seek God's redemptive work. Himself a carrier of the Holy Spirit, he is being used by God's redemptive, re-creative work in my life. To borrow a phrase from C. S. Lewis, as an adolescent and I encounter Jesus together, the pacing-then-leading relationship is never "safe" for me, but it is always good.[16]

Reflecting on Your Journey

☐ How strong was your sense of personal value and efficacy as an adolescent? To what do you attribute that abundance or lack? How did this affect the nurture of your moral self?

☐ As you look back on those adolescent years, what relationships had the greatest impact on your moral choices? What difference did it make to either have or not have pacing-then-leading spiritual caregivers in your life at critical moments of moral decision-making?

☐ What aspects of Travis and Sarah's story stood out as common among the adolescents you serve? Which of the four steps appear to be the most challenging for them as they pursue moral lives? How do you perceive your role at these difficult points?

☐ How do you personally respond, in either thought or feeling, to the idea that your role makes a world of difference yet ultimately you cannot control how an adolescent develops morally? How does this shape your partnership with God as you attempt to provide an environment for the effective nurture of a moral self consistent with his righteousness?

Pressing In

☐ Examine your own heart. Where do you see the rationalizations that parallel Travis and Sarah's at work in your life? Take steps to confess those rationalizations to others and garner support for living efficaciously within the will God reveals to you.

☐ Read Robert Coles's *Moral Intelligence* to gain insight into the social dynamics of the moral development process.

☐ Read Lisa Kuhmerker's *The Kohlberg Legacy* to explore the role of moral dilemmas in the moral education of adolescents.

☐ Ask adolescents to describe the moral tensions of their life on campus, in the home and in the midst of youth culture. Avoid prescriptions for what you think they should do about them; simply listen to their descriptions of the world as they experience it. Discipline yourself for pacing with what lies below the immediate surface of behaviors and words. (Later, you will find these same adolescents soliciting your input, because they experience you as one who understands.)

☐ Rent a video with a clear moral dilemma and watch it with the adolescents in your life. Ask them about their thoughts and feelings in response to the movie. Walk through the characters' interior worlds, looking for ways to highlight each of the four steps of moving from moral belief to moral action. Ask the adolescents to tell not only *what* they would choose in that situation but also *why* they would make that choice and *how* they would be able to execute their decision.

The church has two choices right now. Either we entrench and die, or we take advantage of the incredible new vantage point postmodernism has given us on both the culture and ourselves.

CHRIS SEAY (AGE TWENTY-SIX), PASTOR, UNIVERSITY BAPTIST CHURCH, WACO, TEXAS

Somehow we have managed to take the most incredible story ever told and make it boring and irrelevant. It has taken many decades to do this, but we have accomplished it.

TNL.ORG

I was certain that I knew you
At the tender age of twelve
You'd so often been described by those who said they knew you well
Dark and rugged in your thirties
With a smile as bright as your robe
Every teacher, every preacher,
With the very best intent
Found new ways to hide the mystery replaced by common sense
And to know you was to keep you in my pocket
So easy to hold
It is easy to insist on what is packaged and precise
And dismiss the clear suspicion that you're bigger than we'd like
It is tempting to regard you as familiar in so many ways.

NICHOLE NORDEMAN, "WHO YOU ARE"

I attend a beautiful, traditional old stone church with the finest organ, choir, and music director in my city. I look to few things as warmly as singing great lungfuls of old hymns on Sunday morning and kneeling for that transcendent moment of grace at the communion rail. But I also wonder whether, as Mead put it, "we're speaking a foreign language to younger people," and whether my church is not in danger of withering away. And whether it doesn't deserve that fate if it doesn't get intentional, and soon.

CHARLES TRUEHEART, "WELCOME TO THE NEXT CHURCH"

To find your way in Postmodern Country you need a different eye, ear, compass and map.

GARY PHILLIPS, IN *AQUACHURCH* BY LEONARD SWEET

8

How to Create Space for
Postmodern Spiritual Journeys

Disconnected best described Amanda's body language as she walked into the evening service. Surrounded by the usual trappings of hymnbooks, pews, and a congregation of predominantly middle-aged adults, the usually vibrant late adolescent sat with legs crossed and arms folded. A few mumbled lines of hymns and choruses were the extent of Amanda's attempts to engage her familiar yet foreign surroundings.

After I had completed my sermon as the guest pastor, I moved toward Amanda to thank her for coming. Years ago, while on staff, I had known Amanda as a child who used to swing on my arms and play tag to tease me. Now I only knew a few sketchy details of her life: she had been studying abroad, her goals were to build a professional career in the arts, and her father had left her mother for a younger woman two years ago. I asked Amanda, "Is it hard for you to be here? It seems like your world is very different from this one." Amanda's response was a slight smile, a quiet "Yes, it is" and a hug that said, I believe, "Thanks for connecting with me."

In that brief moment Amanda knew that someone had recognized the distance between church as she knew it and her life as she knew it. As she walked back to her real world my heart was shrouded with profound sadness for her and her generation.[1]

Pacing and Then Leading: The Postmodern Imperative

Like a surfer catching "the big one," I have ridden the wave of youth ministry professionalism for two significant decades. I remember when Youth Specialties' *Ideas* were first published. I attended some of the earliest national nondenominational youth-worker conferences. For over a decade I have been teaching youth ministry in graduate and undergraduate courses throughout North America and in Asia. As the pastor to the student ministries pastoral staff at our church, I continue to live in the world of youth ministry. And after all these years, most of what I know about effectiveness in guiding twenty-first-century adolescent spiritual journeys can be distilled in a simple phrase: *pace, then lead.*

No program overhaul will fix church for Amanda. No quick solution exists to "make church attractive" to Amanda and her peers. In fact, until a spiritual caregiver finds a way to enter Amanda's world—to listen, learn, love and then lead—most of what her local church attempts on her behalf will be useless. Someone has to join Amanda on her real-life Jacob's Ladder of spirituality. Shouting instructions from a distance fails miserably.

Because each journey is unique, dynamic and unpredictable, there are no prepackaged "Ten Steps to Disciplemaking" programs for spiritual caregivers. Help can be found, however, when we explore the types of environments that foster deep spirituality on the postmodern adolescent spiritual journey. These *spiritual spacemakers* offer palatable nourishment for the spiritually hungry, disillusioned, disoriented, disconnected millennial generation. Their practices of spirituality represent an incredible window of opportunity for connecting authentic seekers of spiritual experience with the God who can and must be worshiped in spirit and truth.

Making Space for God

Don Postema asserts, "God makes space for us in the covenant community. We are embraced as children. We belong. We respond by making space for God, by being open in our lives, by living thankfully."[2]

God has made space for us, and he calls us to make space for him. He also moves us to create space for adolescents to engage.[3] We create that space by modeling his embrace, giving them a love that says "You belong to God." We create that space by fashioning opportunities for our children and adolescents to encounter God directly, personally. We create that space by guiding adolescents toward an adult maturity in which they learn to make their own space for God.

The Lilly Endowment funded the Youth Ministry and Spirituality Project, a "spacemaking" experiment for postmodern adolescents. Cosponsored by Youth Specialties and San Francisco Theological Seminary, the project focused on immersing sixteen youth groups across the United States in contemplative practices—"practices that invite a deeper awareness of God's presence."[4] These contemplative practices included meditative reading of Scripture, prayer focused on listening to God, artistic expressions of poetry and painting, and "more traditional spiritual disciplines such as silence, solitude, fasting, and prayer."[5] Ancient models for approaching Scripture and prayer such as lectio divina, the Ignatian awareness examen and centering prayer were employed.[6] Mark Yaconelli explains the rationale for the project:

> Today's popular youth ministry models are creative, dynamic, and fun. Yet something's missing. In a typical youth group, how many kids actually encounter the resurrected Christ? Does our focus on youth directors, curricula, and programs crowd out opportunities for kids to experience God? I think a youth program is effective only when it offers kids the space, tools, and time to encounter God's transforming love.
>
> We often invite kids to live their lives in Christ through our words and lesson plans, but we rarely find ways for them to actually practice this life. *They need us to equip them with the skills to develop a transforming intimacy with God.*[7]

What is the impact of programs that facilitate directly rather than mediate indirectly the Person of God? According to Yaconelli:

> It's changing all of us. As Jen Butler, an associate pastor in Oregon, says, "We shouldn't be surprised it's working so well. It's kind of a no-brainer. If you make the space, the Spirit will come."
>
> Our continuing challenge is to have the courage, trust, patience, and perseverance to set aside that holy space—to invite young people to listen with us for that still, small voice that brings life in abundance.[8]

Spiritual caregivers are spacemakers. How can we make holy space for postmodern adolescents? I will suggest five places where adolescents can "encounter the loving Presence of the ever-patient Christ."[9] The diverse forms by which adolescents practice the presence of Christ in these places

represent a template for spiritual spacemaking:
- ☐ a relational safe place
- ☐ a meaningful learning place
- ☐ an experiential worshiping place
- ☐ an interpersonal prayer place
- ☐ a cultural impact place[10]

A Relational "Safe" Place

Philip Yancey's *What's So Amazing About Grace?* opens with a friend's story of a woman whose concept of church was anything but a safe place.

> A prostitute came to me in wretched straits, homeless, sick, and unable to buy food for her two-year-old daughter. Through sobs and tears, she told me she had been renting out her daughter—two years old!—to men interested in kinky sex. . . . I could hardly bear hearing her sordid story. For one thing, it made me legally liable—I'm required to report cases of child abuse. I had no idea what to say to this woman.
>
> At last I asked if she had ever thought of going to a church for help. I will never forget the look of pure, naïve shock that crossed her face. "Church," she cried, "why would I ever go there? I was already feeling terrible about myself. They'd just make me feel worse."[11]

A dangerous place to confront one's sinfulness cannot be considered a safe place to experience God.

Creating space for twenty-first-century adolescents thus begins with offering them an opportunity to ask questions, wrestle with their fears and come back next week without having everything worked out. They know life is messy—the evidence to support this conclusion is pervasive. They cry out for a place to be a mess and still be loved, to be a mess yet have hope for healing. Postmodern adolescents long for an environment where, together, they can experience the safety of a strong, gracious Father.

Safe leaders create safe places. Relational safety is birthed by spiritual leaders who know what it means to walk with Jesus through their weaknesses, their failures and all the things they are ashamed of. Jimmy Long observes of today's generation of young adults:

> Given the independence of this generation, leaders will need to earn its respect rather than command it. They can do this by showing themselves to be real people who have real hurts. Their compassionate leadership flows

from their hurts, not their persona of perfection. As leaders share their hurts, trust is developed. Xers need people with whom they can identify, since they have been deeply wounded. They do not trust leaders who pretend that they do not make mistakes or that they have no problems. Xers need leaders who can learn from mistakes rather than avoid making them altogether—leaders who can help them work through their problems. Seeing a leader making mistakes frees Xers to take risks. The term *wounded healer* describes a leader of people in the postmodern world.[12]

If such a leader was desirable in the days of the Gen-X adolescent, how much more is there a need for authentically human leaders for the millennial adolescents!

Brennan Manning describes the wounded healer as one who has "been fractured and heartbroken by life."[13] Nearly half of all adolescents are living in broken homes, and the other half know through friendships the pain that results. The damage left in the wake of addictions, sexual promiscuity, pregnancies and abortions, violence and isolation is sufficient that no adolescent can escape the fact that life includes brokenness. They therefore want to see how a real Jesus can touch real brokenness.[14]

The first step toward creating a safe place is *providing safe people as spiritual caregivers.*[15] In past generations we approached adolescents with "Look at our great programs and cool leaders—you need to come and check us out!" In this generation, the message must be "We are broken people finding real hope and healing in Jesus. We want you to come and join us on the journey." This is an invitation to a safe place.

Students also need these safe leaders to help them create *safe communities* for discovering peer spiritual companionship. Large group gatherings, for all of their value in other arenas, do not offer a relationally safe community. Small groups—in a plethora of diverse forms—serve as the primary context for fostering community. The pastor of a rapidly growing church was asked, "Can your church just keep getting bigger and bigger?" His reply: "As long as we keep getting smaller and smaller."[16] Safe postmodern communities will cherish the value of becoming "smaller and smaller."

Leading any type of small group as a wounded healer can be a challenging task. The spiritual caregiver attempts to balance pacing and leading principles with multiple persons simultaneously. Moreover, in order to pace well, adult spiritual caregivers commit themselves to being *among* rather than simply *over* group members. They lead by personhood and relationship rather than by position.[17] If caregivers attempt to lead with "I am the adult, I have something important to teach you, therefore follow my agenda," they are doomed. Adolescents are looking for someone who will live the truth among them before attempting to convince them of the significance of that truth.[18] Hule Goddard observes, "[Postmoderns] are starved for moms and dads, they are craving people who will love them, people who will focus full attention on them and listen to them unconditionally, not because of any motive, but because of the love of Jesus. . . . If you make a place for them in your life, they will come. It doesn't take a great deal of creativity."[19] Safety, not sophistication, is the essential quality of the effective postmodern student ministry leader.

A Meaningful Learning Place

Learning in my generation began when the teacher opened his notes. If he allowed questions at the end or involved us in the learning process, we considered that a great way to make the learning "more personal." Today students expect to begin with their questions. The impersonal is not experienced as truth.

Postmodern Christians with a trust in the Word still remain intense seekers of personal understanding of truth. Knowing what God says is true is one thing; understanding how it makes sense in the complexity of life is quite another.

Meaningful learning of truth begins when that truth is connected to adolescents' personally meaningful questions. Meaningful learning continues as adolescents become engaged in a dialogue between their inner worlds and the Word of God.

Passionately experienced truth. If the truth has not passed through the heart of the spiritual caregiver, then his words communicate only theological information about God or God's Word. Where there is no heart experience of the truth, there is no passion. For the postmodern, no passion signals a lack of personal meaningfulness. Manning ties the experience of passion with the authority of the truth:

> Passion is not high emotion but a steely determination, fired by love, to stay centered in the awareness of Christ's present risenness, a drivenness to remain rooted in the truth of who I am, and a readiness to pay the price of fidelity. To own my unique self in a world filled with voices contrary to the

gospel requires enormous fortitude. In this decade of much empty religious talk and proliferating Bible studies, idle intellectual curiosity and pretension of importance, intelligence without courage is bankrupt. The truth of faith has little value when it is not also the life of the heart.[20]

Manning's word reads like an apologetic for postmodern theological learning.

A passionate experience of God's Word includes a yielding to the authority of his truth. If the caregiver feels "pumped" about theological ideas, even emotionally overwhelmed with their significance, but has not surrendered his heart to God's revealed will, the passion Manning describes remains absent. True passion results in a life that demonstrates integrity in response to God's truth.

Connection to God's salvation story. In Douglas Coupland's defining work, *Generation X,* Claire says, "Either our lives become stories or there is no way to get through them."[21] Claire is lamenting the lack of meaning attached to our daily life experiences.

Andy chimes in, "I agree. Dag agrees. We know that this is why the three of us left our lives behind us and came to the desert—to tell stories and make our own lives worthwhile in the process."[22]

Claire, Dag and Andy understand the vanity of life without a Big Story as a context for meaning.[23] If there is no greater meaning in life than going to school, getting a job, being entertained and trying to survive broken dreams and empty relationships, then each of us is forced to create our own personal narrative. We all need some way to connect the dots of our otherwise random set of life events.

Without a Big Story to make sense out of life and death, we are left with only desperate, individualistic autobiographies of struggles for love and purpose. Sadly, most twenty-first-century adolescents lack knowledge of even the most rudimentary elements of the Big Story of God at work in human history. Precisely these conditions have fostered the proliferation of "designer gods" and "patchwork religions" that characterize postmodernity.

Ron Johnson describes how his church responds in the vacuum that results from the absence of a Big Story:

Postmodern philosophers outside the church preach the "death of the meta-narrative." In other words, they don't believe there is one universal story (like the gospel) that can make sense of life. There is no universal truth. What we're saying at Pathways every week is, "There is a grand story that makes

sense of all your stories, that brings meaning to your life. History really is
going some place, and there is a good ending. You're going to go through a
bunch of pain this side of heaven, but your life here is building toward a great
climax, a life eternally with Jesus Christ."[24]

Teaching from the perspective of the whole Story of God, Genesis to
Revelation, is critical.[25] On the road to Emmaus, Jesus could have given the
two men a couple of theological points or a line from the prophets and then
revealed himself to them. He chose instead to give them a whole picture of
God's plan for redemption. He gave them a rich theological heritage within
which to understand the salvation that was theirs in him.

Systematic, planned teaching sessions should focus on the content of the
Big Story, whether the adolescent hearers are churched or unchurched. While
topical talks still hold an important place in student ministry, postmodern adolescents thirst for a refreshing new understanding of how God moves from
Genesis to Revelation, intersecting their daily routines along the way.

Twenty-first-century adolescents also must discover the connection of
their story to God's Story. To facilitate this connection, spiritual caregivers
must become effective at recounting the discovery of God's redemptive
work in their own stories. The character of God demonstrated in a caregiver's story provides a touchpoint for adolescents to understand how God's
redemptive love can bring meaning to life and death in the present world.

Spiritual caregivers also ought to cultivate the discipline of listening to
adolescents' stories as a central component of their pacing relationships. As
caregivers enter into the unfinished handiwork of God in adolescents' lives,
they can begin to lead students toward awareness of God at work within
them. New questions for meaningful learning are created. New ways of
thinking about life with God are formed. What is God doing? How is he
calling? How can I respond and participate? What does the Word of God
have to say about his will for my response and participation? Posing these
questions with pacing empathy and pacing prayer, spiritual caregivers discover receptive territory for speaking the truth in love.

A picture of this process can be found in Andrew Dreitcer's description
of spiritual direction:

[Spiritual direction] isn't designed to solve particular problems or handle
specific crises. It takes the long view. The spiritual direction relationship
looks for how God is working, calling, prodding, and inviting us to new ways

of viewing with Christ. It focuses on building an intimate relationship with Jesus over a life-time, through all the problems, crises, joys, and blessings.[26]

Finally, twenty-first-century adolescents need Bible teaching in the language of stories. The call for stories has raised legitimate concerns from my generation regarding the role of propositional truth and doctrinal orthodoxy in postmodern culture. With an emphasis on personal meaningfulness and authentic relationship, the core teachings of Scripture and the basic foundations of doctrine could potentially be unwisely discarded as examples of "modern ways of thinking." Christian stories about the impact of Scripture could become the interpretive grid for Scripture, usurping the place of biblical authority in the church.

While the danger is real, such a tragic outcome is unnecessary. God himself, over several thousand years and with multiple authors of sixty-six books, demonstrates how stories can carry truth and how only ultimate truth can give meaning to stories. Teaching the Bible in the language of story does not therefore require a loss of reliance on propositional truth.

When we are teaching Scripture to postmoderns, however, maintaining a tenacious commitment to what the Bible teaches is essential. Teachers must likewise be cautious not to claim as authoritative any content beyond what the Bible reveals. In postmodern culture spiritual caregivers ought to cling with a "life grip" to the core foundations of the Christian faith revealed in Scripture. All other matters of doctrinal nuance must be held much more loosely.[27] Alongside unswerving commitment to biblical authority, however, we should have an equally tenacious commitment to present the Bible in stories as part of the Big Story of God's salvation history.

A biblical vision for life. Postmodern millennials long for a vision worthy of their whole life commitment. Only the Story of God as revealed in Scripture can satisfy that God-created hunger. No vision could be more compelling than one of God at work in them to transform their whole being and through them to reach a lost world.[28]

We internalize the hope of God's vision through a daily experience of being shaped by God's will in the present. Mike Mozley notes that postmodern adolescents "need daily application of how to make it in this world, how this Bible has an impact upon my works and makes sense to my daily situation."[29]

I have noticed that members of the postmodern generation would rather be around me with my family than me alone. Several students have told me, "I want to see how a family works. I love to watch you with your kids." What I thought of as a distraction from quality time with students was actually a contribution to the value of our time together. Postmoderns search for truth that can be *practiced.* Guiding their response to truth, walking them through places of failed obedience to God, and offering practical insights carries more weight than elaborate systematic presentations of theological concepts.[30]

Starting with their questions, leading with a spiritual caregiver's passion, connecting their lives to God's redemptive Story and vision—these characterize a commitment to a holistic relationship of truth with a living God. In the knowing, being and doing that result from practicing these spiritual disciplines in relationship to God's Word and Spirit comes a critical life realization: when I gain a personally meaningful knowledge of truth in relationship to the One who is Truth, I am free indeed (Jn 8:32).

An Experiential Worshiping Place

Recently we gathered 150 postmoderns from our congregation. Our goal: to hear their vision for reaching their generation. We specifically asked them to discuss what a worship experience (note the nomenclature: *experience* rather than *service*) for their generation would look like. Their responses included the following:

WORSHIP!

Free

Interactive

Dancing

Dialogue

Emotional and passionate

Upbeat

Artistic

Elements of orthodoxy

Poetry

Lots of involvement

Joy, liberty

Communion

Respect

Icons, images, symbols

Testimonies
Drama and humor
Student leaders and teachers

Mark Driscoll, a young pastor of a church whose average age is twenty-three, provides a context for understanding the diversity of these responses:

> Worship for the postmodern needs to address the whole person, not just the intellect. The mind must be engaged and taught, not with steps or formulas, but with grand narratives. The heart must be moved to value and live the gospel in all of life. All of the five senses must be engaged to experience God. . . .
>
> Everything in the service needs to preach: architecture, lighting, songs, prayers, fellowship, the smell . . . it all preaches. Being creative is tough work, but we believe art is that region between heaven and earth that connects the two. To experience God is often the highest form of knowing, and the entire worship experience must be more than a presentation about God.[31]

The thread that holds it all together is the emphasis on personal encounter with a living God.[32] Hymns, choruses or popular worship songs sung without passion or encounter with God fail to capture the hearts of this generation. Videos or PowerPoint presentations to add "excellence" fall short as well. Even well-crafted exegetical messages, while interesting, do not inspire response. Creating space for personally experiential worship is crucial.

The diversity of our young people's vision for their generation signals the necessity of creating multiple spaces for worship. Relying on the same tried-and-true choruses on overheads in the youth group, the same routine of family Bible readings and prayer requests, and the same teachings on choosing a devotional routine will likely fail to prompt the depth of personal encounter sought by postmodern adolescents. If it is not living, dynamic and personally engaging, it will be experienced as religion without relationship.

Entire books have been written on this subject; here I highlight just three key principles for spiritual caregivers wanting to pace and then lead adolescents to experiential worship.

1. *Expose adolescents to diverse worship experiences.* The modern institutional church developed tight patterns of worship that were handed down

from generation to generation—just ask the first person to suggest guitars or drums in a traditional church! The postmodern church will not ask, "What does a worship service look like?" It rather asks, "What else can we incorporate into our worship experiences?"

Students benefit significantly from intentional encounters with Christians whose public and private worship varies from their own. They gain breadth in worship as they engage "knowing" approaches to worship (reading of Scripture and liturgy), "being" approaches (silence and celebration) and "doing" approaches (dance, use of symbols and the visual arts). Adolescents find depth in worship as spiritual caregivers coach them through a discovery of their own rhythm for their personal worship of God.

2. *Provide resources for creating personal worship experiences.* Model new Bible study methods, introduce them to CDs or stories that will prompt encounters with God, teach them how to journal in a style that fits their personality. Form a worship dance team or a worship arts community within the church. Cosponsor a coffeehouse where young artists can share poetry, short stories, music and interpretive dance. Offer worship nights or retreats where private solitude and corporate reflection leads to an intergenerational receptivity to the presence of Christ. A family can visit churches whose worship experiences, while vital and rich, contrast greatly to its own home church. All these possibilities find their stimulus in the question "What could I do to broaden and deepen an adolescent's personal encounter with God?" It is a question spiritual caregivers must not neglect.

3. *Facilitate connections between head, heart and hands in worship.* How we understand worship speaks volumes about our concept of God. True worship is not a planned event. True worship is a particular moment in the history of a relationship with God. Treating worship as if it were something to do in order to focus on God before we teach or as simply "the right way" to show God that we love him is woefully inadequate. Paul implored the Christians in Rome to offer themselves as "living sacrifices." Adolescents want guidance for how all of life can be experienced as a form of worship. A compartmentalized approach to worship fails to capture the heart of God for a worshiping people. When the spiritual discipline of intentional, experiential worship appropriately relates to knowing, being and doing, the resulting whole-person encounter of the Whole Person of God will, by definition, transform the worshiper.

The act of intentional, focused worship powerfully shapes the postmodern adolescent's view of God. Spiritual caregivers should help students discipline their worship with biblical teachings on who God is and how he relates to his people. The significance of this challenge in postmodernity surfaces in these comments:

> The worship-based models in the postmodern setting are saying, "We're not going to expect you to choose Christianity based on a presuppostion or an idea or a concept, but on the person of Christ and the people of Christ. So you have to respond and choose Christianity in the context of community, not within the context of abstract ideas."[33]

As people encounter Christ in community rather than proposition, we come closer to engaging his heart. However, we must avoid reinterpreting Christ through our worship experience without reference to his scriptural self-revelation. Like learning through stories, the discipline of experiential worship requires a heightened attentiveness to the authority and clarity of biblical teaching.

An Interpersonal Prayer Place

Jesus' disciples asked him, "Lord, teach us how to pray" (see Mt 6:9-13; Lk 11:1-4) His response presents a radical theology of prayer. To a people who perceived God as a transcendent deity distantly presiding over a religious empire, Jesus says, "When you pray, begin with 'Our Father.' " Jesus shows us an embracing, loving Father calling his children to intimate relationship. Prayer, for Jesus, consists of dialogue within that relationship.

Don Postema reflects on the interpersonal nature of God's design of prayer:

> Prayer is an act by which we open ourselves to God's presence, break up our hard hearts to receive the refreshing shower of God's gifts, to be embraced by Christ' love, to be filled with the life of the Spirit. . . .
> Prayer is taking time to let God recreate us, play with us, touch us as an artist is making a sculpture, a painting, or a piece of music with our lives, making us "poets of the Word."[34]

Prayer is at its best when it engages the heart of the child with the heart of the Father. Our goal thus becomes teaching postmodern adolescents how to be children who respond to a Father's request to spend time together.

How do spiritual caregivers teach postmodern adolescents to pray? First, the caregiver develops a rich prayer life. Early-first-century Jewish models for prayer had been handed down by the Pharisees, self-appointed trustees of the religious empire they perceived God to be ruling. Jesus' disciples asked him to teach them to pray because they had never been exposed to an authentic walk with the Father. The greatest draw to prayer comes from being exposed to the real thing. Spiritual caregivers should thus begin with an honest evaluation of their own prayer life.

Second, spiritual caregivers mentor adolescents in the heart and art of prayer. Based on the theological conviction that God is a speaking and listening God, Leanne Payne offers the following model for daily prayer. The basis of the model is the very prayer Jesus taught his disciples:

Meditation on the Scriptures (listening to God through his written Word)
Praise and thanksgiving: "Our Father, who art in heaven,
    hallowed be thy Name."
Intercession: "Thy kingdom come, thy will be done, on earth
    as it is in heaven."
Personal petitions: "Give us this day our daily bread."
Repentance and forgiveness prayers: "And forgive us our trespasses,
    as we forgive those who trespass against us."
A full committal of ourselves and our day to God: "And lead
    us not into temptation, but deliver us from evil.
    For thine is the kingdom, and the power, and the glory,
    forever and ever. Amen."[35]

Payne begins and ends with listening prayer. God speaks through his Word. We respond to a Father who is intently, intimately listening. Then we listen for him to speak into our hearts, perhaps through the Word, our thoughts, our intuitions or even the world around us.[36]

Third, spiritual caregivers create a culture of interpersonal prayer. Imagine a college freshman struggling in his first semester away from home. His grades are slipping. He is down to his last two dollars—and there are six days before his next paycheck. The group he had hoped would be his primary social group has suddenly grown cold toward him. A part of him really wants to tell his parents, while another part really wants to avoid disclosing all of this to them. Now, as a participant in an interactive story, imagine each of these "rest of the story" scenarios.[37]

Scenario 1. He calls his parents. They are cordial, thankful he has called. They exchange bits of information about their worlds, but nothing personal. When the father asks, "Is there anything you need, son?" the son hesitates. He finally responds with a weak "I'm doing OK." His parents seem pleased with his answer, though Mom does ask if he has been eating well. He assures them that he has, although money has been tight. The son then adds, "I could use a little help, maybe just ten dollars to get me to the next paycheck if that's OK."

Scenario 2. His parents call him and leave a message for him to return the call. When he does, they seem thrilled to have a chance to catch up on his world. His parents articulate the feelings they have been experiencing since he left for school—they want him to know the mixture of joy and sadness they have felt as they reflect on how much he means to them. When the father asks, "How are you doing?" the son hesitates. He finally responds with a weak "I'm doing OK." The mother responds, "You sound like you are not OK—you seem sad. I am concerned about you." The father adds, "You know, son, we want to know how you are *really* doing. We want to be there for you, even if that means we need to change our plans to come and visit you this weekend." Tearfully, the son discloses the sense of despair he is experiencing.

The first scenario represents the prayer environment adolescents often experience in home and church. The second scenario pictures a culture of interpersonal prayer.

Spiritual caregivers are not primarily pacing with and leading adolescents toward a Christian lifestyle. Rather, we are moving them into an ever-deepening love relationship with the triune God. Andrew Kuyper, in *To Be Near unto God,* writes, "The heart of him who fears God does not rest until it has come to such a conscious fellowship with its God, that between itself and the heart of God there is mutual knowledge, the one of the other—even the clear sense that God has knowledge of us and we of Him."[38]

All relationships move toward intimacy through increasingly meaningful communication. When the communication is between humanity and God, we call it prayer. Such interpersonal prayer cannot be neglected as a core spiritual discipline for the postmodern sojourner.

A Cultural Impact Place

How will the safe communities of the postmodern church embrace those who do not belong to the household of faith? Kevin Offner observes,

> The greatest apologetic for Christianity is not a well-reasoned argument but a wildly loving community. Our Lord did not say that they will know us by our truth—as important as this is—but by our love. At the very heart of the gospel is not a proposition but a person, Jesus Christ, who is made manifest in and through his called-out ones in their life together.[39]

That apologetic cannot be communicated apart from an extension of the community into the broader culture. The postmodern spiritual disciplines of relational safety, meaningful learning, experiential worship and interpersonal prayer must manifest themselves in a "go" rather than a "come" model. Postmodern adolescents are eager to assume the challenge of "taking Christianity to the streets."[40]

Because millennial adolescents thirst for authenticity, conceive of spirituality as a whole-life reality, and hold onto the broken heart of God for the world without isolating themselves from that world, this generation possesses a unique capacity for living out the call to a ministry of reconciliation. Dean and Foster believe the very nature of adolescence prepares them for success:

> Developmentally, youth are capable of extraordinary commitment to someone who believes in them, of ridiculous fidelity to a cause worthy of their total commitment. God did not choose a teenager to bear salvation to the world by accident. Who else would agree to such a plan? While the coming of Jesus Christ in a virgin's womb is the unrepeatable mystery of God, God invites all of us to become Godbearers—persons who by the power of the Holy Spirit smuggle Jesus into the world through our own lives, who by virtue of our yes to God find ourselves forever and irrevocably changed.[41]

The spiritual discipline of Godbearing is a mantle to be carried by postmodern adolescents in the midst of their own generation and the one to follow. Because only they can carry this mantle, spiritual caregivers must find ways to challenge them to "a cause worthy of their total commitment" and express belief in their capacity to bear God in a postmodern world.

Beyond service projects. The acts of doing alone, however, miss the mark for creating space for God's transforming work in these reconciling world-changers. As we have seen, postmodern adolescents crave meaningful interpersonal experiences that call for investment of their individual resources. Leaf-raking, car washes, large outreach events and summer mission trips all make some contribution toward developing students in service and ministry. In the end, however, none of these activities in themselves have the power to shape the next generation of leadership. Churches, parachurch ministries, families and small group leaders should seek to infuse the values mentioned below into acts of service.

To mature spiritually, students require active, authentic expression of their personal interests, natural abilities and spiritual gifts. Christian community cannot be fully experienced as community until the adolescents' presence and participation are required. Fun games, competition and icebreakers are thus being superseded by artistic expression, music, drama, personal reflections, use of technology to serve, and experiments with new ideas. The most compelling ideas require multiple perspectives to design and diverse gifts to execute.

In the midst of a highly diverse world, postmoderns seek opportunities for synergy—contributing one's part to something that becomes greater than the sum of all the parts. Consider the postmodern world of sports. In my generation, the Iron Man competition was the ultimate sports challenge. Distance running followed by a lengthy swim followed by a bicycle road race resulted in the crowning of one exalted champion. The epitome of extreme endurance and success in postmodern sports is the Eco-Challenge. In the Eco-Challenge, the whole team has to stay together and work together every step of the way, for the sake of both safety and progress. For more than a week, teams cross deserts, scale mountains, hack through dangerous forests, swim in shark-infested waters and battle the elements not so much to finish first as to survive—together.[42] The Eco-Challenge has been described as "a vast world of incredible beauty fraught with hidden dangers, a limitless choice of pathways and solutions, a goal that seems clear and grows fuzzy as one proceeds but is nevertheless attainable by a tight group of people working together, relying on one another."[43]

The Eco-Challenge is a powerful metaphor for a means for postmodern adolescents to take ownership of the call to spiritual leadership in their generation. Rather than asking an individual student to do heroic work against the tide of cultural resistance, spiritual caregivers join with adolescents in building a team to reach their common goal: adult Christian maturity and leadership in the midst of their generation. Caregivers realize the postmodern culture of the "youth way" is a "vast world of incredible beauty fraught with hidden dangers, a limitless choice of pathways and solutions." They understand that while there is a "goal that seems clear," in the messiness we call life the goal "grows fuzzy as one proceeds." These caregivers are confident that the goal is "nevertheless attainable by a tight group of people working together, relying on one another" and submitted to the purpose, presence and power of God at work in their lives.

In this vision, students' presence and participation are essential. Moreover, the adolescent's personal, direct encounter with God in the midst of the team matters—the strength of the whole requires the strengthening of the parts.[44]

In the spiritual challenge of pacing and then leading adolescent spiritual journeys, the true victory lies in seeing an adolescent become a spiritual caregiver in her own generation. When she is investing herself in the lives of her peers, opening the Scriptures and sharing Jesus on her friends' trek to Emmaus, an indigenous redemptive work of God in a postmodern, sensate culture has truly begun to emerge. Nothing less should constitute the missionary vision of adult caregivers engaged in bicultural relationships with postmodern pilgrims in progress.[45]

Creating Space for God in a Postmodern World

In spite of the significant challenges of postmodern culture, the shift from modernity brings with it many welcome changes. Postmodernity brings a heightened awareness of spirituality and mystery, a greater desire for personal intimacy, a deeper appreciation of and tolerance for cultural diversity, more patience for complexity and process in human relationships, enhanced attentiveness to experiential ways of learning, broader openness to the exchange of new ideas, and greater understanding of the interconnectedness of the global village. These changes will all contribute to the growth of Christian evangelism, mission, education, youth ministry and counseling ministries around the world. More specifically, these characteristics of postmodernity provide magnificent present-tense entry points for bringing the reality of Jesus' life into youth culture.

Maximizing those entry points cannot be accomplished through institutional initiatives. Pastor Chris Seay articulates the suspicion the millennial generation has regarding our institutional efforts: "It's not that we don't trust God; it's that we don't trust the institutions. They've let us down."[46] The best examples of postmodern churches are yet to come. When they do emerge, they will look more like Chris Seay or Amanda than like me. The future spacemakers for a post-Christian, postmodern youth culture are still wading through it themselves; that's why they will be the most qualified to lead the rest of us.

Our role for now is to pace and then lead them into a full authenticity of life with God, to provide places to foster their intimacy with him. Even now, if we are pacing and leading well, we will find ourselves following them as they lead the way in the ministry of reconciliation to a postmodern generation.

Reflecting on Your Journey

☐ In the past month, how would you describe the space you have created for God? Relatively, is it the size of

a large room

half of a large room

a one-foot-square tile on the floor of the room

a napkin lying on the tile on the floor of the room

a one-inch-square design imprinted on the napkin lying on the tile on the floor of the room?

☐ What are the biggest external hindrances you face in creating space for God? What are your most significant internal hindrances?

☐ Of the five places of postmodern spiritual disciplines, where would you say you are experiencing the most depth in your own spiritual life? Where are you experiencing the least depth? To what do you attribute this lack?

☐ Complete the following sentence: The most difficult place for me to provide for the adolescents in my life is_____
_____because_____.

☐ What do you find to be the correlation between your own spiritual life and the cultivation of spiritual depth in the lives of the adolescents you love? What does this suggest about the nature of spiritual leadership?

Pressing In

☐ What about our relationships with God makes it difficult to cultivate relational space for deepening intimacy? How can we begin to address this struggle?

☐ As you read the chapter, what stands out as an issue you need to explore more thoroughly? Seek resources in persons and books, including the Holy Spirit and the Scriptures, to expand your understanding regarding this topic. As your insight increases, ask God to help you translate your learning into meaningful spiritual experiences for your adolescents.

☐ Plan your schedule for the next three months, beginning by scheduling a "God day" away. Before you allocate discretionary time to hobbies or events, consider how you could create a day for building your friendship with God. Ask a few friends, including adolescents, to pray for that day, and report back the results.

☐ Lean into the safe community God has provided for you. If you do not have one, pray diligently to discover such relationships. Covenant with those who make up your safe community to seek increasing levels of authenticity and intimacy. Determine not to settle for shallow relationships with God's people, lest you hinder your journey into the depths of his love for you.

☐ Read Dean and Foster's *God-bearing Youth Ministry* for a renewed vision of the call to incarnate spiritual life in the midst of adolescent reality.

☐ Take the adolescents in your life on a "God day" away for silence and solitude. Fast and pray all day, spending time both together and apart. In the evening celebrate what God did during the day, with a meal and a time of sharing.

Section 3

Exploring the Terrain of Adolescent Journeys

Preparing for Your Journey

As you prepare to read chapters nine to eleven, ask God to move the learning through your mind and heart into the very depths of your soul. Pray that God will speak truth and grace into your life concerning the following questions.

☐ If you could watch a video that condensed the adolescent growth process from ages twelve to twenty-two, what would you observe? What themes, patterns and story lines would emerge consistently in all adolescents?

☐ How does personal development (physical, emotional, mental, moral, social) interface with spiritual growth? How does God weave spiritual transformation into the fabric of adolescent maturation?

☐ How do adolescent relationships and experiences shape the identity of a soon-to-be adult?

☐ How does the role of the spiritual caregiver evolve over the years of maturation from early adolescent to young adult?

☐ What expectations should you have for personal maturity at each phase of adolescent development? How does this inform your approach to spiritual nurture?

☐ How have your own adolescent experiences and relationships continued to affect your engagement of adolescents in their real-world lives? Where have your past hurts or failures caused you to be reactive to adolescents' journeys? What issues do you need to be aware of as you enter pacing-then-leading relationships with adolescents whose pain mirrors that of your own past?

In junior high, who you are is not so much defined by who you are, but by the person sitting next to you in the cafeteria [glancing at his best friend, the nerdy Paul] . . . a scary thought.
KEVIN ARNOLD, *THE WONDER YEARS*

The rush to grow up has blurred the distinction between being preadolescent and being adolescent. The growing-up-too-fast syndrome has produced preteeners who experiment too soon with behaviors traditionally associated with the teenage years.
DAVID LYNN, "THE NEW ADOLESCENCE"

I don't recall having sexuality pushed in my face when I was 10 or 11. But I have a younger half-sister who is 11 years old, and she's a very big fan of Britney Spears and the Spice Girls, and she tries to emulate them in the way she dresses and the way she acts. . . . I see her wanting to wear clothes that I would never have considered wearing. I don't remember going through that at her age.
CHU HUI, AGE NINETEEN, IN "THE END OF INNOCENCE"

Jeffrey, a 13-year-old eighth grader from Long Island, said that of his group of five friends, two are already sleeping with their girlfriends. They are not behaving promiscuously, he states, since these are "long term" relationships—each having lasted for "at least one month."
NINA DARNTON, "*THE END OF INNOCENCE*"

No, no. I've been there before. It was hard enough the first time.
FROM THE MOVIE *BIG;* TOM HANKS'S ADULT GIRLFRIEND'S RESPONSE TO HIS REQUEST THAT SHE JOIN HIM IN GOING BACK TO BEING A THIRTEEN-YEAR-OLD

I praise you because I am fearfully and wonderfully made;
your works are wonderful,
I know that full well.
PSALM 139:14

9

Early Adolescence

"We're Not in Kansas Anymore"

*T*he Foothills Parkway lies a half-hour's drive from my home. Located ten minutes from the Great Smoky Mountain National Park, the parkway leads to an overlook that provides a dramatic view of the diverse topography and landscapes of east Tennessee. From the overlook one can observe mountain peaks, mountain ranges, ridges, valleys, coves and plateaus in a natural 360-degree theater. The scenery is magnificent. Making the experience even more enjoyable are panoramic pictures placed at strategic points around the circular overlook. Each of these pictures identifies precisely what is being seen as one gazes in a particular direction. Peaks and valleys are named, towns labeled, landmarks highlighted. The view is therefore not only breathtaking but informative as well. As I follow the pictures around the circle I acquire new perspectives about where I have been and where I am going in my Tennessee travels.

Spiritual caregivers need such a panoramic view of the topography and landscape of the adolescent passage of the human spiritual journey. This chapter and the following two seek to provide this overview. Insight is offered on how to pace and then lead adolescents during early, middle and late adolescence. Perspective will emerge from seeing adolescence as a multifaceted yet coherent experience designed by God to metamorphose children into adults. The coherence of the adolescent experience is expressed in the following three assumptions which underpin each chapter's description.

1. *Adolescence is primarily an interpersonal research project that seeks to answer the question "Who am I?"* Adolescents are wholly engaged in the process of developing a sense of identity separate from their parents. Les Parrot III explains:

> Achieving a sense of identity is the major developmental task of teenagers. Like a stunned soldier in a state of confusion, sooner or later, young people are hit with a bomb that is more powerful than dynamite—puberty. Somewhere between childhood and maturity their bodies kick into overdrive and fuel changes at an alarming rate. With this acceleration of physical and emotional growth, they become strangers to themselves. Under attack by an arsenal of fiery hormones, the bewildered young person begins to ask, *"Who am I?"*
>
> While achievement of a meaningful answer to this question is a lifelong pursuit, it is the burning challenge of adolescence.[1]

The adolescent's pursuit of a sense of self is lived out through her daily relationships with peers, parents and other significant adults. She looks primarily to those relationships to find a working definition of who she is. If the adolescent is breathing and alert, one can assume that she is assessing the current status of her self-definition.

2. *Adolescence is a time of transformation, not just a time of transition.* Moving from grade school to middle school or junior high to high school in a span of two to three years calls for transition at a staggering pace. More dramatic, however, are the physical, mental and emotional changes, and therefore spiritual transformations, occurring in the adolescent's life. To understand an adolescent one has to begin from the point of view of a person whose mind and body are evolving into a form alien to all of his previous experiences just as all of his relationships are becoming exponentially less familiar and more complicated.[2] Add to this his obsession with the question "Who am I?" and the "bewildering" aspects of a young person's experience suddenly seem well within the range of normal.

3. *Adolescent spirituality is integrally woven into the fabric of whole-person growth.* This assumption is a natural corollary to the whole-person spirituality described in chapter three's discussion of a theology for pacing and then leading. Catherine Stonehouse, in *Joining Children on the Spiri-*

tual Journey, relates human development and spiritual maturation:

> The spiritual journey is not a path separate from the rest of life, walked by
> one's spirit. It is the path of everyday living where God meets and walks with
> us, where we respond to God with our whole developing self. The journey
> begins at conception and continues until we no longer walk this earth. Every
> portion of the journey is important because we learn and who we become
> along each section of the way influences what we see, hear, and become in
> the future.[3]

The adolescent spiritual journey is inseparable from the adolescent developmental journey. Adolescent spiritual maturation "occurs within the
matrix of human developmental processes—physical, intellectual, emotional, social, moral."[4] To nurture spirituality is to nurture the whole person
in relationship to God.

Along the way caregivers will find themselves guiding adolescents' nav-
igation of the physical demands of rapidly transforming bodies, the intellectual challenges of postmodern "radical pluralism,"[5] the emotional throes
of feeling inferior or undesirable, the social barriers of cliques that indis-
criminately exclude and the moral dilemmas of a sensate "youth way."
Spiritual caregivers best serve adolescents when they pace and then lead
adolescents to a discovery of God at work in the midst of their entire being.
By doing so, caregivers enable the adolescents to engage God in those
same real-life places.

The first view presenting itself is a wide-angle portrait of early adolescence, the initial excursion on the adolescent journey.

Something's Changed

"Delightful." For thirteen years Karl and Mary had repeatedly heard this
adjective from teachers, pastors, coaches and neighbors applied to their
daughter, Tameeka. The warm smile, the pleasant manners and the eager-
to-please enthusiasm Tameeka brought into every social environment had
been a source of tremendous joy and pride for her parents.

"Dreadful." This is the only word that comes to mind when Karl and
Mary recall last weekend with Tameeka. She came home on Friday in one
of her recently acquired "moods." Sullen and quick to criticize, Tameeka
seemed to be angry with her mom for simply breathing the same air. Hoping to ease the tension that afternoon, Mary reminded her that the family
was going to spend the weekend at a cousin's beach house, a place

Tameeka had always loved to go. Tameeka's only response was "Can Elyse go too?" When Mary denied her request, Tameeka rolled her eyes, breathed a heavy sigh and protested, "This is going to be *so* boring."

She was wrong. The weekend had very few boring moments. Both days were filled with confrontations over Tameeka's critical comments and her never-ending requests to do something *fun—fun* being defined as whatever they were not doing at the moment. By the time they were packing the car to return home, Karl angrily announced that there would be no more family getaways until Tameeka left for college. As they finally pulled in their own driveway, Mary turned to the pouting teenager in the back seat and asked, "Who are you, and what have you done with my daughter?"

Not every thirteen-year-old hits the wall of puberty with the same abruptness and force of impact as Tameeka. For some the initiation is more gradual and less dramatic. For others the intensity of early adolescence is as deeply felt but more indirectly manifested, perhaps in stomachaches, problems with academic concentration or social withdrawal. In every case, however, the initial experiences of becoming an adolescent profoundly rock the no-longer-child's inner world. One life traveler who had recently reached the adolescent passage of her journey used these words to describe the impact:

> Every day, just about, something new seems to be happening to this body of mine and I get scared sometimes. I'll wake up in the middle of the night and I can't go back to sleep, and I toss and I turn and I can't stop my mind; it's racing fast, and everything is coming into it, and I think of my two best friends, and how their faces are all broken out, and I worry mine will break out, too, but so far it hasn't, and I think of my sizes, and I can't get it out of my head—the chest size and the stomach size and what I'll be wearing and whether I'll be able to fit into this kind of dress or the latest swimsuit. Well, it goes on and on, and I'm dizzy, even though it's maybe one o'clock in the morning, and there I am, in bed, so how can you be dizzy?
>
> Everything is growing and changing. I can see my mother watching me. I can see everyone watching me. There are times I think I see people watching me when they really couldn't care less! My dad makes a point of not staring, but he catches his look, I guess. I'm going to be "big-chested"; that's how my mother describes herself! I have to figure out how to dress so I feel better—I mean, so I don't feel strange, with my bosom just sticking out at everyone! I have to decide if I should shave my legs! I will! I wish a lot of the time I could just go back to being a little girl, without all these problems and these decisions![6]

Welcome to early adolescence—we're definitely not in Kansas anymore.

Fasten Your Seatbelt

Pacing with the life of a twelve- to fourteen-year-old can be like riding on an airplane that has just begun to encounter moderate to severe turbulence. A seasoned air traveler, at such times I still have the feeling of being hurtled into an uncomfortable, unsafe place. As one who loves to be in control, I despise the fact that I have no control over the speed or direction of the airplane. If the turbulence lasts for quite a while, I become frustrated that I have no idea when the next hard bounce will hit or how long it will be until the ride becomes smooth.

In the midst of my anxiety, I begin to notice that my fellow passengers are responding in a variety of ways, some with patience, others with panic. (Unfortunately, those who are in a panic agitate me more than those who are patient calm me.) As I brace myself physically, mentally and emotionally for the next hard bounce, I remind myself that the plane was built to endure this, the pilot knows exactly what he is doing, and this will not last forever. I am further relaxed when I recall the numerous times I have endured turbulence on a flight that eventually reached its destination safely.

Now imagine that I had never been on a plane before. I have heard about turbulence, even watched a movie about it once; still I have never experienced for myself being shaken and rattled at five hundred-plus miles per hour, thirty thousand feet above the ground. The people seated near me seem to be about to panic—and I know they *have* flown before. I am uncertain how to tell what is routine and what is dangerous turbulence. Furthermore, the pilot says nothing except that the flight attendants should sit down and fasten their seatbelts. *Wham!* The plane drops suddenly, a woman across the aisle shrieks, and we just keep on going. "Somebody slow this thing down!"

Say hello to the inner world of the early adolescent. Lacking sufficient life experience and often sensing that their world is hurtling out of control, these young lives need the reassurance that they are safe, that they were made to be able to endure this, and that God, the One who *is* in control, knows exactly what he is doing. They need seasoned spiritual caregivers sitting in the seats next to them, listening to what they feel, explaining what is happening and sharing stories about riding out this turbulence on their own journey to maturity.

Tameeka's parents, her small group leader at church and her drama coach each have a unique contribution to make as calming influences in her turbulent inner world. The worst-case scenario would be for these potential spiritual caregivers to pull back or give up on the process. Like the screaming woman across the aisle, adults who pull away communicate to adolescents that they have reason to believe they should be afraid. Pacing with Tameeka communicates the opposite message: "I have been here before. I am with you here now. With God's help we will get through this just fine. In fact, you can relax and enjoy the journey God has planned for you." Leading Tameeka thus begins with learning to celebrate both her self and the God-created process she has entered as God's gifts to our world and hers.

Who Is This Person?

Spiritual caregivers seeking to pace with early adolescents have a particularly challenging road ahead. The older one becomes, the less clearly one remembers what it was like to be a thirteen-year-old. In light of this, I have often assigned adult caregivers the task of answering the question "What was I like in seventh grade?" The exercise brings to mind a lot of humorous stories (humorous now, not so humorous then) about embarrassing and awkward moments, outrageous wardrobes and a plethora of naïve perspectives on issues such as parents, sex and God. In the midst of the humor, however, one can almost universally find sadness. In fact, in the years I have asked hundreds of adults to describe their seventh-grade selves, only about 2 percent have remembered that year of life as a generally positive experience.[7] Early adolescence is a challenging time to live; and a challenging moment for spiritual caregivers to pace in relationally meaningful ways.[8]

No one, especially a young teenager, wants to be thought of as merely a specimen of his developmental stage. Adult caregivers must reject "all junior highers are like that" thinking. *All early adolescents are individual persons, growing at an individual pace, in uniquely individual ways.* Gaining insight into what happens as a twelve year old exits childhood via the on-ramp of adolescence must therefore always be examined through a lens of respect for individuality.

With that respect in place, caregivers can draw on developmental insights to pace with early adolescents' experiences. By relationally fastening their seatbelts and riding it out with these wonderful, often overlooked children of God, caregivers earn the privilege of leading them, in the midst of the turbulence, toward God's embracing presence, purpose and power. As they learn who they are and lead them toward who God has called them to be, spiritual caregivers will discover that there is much to celebrate in the lives of God's amazing works-in-progress we call early adolescents.

The Dance: Portrait of the Work in Progress

For a vivid portrait of the developmental path of early adolescents, caregivers should attend a junior high dance. Most of the participants stand awkwardly on the side, anxiously weighing the social risk of appearing interested in a potential dance partner against the social risk of staying put as a wallflower. Huddles of guys bargain over who should ask, "If Jeff wanted to dance with you, would you say yes?" Flocks of girls glance nervously toward the huddles of guys, living vicariously off the energy of the electricity between Jeff and their peer who is the object of his infatuation. The couples who are dancing betray the bad joke of early adolescent physical development: the girls are as much as six inches taller than the guys. Though no one seems to notice, the guys are painfully aware that the imposing effect of the girls' height is nothing compared to the emotional intimidation they feel. Mimicking behaviors they have observed in music videos, movies and their older siblings, the students struggle through the evening, feeling more relieved than excited when the dance has concluded.

The surrealistic nature of a junior high dance results from the in-between nature of early adolescence. Some bodies are in high gear in primary sexual development. Others clearly are not. Those who are more physically developed lack confidence in how to live within bodies that create a false appearance of internal maturity. Those who are less developed are even less confident; feeling that they look like children when they should look like men and women, the late bloomers are uncertain of how to relate to their more advanced peers.

The impact of the onset of physical puberty cannot be overstated. Early adolescents are not simply making a transition, they are being transformed. The transformation can at times seem too much for both the young teenager and the adults who care for him. Judy Blume captures the overwhelming nature of puberty with the character Tony in *Then Again, Maybe I Won't:*

Oh-oh . . . here it comes! I was right the first time. What'll I say? Nothing. I won't say a word. I'll let him say it. I sat down on my bed. Pop pulled my desk chair over and sat close to me. He looked around for a while, rubbing his hands together, almost like he was praying.

"Uh Tony . . ." he finally said.

"Yes, Pop?"

"Uh . . . well . . . now that you're in seventh grade there are things you should know about." While he was talking Pop cracked each of his knuckles.

"Yes, Pop?"

"Oh . . . I don't know . . . maybe Ralph should be the one to talk to you. He's a lot closer to your age." Pop stopped talking and looked around my room. Then he coughed a little and started again. "You see, Tony . . . there are things you should know about girls and about babies and about . . . look Tony, do you know anything?"

He doesn't know about my dreams, I thought. This has nothing to do with what I've been thinking about. He doesn't know. He's more scared than I am.

"Tony . . . I asked you, do you know anything?"

"Sure Pop," I said.

"You do? You know about babies . . . how they're made?"

"Sure Pop. Since third grade."

"You're positive you have the right information?"

"Sure Pop."

"Do you know other things, too, Tony?"

"Sure Pop. A lot."

My father looked relieved. "Well," he said, "thing to remember is that I'm here to answer all your questions."

"Okay Pop. I'll remember."

He rubbed his hands again. "I don't know, Tony . . . I feel like I should say more. Your mother thinks there's a lot for you to learn, but I don't know what to tell you. I never told Vinnie or Ralph anything. I don't even know how Vinnie learned. From his friends I guess. And Vinnie told Ralph. So I'm not too experienced when it comes to discussing the subject. But listen, Tony . . . man to man . . . you can always come to me." . . .

The next day my father handed me a book called *Basic Facts About Sex*. He said I should read it in my spare time and if I have any questions I should come to him. There's a whole section on wet dreams and another on masturbation. Maybe they do know about me after all! My stomach jumped around so bad I had to take a pill.[9]

No wonder so many of us have selectively forgotten our own early adolescence!

A New View of Me

If bodies were all that were changing, the equation of puberty would be much simpler. The most dramatic changes, however, cannot be accounted for with a tape measure. Somewhere along the path of early adolescence the mind begins to transform itself as well. David Elkind describes this transformation as learning to think in a new key:

> The new thinking abilities are like a Copernican revolution in the way young people see themselves, others, and the world in general. And these new thinking abilities strongly color how young people adjust to the changes in their bodily configuration and appearance. For example, the self-consciousness so common in the early teen years is a result of a change in thinking and not just a product of the physical changes (or lack of them) themselves.[10]

The "new key" combined with inexperience in handling this recently acquired capacity results in early adolescents' being idealistic, critical, argumentative, self-conscious, self-centered and inconsistent in their feelings and choices.[11] Contrary to Mary's fear that an alien had replaced Tameeka, much of what she was observing was simply the emergence of her daughter's new way of thinking.

Take a rapidly changing body—including a set of hormones working overtime to fuel primary sexual maturity—then add a new way of thinking that gives rise to a preoccupation with how others see you, and you have a recipe for emotional distress. Mary and Karl might feel relieved to know that Tameeka's moodiness is indicative of the level of emotional energy required to navigate early adolescence. By analogy, imagine taking Tameeka when she was a compliant six-year-old and putting her through a physically and mentally exhausting outdoor stress/endurance experience for eight hours. Now, imagine Karl and Mary asking her to come to the dinner table and be as carefree and pleasant as she has always been. Of course she would not be able to do so, and her parents would understand that. "After all," they would agree, "look at what she has been through today."

While Tameeka is responsible to make choices that are consistent with being a thirteen-year-old (choices such as making an effort to be a part of the family rather than punishing the family for her bad mood and being respectful even when she feels emotionally out of control), Karl and Mary can ease the tension by first empathizing with her daily stress/endurance test. Beginning to define herself in a new body, thinking in a new key and being overly sensitive to the remarks and actions of others is enough to drive anyone to the edge—especially when she spends the entire day surrounded by early adolescents enduring the same transformation!

Peer Pressure Points

The net effect of all these changes creates a junior high school social environment that can be very intimidating. Vying for peer acceptance to validate their sense of belonging and value in the uncharted waters of adolescence and youth culture, students maneuver, manipulate and manhandle one another emotionally. As a result, students are excluded, feel betrayed and may have a sense of being "losers."[12] Ironically, the "winners" do not fare much better than those on the outside of the social cliques. They feel insecure because they know that if the social currents shift, they too may find themselves drifting alone, set loose by more dominant members of the group. "Outside" is the loneliest place to be in the early-adolescent world. Not belonging calls into question an eighth grader's personal worth in the new world that his body and mind have forced him to enter.

Making important decisions, particularly those involving moral implications, can be extremely challenging in the midst of early-adolescent socialization. In the early teen years, having not completed their transformation into a new key of thinking, adolescents still reason in fairly defined categories of right and wrong. The standards typically come from the teachings of their childhood. Early adolescents still experience a strong gravitational pull toward the morals of their parents.[13] The impact of a sensate worldview on the home and youth culture, however, is the bad news of this gravitational force.

On the home front, parents too often fail to model or transmit the moral standards we as Christian spiritual caregivers desire for our adolescents. Consequently, a large percentage of early adolescents make moral choices consistent with the morality of their parents yet inconsistent with the moral standards of God. Furthermore, parents, even those who do espouse higher moral standards, increasingly are impotent as protectors of their children's moral innocence.[14] Stressed with work, financial debt, hurting or broken marriages, and immersed in pursuit of the immediate payoffs of a sensate culture, these parents do not take time to monitor their children's media consumption. Nina Darton, in a *Newsweek* article titled "The End of Innocence," relates this example of parental abdication of the responsibility to protect:

> A 16-year-old Houston girl was baby-sitting for two boys, 6 and 9 years old. The kids were glued to the George Michael "I Want Your Sex" video on MTV. Singing along, the boys came to the words "sex with you alone." The younger one looked a little puzzled. "What's that thing when it isn't alone, when lots of people do it?" he asked. "A borney?" "No," his brother shot back contemptuously. "You're so dumb. It's an orgy." Even the babysitter— who thinks of herself as "pretty sexy," has already "had sex" with one boyfriend and "fooled around" with several others—was shocked. "At that age, I never even heard of anything like that, " she said. "I didn't know about that stuff until at least sixth grade."[15]

On the cultural front, the "youth way" bombards young children, preteens and early adolescents with tidal waves of sensual misinformation and morally impoverished impressions of life. The ethos of the culture begins to exert an increasingly powerful pull as teenagers move toward middle adolescence, a time when they will be choosing more for themselves than their parents. The early adolescents who carry too much information, who have been exposed to too many sensual images and who lack moral guidance from a pacing spiritual caregiver are set up to implode under the pressures of peer socialization. Exemplifying this tragic acquiescence to a sensate culture, one thirteen-year-old remarked, "Hey, my own *life* is R-rated, so why shouldn't I be able to go see an R-rated movie?"[16]

The emerging need to find a new place for the "new me" in the new environment of "teendom" leads to the stressful realities of peer pressure, no matter what one's home experiences may have been. The social and cultural elements of that new environment intensify the weight felt by early adolescents committed to walking the Jesus way in the midst of the youth way. Pacing and then leading them in the twenty-first century therefore demands our careful attention to the tense intersection of internal needs and external forces. Relief from peer pressure begins with being understood and accepted by a spiritual caregiver. Relief continues as the caregiver leads by offering guidance and providing support for an "in the world but not of it" calling. Each early adolescent's journey will be as distinct as her personality, family background, friendship experiences, level of immersion in the youth way and personal relationship with God. Pacing and then leading will include helping those with G-rated lives as well as those with R-rated lives learn to live in the embrace of grace, a force that exceeds the pressure of the weight of the world (1 Jn 4:4).

Principles for Nurturing Early Adolescent Lives

Pacing and then leading early adolescents has been portrayed thus far as challenging, wonderful, scary, overwhelming, filled with celebration and dynamic. In some sense all spiritual caregiving is marked by these qualities. The uniqueness of the age group lies in the remarkable transformation that occurs within a few short years or, in some cases, months. The five principles below are designed to guide spiritual caregivers in their pacing and leading in the midst of this life passage.

1. Assist them in building supportive peer group friendships. Friendships represent emotional life support for junior high students. David Veerman observes, "Early adolescents can seem obsessed with their friends, forming tight cliques, writing copious notes, and talking incessantly on the phone. Friends are important because fragile egos need acceptance, affirmation, and a place to belong."[17]

Having adult spiritual caregivers is not enough to enable the full maturation process of early adolescents. Without peers a child is hindered from taking steps away from parental dependence toward adult independence. Early adolescents *need* peers who accept and support them if they are to grow into a mature sense of who God made them to be.

Early adolescents particularly need assistance because they naturally gravitate to the safest, most comfortable peer group available. Their fragile egos make them reluctant to move out of contexts where they find acceptance, even if their parents see those contexts as potentially damaging. This is why when working with an early adolescent whom you believe to be "running with the wrong crowd," simply telling her why she should not be with that group fails to enable her to let go. She will need additional assistance in forming new friendships where acceptance is offered and experienced.

Gatherings of same-sex companions who enjoy the same types of activities are the safest contexts for early-adolescent friendships. Finding a same-sex group of friends who share enjoyment of camping, mountain biking, jazz dance or soccer enables the young adolescent to build an affiliation as a runway to friendship. Not yet prepared for the more intimate relationships of middle and late adolescence, junior highers tend to relate in and through activities. Helping them build friendships therefore means identifying places where they go to do things with others.

Early adolescents do experiment with opposite-sex relationships, but they are ill-equipped to deal with intimacy. They may "go with" a guy or girl (and, sadly, even become sexually active), but the relationships are more about gauging one's level of social acceptance than about true interpersonal exchange—the formation of a mature individual self simply has not occurred. As a result, most "dating relationships" have a life span of weeks rather than months.

An early adolescent's relationship with God often mirrors the feedback he believes he is receiving from his peers. He needs comfort when failed peer acceptance has led to a sense of abandonment by God as well. He needs truth spoken into those places so that he can be exposed to the unconditional love of the Creator and Redeemer—the only authoritative ground we have for establishing our sense of identity. The early adolescent's need is neither sin nor weakness. His need for acceptance from God *and* human friends is an inherent aspect of the God-created maturation process.

2. Create learning experiences that emphasize "doing the faith" in response to God's love. The entry point for early-adolescent spirituality is *doing*. They love being active, working in teams, practicing new skills and finding concrete ways to express their faith. For truth to become real, it must have a tangible means of being experienced. Teaching an early adolescent a biblical principle and then praying that she will learn to apply that truth falls far short of meeting her needs.

Sunday school teachers, confirmation class leaders and other teachers of this age group often become frustrated with them. The instructing adult grows impatient with their short attention span, desire for activity and lack of interest in pursuing knowledge. The problem in these settings, of course, is not the early adolescent but rather the expectations of the adult.[18] Early adolescents require concrete examples of faith in action, specific illustrations and applications of biblical truth in their real world, and opportunities to practice the skills required to fulfill their commitment to obedience. They need active learning experiences that become their own personal illustrations of what it means for them to call themselves Christian.

Group service projects, meals prepared for those in need, dramas and concerts, CDs reviewed by small groups to identify the lyrics' truths and lies, or inductive Bible study in teams to discover what God says about forgiveness are examples of how early adolescents make meaning in their faith. Each of these examples involves acting in response to who God is— and doing so with their friends. In the doing together comes the opportunity for learning. When spirituality is treated as a spectator sport, early adolescents will fail to learn the reality of Jesus.

3. Provide them with meaningful adult interaction in their daily lives. Early adolescents remain dependent on their parents and other significant adults. Not able to drive and usually unable to earn much money by working, they have only limited freedom to explore the world on their own. At this age they are still very comfortable with adults' presence and involvement in their group activities, though at times they do want to show their friends that they are "independent." Wise adults will take advantage of these factors before the currents of middle and late adolescence sweep young ones further toward adulthood.

Early adolescents, particularly males, are much more comfortable doing things in a group than sitting down to have an individual talk with an adult. In the midst of driving to the game or pitching the tent the spiritual caregiver will find rich opportunities to pace with the seventh grader's world. As the outcome of the game or the events of the weekend are reviewed, the caregiver will encounter fertile ground for leading into a discussion of God's presence and purpose in the seventh grader's world. Meaningful dialogue will happen in the midst of and following *doing with.*

4. Create opportunities for them to make contributions that highlight their individual value to others. When I was a counselor at a camp for junior-high students, the camp-out night was the highlight of my week. Teaching Bible studies, planning recreational activities and keeping watch over my cabin of seven boys provided many opportunities to build meaningful relationships. Nothing, however, compared with camping out. To clear a spot for the tents, gather firewood, prepare meals and monitor the campfire, we would divide ourselves into teams. Each team had its own responsibilities, tasks that were necessary for the success of the group. Everyone had a role and everyone's role was essential.

Early adolescents crave healthy team experiences. Being on a team lessens the self-consciousness of individual responsibilities and heightens affirmation for one's efforts. A team lessens the emphasis on individual giftedness and heightens the emphasis on cooperative effort. A team, when well developed, is a safe place to be.

Spiritual caregivers have many opportunities to create a sense of team among the early adolescents they nurture by delegating responsibilities, overseeing team cooperation and progress, affirming success and working through failures. Failure by spiritual caregivers to provide adequate support or challenge will, of course, disable the early adolescent's attempts to make his or her distinctive contribution. Patience, attentiveness and concern for both the person and the assigned responsibilities are required for maximizing each member's efforts.

Adolescents with special talents often gain the inside track in contributing to a team. Outstanding athletes, musicians and students find opportunities to express their abilities in a variety of school and community activities. Highly competitive environments, however, are not always ideal places for contributing. The drive to win and the pressure to perform may creep in, causing the early adolescent to feel affirmed only when she "gets it right." The truest value of a person's contributions is not based on excellence of performance but on excellence in the use of her abilities to make a difference for others.[19]

5. Communicate clear moral boundaries and behavioral expectations. Early adolescents require concrete, specific codes of conduct. They need unclouded teaching on biblical truths concerning sexual morality, being truthful, taking responsibility for sins, being ethical and fair in schoolwork, and guarding their bodies against drugs and alcohol abuse. Alongside these guidelines, they also need practice in how to make decisions. What do I do if I'm sleeping over at my friend's and he has access to pornographic videos? What if I know that my friend is cheating on an exam and the teacher confronts me? What if I have lied to my parents and God convicts me of that sin—do I have to tell them? What if a friend is about to have an abortion—do I have to tell someone to protect the baby's life? Real-life questions that engage adolescents in theological reasoning are critical to the formation of decision-making skills.

While mature moral reasoning does not emerge until middle to late adolescence, the rudimentary attitudes, concepts and skills for adult decision-making can be shaped in early adolescence. Given the complexity of their cultural milieu and the lack of protection many junior highers are afforded from the sights and sounds of a sensate youth way, it is not only expedient but necessary to begin training for adult moral decision-making.

The Impact of the Early Adolescent Years

Inside every high school student, college student and middle-aged parent resides an "inner early adolescent." What happens in the years of junior high makes a profound impact on the rest of one's life. Consider one man's account of living with his "inner early adolescent" view of self as his constant companion:

> It wasn't easy to pay attention in French class. Our yearbooks had just been passed out, so while the teacher droned on, we were quietly signing books and passing them around the room.
>
> Mine was somewhere at the back of the class. I couldn't wait to get it back. What would my friends say of me? Would there be words of praise? Admiration? When class was over, I quickly found my yearbook and flipped through it with anticipation. And then it caught my eye: someone had written large words across the last page of my book: HI THERE, UGLY!
>
> I had never really considered whether or not I was "good looking," but now I knew. I was ugly. If someone at the back of that grade-seven class thought I was ugly, there were probably many others who agreed. I studied myself in the mirror: big nose, pimples, slightly overweight, not muscular. Yes, it must be true, I thought. I'm ugly. I told no one any of this. There seemed to be no need. It was a fact: I was ugly.[20]

From this point on, the man carried a sense of ugliness; twenty years later he found that it was affecting his marriage.

> Finally one day my wife asked, "Why is it that you never look at me when I say that you're handsome?" I decided to tell her about the yearbook and my conclusions. "You can't believe that! It's wrong! Somebody who didn't even know you in grade seven can't be taken seriously! I know you, I love you and I chose to marry you. I think you're handsome and I think I've proved that." So, was I going to believe my wife . . . or that old graffiti?
>
> I thought about that question for a long time and about how God doesn't make junk. Who was I going to believe? I chose to believe my wife and God.
>
> I still have a big nose. At age thirty-four, I even still get pimples! My hair has begun to recede and you could probably find people who would say that I am ugly. But I'm not one of them! As time goes on and I listen more and more to those who love me, I know that I am beautiful . . . or should I say, handsome.[21]

Pacing involves listening to early adolescent hearts; leading then connects those impressionable hearts to a God-view of their maturing selves. Simple, loving acts of *doing life with* early adolescents let us penetrate the graceless world of junior high with the Father's embrace of grace. That embrace communicates, "God loves you just the way you are—I know, because he lets me share in his love for you." The message is relevant for today and the rest of their lives, because as time goes on we all listen more and more to the people who really love us.

How blessed is the early adolescent who learns in meaningful, personal ways that God is the One who loves him most!

Reflecting on Your Journey

☐ Do you recall ever feeling like Tony (the Judy Blume character) as an early adolescent? Do you recall ever feeling like Tony's dad as a spiritual caregiver of an early adolescent? What makes it so difficult for adults and early adolescents to connect on deeply personal issues such as sex, emotions and peer relationships?

☐ Describe yourself as a seventh grader. What did you look like? What mattered to you the most? When did you feel excited? When did you feel scared? What were your family relationships like? your peer relationships?

☐ What impresses you as the most significant challenges of being an early adolescent—in any generation?

☐ Given what you have been learning about postmodern sensate culture, how are today's early adolescents' challenges similar to or different from your experiences of growing up?

☐ How do you personally feel about early adolescents? How effective do you feel you have been in your pacing-then-leading relationships with early adolescents?

☐ What have you read in this chapter that will shape your future relationships with persons at this stage in life? Pray for discernment and wisdom as you consider how to pace with more attention and lead with more accuracy in the lives of early adolescents.

Pressing In

☐ Sit with God for a while and reflect on the early adolescents in your past and present world. What new perspectives or attitudes does God seem to be birthing in you? How does he want to transform you so that your relationships with early adolescents will be transformed?

☐ Ask your parents to help you remember your early adolescent years. Take a journey through yearbooks, scrapbooks and "artifacts" of those years. What do you see? Where do you see God at work? What does this reflective stroll teach you about God at work in your life? How does this shape your view of your role in partnering with God in present early-adolescent lives?

☐ Read David Veerman's *Reaching Kids Before High School* to gain a more comprehensive portrait of the early-adolescent years.

☐ Watch reruns of the television show *The Wonder Years*. Look for examples of early-adolescent thinking, feeling and experiencing. Consider how the cultural shifts that are occurring in the present generation are reflected in these examples.

☐ Take a fifteen-year veteran junior high or middle school teacher to lunch. Ask the teacher to describe constants and changes they have observed through their years of teaching. Ask: What do you believe your students need most from parents and significant adult others? Be sure to affirm the teacher for his or her immeasurable impact on students' lives.

☐ With a Bible, pen and journal spend several hours in pacing prayer with God concerning the early adolescents in your life. Listen for his heart, be paced with by him, and follow his leading as you walk with him into the world of students for whom he died.

The big question of adolescent life—the unspoken question that teenagers are constantly asking each other and constantly answering— is: Are you one of us or one of them? If you're one of us, prove it. Prove it by showing you don't care about their rules. Prove it by doing something—a tattoo would be nice, a hole through your nose even better—that will mark you irrevocably as one of us.

JUDITH RICH HARRIS, *THE NURTURE ASSUMPTION*

We accept the fact that we had to sacrifice a whole Saturday in detention for whatever it was we did wrong. But we think you are crazy to make us write an essay telling you who we think we are. You see us as you want to see us, in the simplest terms, with the most convenient definitions. But what we found out is that each one of us is a brain, and an athlete, and a basket case, and a princess, and a criminal. Does that answer your question? Sincerely Yours,
The Breakfast Club

FROM THE FILM *THE BREAKFAST CLUB*

"I don't want to be reached. I don't want to be loved!" declared seventeen-year-old Ziggy. When asked why he felt that way he said, "'cause when I needed it, nobody was there. Do you hear me? Nobody was there. So, I don't want it now."

SCOTT LARSON, *RISK IN OUR MIDST*

I pray that out of his glorious riches he may strengthen you with power through his Spirit in your inner being, so that Christ may dwell in your hearts through faith. And I pray that you, being rooted and established in love, may have power, together with all the saints, to grasp how wide and long and high and deep is the love of Christ, and to know this love that surpasses knowledge—that you may be filled to the measure of all the fullness of God.

EPHESIANS 3:16-19

10

Middle Adolescence

Whose Am I?

*T*o understand life as a middle adolescent one need travel no farther than the nearest high school campus. On a campus filled with classes, courses, clubs and courtship, even the casual observer would discover a well-established social order that directs the conversations and behaviors of all campus members. "The Most Mature Thing I've Ever Seen," a reminiscing entry in *Chicken Soup for the Teenage Soul,* vividly portrays the presence and power of these palpable yet unseen forces of peer socialization:

> Every student at Monroe High School knew about it. Nobody did it. Nobody.
>
> Lunchtime at Monroe High School was consistent. As soon as the bell that ended the last morning class started ringing, the students swarmed toward their lockers. Then those who didn't eat in the cafeteria headed with their sack lunches toward the quad. The quad was a large, treeless square of concrete in the center of campus. It was the meeting-and-eating place.
>
> Around the quad the various school cliques assembled. The druggies lined up on the south side. The punkers were next to them. On the east side were the brothers. Next to them were the nerds and brains. The jocks stood on the north side next to the surfers. The rednecks were on the west side. The

socialites were in the cafeteria. Everybody knew their place.

This arrangement did create some tension. But for all the tension generated on the perimeter of the quad at lunchtime, it was nothing compared with the inside of the quad.

The inside was no-man's land.

Nobody at Monroe walked across the middle of the quad. To get from one side to the other, students walked around the quad. Around the people. Around the stares.

Everybody knew about it, so nobody did it.

Then one day at the beginning of spring, a new student arrived at Monroe. Her name was Lisa. She was unfamiliar to the area; in fact, she was new to the state.

And although Lisa was pleasant enough, she did not quickly attract friends. She was overweight and shy, and the style of her clothes was not . . . right.

She had enrolled at Monroe that morning. All morning she had struggled to find her classes, sometimes arriving late, which was especially embarrassing. The teachers had generally been tolerant, if not cordial. Some were irritated; their classes were already too large, and now this added paperwork before class.

But she had made it through the morning to the lunch bell. Hearing the bell, she sighed and entered the crush of students in the hall. She weaved her way to her locker and tried her combination three, four, five times before it banged open. Standing in front of her locker, she decided to carry along with her lunch all of her books for afternoon classes. She thought she could save herself another trip to her locker by eating lunch on the steps in front of her next class.

So Lisa began the longest walk of her life—the walk across campus toward her next class. Through the hall. Down the steps. Across the lawn. Across the sidewalk. Across the quad.

As Lisa walked she shifted the heavy books, alternately resting the arm that held her light lunch. She had grabbed too many books; the top book kept slipping off, and she was forced to keep her eye on it in a balancing act as she moved past the people, shifting the books from arm to arm, focusing on the balanced book, shuffling forward, oblivious to her surroundings.

All at once she sensed something: the air was eerily quiet. A nameless dread clutched her. She stopped. She lifted her head.

Hundreds of eyes were staring. Cruel, hateful stares. Pitiless stares. Angry stares. Unfeeling, cold stares. They bore into her.

She froze, dazed, pinned down. Her mind screamed, No! This can't be happening!

What happened next people couldn't say for sure. Some later said she dropped her book, reached down to pick it up, and lost her balance. Some claimed she tripped. It didn't matter how it happened.

She slipped to the pavement and lay there, legs splayed, in the center of the quad.

Then the laughter started, like an electric current jolting the perimeter, charged with a nightmarish quality, wrapping itself around and around its victim.

And she lay there.

From every side fingers pointed, and then the taunt began, building in raucous merriment, building in heartless insanity: "You! You! You! YOU!"

And she lay there.

From the edge of the perimeter a figure emerged slowly. He was a tall boy, and he walked rigidly, as though he were measuring each step. He headed straight toward the place where the fingers pointed. As more and more students noticed someone else in the middle the calls softened, and then they ceased. A hush flickered over the crowd.

The boy walked into the silence. He walked steadily, his eyes fixed on the form lying on the concrete.

By the time he reached the girl, the silence was deafening. The boy simply knelt and picked up the lunch sack and the scattered books, and then he placed a hand under the girl's arm and looked into her face. And she got up.

The boy steadied her once as they walked across the quad and through the quiet perimeter that parted before them.

The next day at Monroe High School at lunchtime a curious thing happened. A soon as the bell that ended the last morning class started ringing, the students swarmed toward their lockers. Then those who didn't eat in the cafeteria headed with their sack lunches across the quad.

From all parts of the campus, different groups of students walked freely across the quad. No one could really explain why it was okay now. Everybody just knew. And if you ever visit Monroe High School, that's how it is today.

It happened some time ago. I never even knew his name. But what he did, nobody who was there will ever forget.

Nobody.[1]

Disengaged from the context of middle adolescence, this story might seem to be much ado about nothing. After all, the girl simply fell down; the unknown rescuer didn't actually save Lisa's life. Yet in a very real sense, the hero of the story did rescue Lisa's life. On her first day at Monroe, Lisa had come face to face with an unconsciously self-inflicted social death. Her choice to walk across the quad prompted the entire campus to conclude, "She is not one of *us*."[2] Her physical fall only served to pump up the volume of the message. As the young man reached for Lisa's hand, she was hanging by her relational fingernails, quickly losing her grip on the slippery cliff of social acceptance. The brave, compassionate young stranger provided Lisa with a handhold by which she could begin to pull herself out of danger. She knew it, the young hero knew it, and so did everyone else in the quad.

Peer socialization undeniably dominates the lives of middle adolescents. Spiritual caregivers entering relationships with high school students quickly discover its presence and power. When caregivers also understand the role of peer socialization in the maturation process, they are empowered to pace with high school students and then lead them to overcome rather than be overcome by the social forces of middle adolescence.

Crossing the Social Bridge

What began in early adolescence as reactive, sporadic attempts to gain an identity separate from one's parents becomes a proactive, focused lifestyle in middle adolescence. The fifteen to eighteen year old feels an increased urgency to be "my own person." Like a bridge, the high school years provide a path between the primarily parent-ordered world of their childhood lives and the self-ordered world of their young adult lives (see figure 7).

The anticipation of the other side urges the teenager onward, toward the establishment of his own place in the world. In the crossing, however,

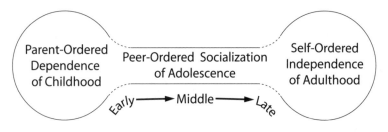

Figure 7.   Individuation

childhood needs for parents as a source of security are not erased. Adolescents lacking parental nurture, discipline and guidance are at great risk during the high school years. Even with good parenting, however, living "between the times" often causes internal tension between teens' most consistent need, parental love, and their growing need, a sense of self individuated from parents.

This tension played itself out vividly during a retreat for high school students and their parents. Haley, known within the church as a personable but rebellious fifteen year old, approached me to ask, "Do we have to sit with our parents?" The strained expressions on the faces of her friends Elizabeth and Carmen suggested that Haley was expressing their sentiments as well as her own. Each of these sophomores had agreed to attend the retreat only after they were assured that at least one other member of the trio would be present. Now, as they surveyed the hotel meeting room, they were confronted with the socially threatening possibility that they would be separated from each other in order to be seated with their parents.

"No, it isn't necessary to sit with your parents. You and your parents will be together later, but to start the meeting you can sit wherever you like."

The three accepted my response with a collective "Whew!"

Soon students and parents began to fill the room. The adolescents typically sat near their parents, but only when they could sit *next to* their friends. We launched our program with our own version of the game show *Family Feud* and then continued with a parent-teen adaptation of *The Newlywed Game*. Questions like "At what age will your mom say that she was first kissed by a boyfriend?" and "What kind of music did your dad listen to when he was your age?" led to lots of laughter and good-natured teasing. By the end of the games, when we moved into a family devotional time, the students had unconsciously migrated to join their parents. The shared experiences of playing and laughing together had transformed that generic meeting room into a socially safe haven for parent-teen interaction.

To see adolescents and parents having fun together did not surprise me. Our youth ministry leadership team had prepared a retreat that was user-friendly for both age groups. I was thoroughly surprised, however, by what I observed after the meeting. As students headed out to the recreation area and parents gathered around the coffeepot, I saw a small huddle in the center of the room. The group, a mixture of parents and adolescents, was engaged in animated conversation, reviewing the highlights of the evening's events. In the middle of the group sat Neal, the father of two high school students. On his lap, with both arms lovingly locked around his neck, sat his affectionate daughter Haley.

Haley's behavior on the first night of our retreat epitomizes life on the bridge between two worlds. Her behavior read like a slogan for middle adolescence: "Let me go—but not too far." Herein lies the purpose for an adolescent social structure. Peer groups at their best do not supplant parents; rather, they supplement them by providing a relational bridge for safely learning how to become independent.

Individuation: Recognizing Me

Two life-changing events dominate the landscape of middle adolescence: getting a driver's license and graduating from high school. Like booster rockets, the license and diploma propel the "ready or not, here I come" adolescent into an increasingly adult world. The widening opportunities and the coinciding increase in responsibilities alter forever the adolescent's way of life. Anticipating and absorbing the profound impact of these two externally life-changing events alone would be sufficient reasons to consider the middle adolescent years a crucial passage. The legal right to operate a moving vehicle and the legal end of compulsory education, however, only add fuel to an already hot pursuit of a mature sense of self.

A mature adult self recognizes *This is who I am,* apart from reliance on others for self-definition. David Elkind uses the terms *differentiation* and *integration* to describe the functional processes of a successful journey to this highly prized adult self:

> Growth by *integration* is conflictual, time-consuming, and laborious. A child who is acquiring the concept of squareness, for example, must encounter a variety of different shapes before he or she can separate squareness from roundness or pointedness. In addition, the child must see many different square things such as boxes, dice, sugar cubes, and alphabet blocks before he or she can arrive at a higher-order notion of squareness that will allow him or her to differentiate square from all other shapes and to integrate all square things, regardless of size, color, or any other features, into the same concept.
>
> The principles of differentiation and integration operate in the social realm as well. To acquire a consistent sense of self, we must encounter a great number of different experiences within which we can discover how

our feelings, thoughts, and beliefs are different from those of other people. At the same time, we also need to learn how much we are like other people. We need to discover that other people don't like insults any more than we do. As a result of this slow process of differentiating ourselves from others, in terms of how we are alike and yet different from them, we gradually arrive at a stable and unique perception of our self.[3]

The adolescent's social context provides the natural habitat for the nurture of a fully formed self. *Who am I?* is largely answered in the interpersonal environment of peer interaction. In the midst of these daily interactions, the middle adolescent continually reflects to herself, *How am I like you?* and *How am I unlike you?*

Compelled by the desires both to differentiate herself from her inherited identity and to prepare herself for the quickly advancing horizon of adulthood, the high school student forms tight friendships. These friendships are serving a dual purpose. First, they provide the context for differentiation and integration as explained by Elkind. Differentiation and integration cannot be accomplished by loosely associating oneself with a large group of people. Without close friendships, the high school student is not fully empowered to experiment with his individual thoughts, feelings and goals.

Middle adolescents need a place to try out new ideas about themselves. This place must be interpersonally safe. That is the second role of friendships: to serve as a "safe house" on the intimidating bridge to an adult self. Lisa's lack of a safe house left her completely vulnerable at Monroe High School. Without Elizabeth and Carmen, Haley likewise would have lacked a context for being adolescent. In a very large world, a close group of friends means not having to be alone on the journey.

Being on the bridge to adulthood is scary. Believing that one is alone on the bridge is terrifying. Lisa's rescuer and Haley's two friends allowed Lisa and Haley to affirm, *I am like this peer group,* on the path to independently proclaiming, *This is who I am.*

Friendships thus become the most emotionally prized part of a high-school student's world.[4]

Mirror, Mirror in the Hall

Steve Patty, in *Reaching a Generation for Christ*, characterizes the high-school student's life perspective as a "relational lens."[5] The middle adolescent looks at every experience through the lens of personal relationships. In the end, however, he is primarily gazing at himself. Enabled by a deeper maturation of "new key" thinking, the middle adolescent is able to take the perspective of others' views of him. He can imagine what the other students in the hallway, the cafeteria or the gym are thinking about him as they observe his appearance, social skills, level of social success and every other aspect of himself that he considers relevant to his incomplete identity process. Elkind helps us understand:

> Because teenagers are caught up with the transformations they are undergoing—in their bodies, in their facial structure, in their feelings and emotions, and in their thinking powers—they become self-centered. They assume that everyone around them is concerned about the same thing they are concerned with, namely, themselves. I call this assumption the *imaginary audience*. It is the imaginary audience that accounts for the teenager's extreme self-consciousness. Teenagers feel that they are always on stage and that everyone around them is as aware and as concerned about their appearance and behavior as they themselves are.[6]

One observer of high school behavior concludes that middle adolescents think in these terms: "I am not who I think I am, I am not who you think I am, I am who I think you think I am."[7]

The deeply felt need for peer affirmation and acceptance coupled with the imaginary audience can be overwhelming. The power of these combined forces was evidenced to my wife and me as we listened to high school juniors Erin and Kelley. The friends attended an exclusive, all-girls private school. The academy required a particular uniform with no variances allowed. Erin and Kelley confided in us about their extreme self-consciousness at school. Erin said she felt as if every time she walked down the hall all the other girls were staring at her and making judgments about how she looked and where she fit in socially. Kelley added that the two suspected that everyone in the school looked at them as weird because of their virginity. Both girls had the constant sense that they were being examined and found wanting on the scales of their peers' social judgments.

Pacing with middle adolescents requires coming alongside these "mirror, mirror in the hall" experiences. Because of the need for self-definition and the role of peers in their lives, the critiques of the observing peer public, whether factual or imagined, are very real to them. Moreover, their very real thoughts and feelings about how others are perceiving them are powerfully forming the answer to *Who am I?*

Embracing the Truth

"People do not see the world as *it* is; they see it as *they* are."[8] For middle adolescents, perceptions of the truth of Christian faith are deeply affected by peer relationships. If a high school student gains acceptance in a peer group including members who have authentic, growing relationships with Christ, then the student gains a very positive view of what it means to follow him. If, however, a student moves into a peer group primarily disinterested in or antagonistic toward the gospel and Christ, the student will likely begin to develop negative perceptions of the call to Christ.

Let me be clear. I am not suggesting that either salvation or sanctification in middle adolescents is dependent on peer socialization. We are saved, sustained and sanctified by grace. I am, however, suggesting that peer relationships are critical components in the maturation of middle adolescent faith. The spiritual needs of a high school student *in relationship to his peers*, to be accepted, to be embraced as valuable, to hear messages of affirmation and to have a safe social haven, are real.[9]

Adolescents generally conform to the social contexts of peers with whom they find acceptance. Almost universally adolescents fit themselves, either by design or default, into some peer group.[10] To fail to do so severely impedes identity formation. Peer groups take on a defined, less permeable form once teenagers move into middle adolescence. Judith Rich Harris observes:

> In high school it is far more difficult to move into or out of a clique. By the time kids get to high school, most of them have been "typed" by their classmates and by themselves. The temporary cliques of earlier years have solidified into fairly rigid social categories based not on demographics alone: *now they reflect the personalities, propensities, and abilities of the people who belong to them.*[11]

Pacing and then leading middle adolescents requires a healthy respect for the presence, power and purpose of peer groups. Because beliefs can ultimately be shaped by behaviors, being in a peer group for an extended time has the potential to meaningfully change a student's life. It is not only that middle adolescents create peer groups; they are themselves being "created" by those groups.

The question *who am I?* is therefore largely answered in high school by *whose am I?* Whether the group is a team, clique or boyfriend, peer relationships become a primary source of self-definition. The reasoning goes, "If this is who accepts me and where I feel I belong, then *who they are must be who I am.*"

Principles for Nurturing Middle Adolescent Lives

"Teach them how to make Christian choices. Make sure they know the Bible. Keep them out of trouble. Graduate them with a 'good testimony.' " These are the goals of high school ministry based on growth by addition and subtraction. The pacing-then-leading model of spiritual caregiving, however, desires nothing less than whole-person transformation. The spiritual caregiver of a middle adolescent has the extraordinary privilege of walking alongside a young person moving from the childish faith and ways of early adolescence into the first stages of truly adult Christian maturity. To guide the caregiver's incredible journey, four comprehensive principles are listed below.

   1. Mentor the middle adolescent toward authenticity and depth in her close relationships. Navigating the social structures of high school often leads to unhealthy styles of relating. Students attempting to gain acceptance or fend off rejection may develop inauthentic, immature approaches to communication, conflict resolution and relational commitment. Those failing to mature through these patterns become much more susceptible to peer pressure. Never learning what it means to *bond* relationally, they reactively *band* together in peer groups or dating relationships.[12] As a result, they are ill-prepared for the level of intimacy required for healthy late adolescent and early adult relationships. With the numbers of students growing up in divorced homes, the false messages of youth cultural media concerning love and intimacy, and the increasing splintering of society due to postmodernity's sacred commitment to pluralism, spiritual caregivers are needed now more than ever to mentor healthy relationships.

   Interest in opposite-sex relationships emerges quickly as high school students transition rapidly out of the same-sex groupings of early adolescence. By their sophomore year, students spend more time in same-sex dyads or triads. As juniors, they begin investing more time in mixed-sex groups. For many seniors, the preferred social environment is with a single person of the opposite sex.[13] Therefore much of the guidance high school students need relates to maturing in opposite-sex relationships. Learning how to deal with too much or too little attention from a member of the opposite sex, how to communicate with opposite-sex friends and dates, how to work through the emotional rollercoaster ride of high school opposite-sex relationships, how to be godly within the confusing physical, emotional and mental whirlwind of sexual attraction, and how to make friendship a higher value than dates are among the many ways middle adolescents need to experience growth.

When Ann, a sophomore student ministry leader, began dating Mike, a non-Christian, I became very concerned. Mike was handsome, athletic, popular and very attracted to Ann. His attention felt great for Ann's self-esteem, but she was torn because her heart knew this was not OK in God's eyes. As the relationship progressed, so did Ann's internal tension.

Recognizing that she was in trouble, my wife and I prayed for insight on how to help her. We resisted a "telling" model, because she already knew something was wrong. We decided instead to pace with their relationship. We got to know Mike, who did not attend our group. We asked them out on a double date. As we paced our relationship with theirs, Ann soon began to talk with us about her areas of disappointment with Mike. Being with Mike alongside our marriage, the type of marriage Ann wanted to have one day, opened her eyes to what was missing. Soon we were leading her through the process of breaking up with Mike and renewing her commitment to follow God's will in her relationships.

Giving students information and principles for healthy relationships is helpful. Without the listening, loving and modeling of pacing and then leading them, however, they are left with insufficient resources for the complexity of their relational world.

2. Assist them in learning to own, experience and appropriately express their emotions. The transition from primarily same-sex groups to mixed-sex groups to opposite-sex dating relationships in three years is staggering. Add to this the final stages of physical puberty, the tension of campus social structures and the rapid acceleration of adultlike responsibilities, and what do you get? A lot of emotion!

Middle adolescents are more experienced in handling intense emotions than early adolescents, but familiarity does not guarantee effectiveness. Heavily affected by the levels of satisfaction they are experiencing relationally, middle adolescents' emotions can vary greatly within a short span. As they move rapidly from one relational context to another, their emotions are often short-lived but intense.[14] For instance, consider this brief excerpt from a fictional junior's day:

Jim leaves his biology class at 11:55. Since 11:40 he has been riding an emotional high. Janet, the girl he has been flirting with for weeks, winked at him after he passed her a note in class. On the way out, he says to her, "I'll see you tomorrow." Her reply, "I hope so," has moved him to euphoria.

As he walks down the hall, however, he discovers Frank standing directly in front of his locker. Frank is the star running back of the varsity football team, while Jim is a second-string junior varsity defensive back. A couple of times in spring practice Frank flattened Jim. Since then, whenever he sees Jim he calls him "Pancake."

Jim, feeling embarrassed and intimidated, decides to hold on to his books as he goes to lunch. His mood is dampened, but not ruined; the memory of Janet's flirtatious wink and her sweet "I hope so" still carries the day.

Surprisingly, Janet walks by Jim as he stands in the cafeteria line. Outside the context of the biology classroom, he feels relationally naked. How should he respond to her now? He wants neither to risk being too cool and ignoring her nor to be too assertive and have her ignore him. He gets out a weak "Hey, Janet."

His heart leaps when she smiles in return; but then he returns to earth as she asks, "Why are you carrying your books to lunch?" She seems to accept his lame excuse, but as she turns to leave, he suddenly lacks an appetite for his food.

Why do I have be so stupid? he berates himself. Deciding that his low-rent image cannot afford to be seen holding his books in the lunch line, he decides to walk back to his locker. On the way, Frank greets him with "Hey, it's Pancake!"

Jim tries not to make eye contact with Frank—he just wants to be invisible until he can get to the end of the day. Unfortunately, it is only 12:30.

Pacing with high school students begins with giving them permission to *experience* their emotions. Jim needs a spiritual caregiver to help him normalize what he is feeling. As Jim begins to accept that what he feels is normal, he can begin to *own* those emotions and address the root of his feelings. He can admit that because he sees himself as inferior to guys like Frank, he is feeling fearful of Janet's rejection. He can also own his anger at himself for not knowing how to relate to Janet.

The spiritual caregiver can talk with Jim about how he, as an adult, is still learning to deal with his own feelings of inferiority, fear of rejection and anger at his failures. Leading Jim will involve guiding Jim in his *expression* of his emotions. This will include praying those emotions to God in dialogue with his Spirit and Word and discussing ways to release what is bottled up inside through physical activity or journaling or talking to friends.

Whether it is experimenting with substance use or exploring sexual activity or deceiving parents or escaping through violent movies and music, many of the behaviors we teach Christian high school students to avoid are in fact reactions to their intense, varied emotions. Maturely working out emotional stress is therefore an important aspect of guiding middle adolescents toward adult spiritual maturity, in their thoughts, feelings and actions.

3. Model moral maturity, teach moral skills, and nurture maturing moral reasoning.[15] In the "just do it" sensate culture, "just say no" campaigns prove rather impotent. Morality cannot be taught through sound bytes, whether in the popular culture, the home or the church. Middle adolescents must encounter moral issues the way everything else meaningfully enters their lives: relationally. They need spiritual caregivers who embody the virtues of Christian character, not just the rules of Christian conduct.

Middle adolescents further require skills for keeping moral commitments. Many high school students go beyond sexual boundaries or use marijuana because of a lack of relational and social skills. Insecure in their feelings about themselves, unable to dialogue with their friends about their fears, unconscious of the danger of being with the wrong people in the wrong place at the wrong time, and untrained in using leisure time to build confidence in themselves and God, students get swept down the path of least resistance.

Middle adolescents, like early adolescents, must have a knowledge of the key truths of Scripture and the boundaries of godly moral behavior. However, they require more interaction in moral thinking processes than younger adolescents. The *why* question becomes more important than the *what* question as the complexity of their reasoning develops. During a Bible study on sexuality, one honest high school junior said, "We all know what the Bible says about sex—but tell us the truth about it." Her need, like the majority of her peers, is to encounter the truth of the Bible as meaningful truth in her own life.

Meeting the cry for meaningful understanding of the truth begins as a relational caregiver paces with what students are thinking and feeling. By listening not only to what the adolescent believes but also *how* he came to that conclusion, the spiritual caregiver discerns where his ways of thinking about himself and God should be affirmed and where he must be corrected. Having understood the *structure* of his moral reasoning rather than merely identifying the *content* of his moral beliefs, the caregiver can then lead the teenager not only to moral truth but also toward more mature moral thinking about the truth.[16]

The need for engagement of moral thinking cannot be overstated given the prevalence of a youth-way approach to moral reasoning that is blatantly antithetical to the mind of God. High school students are capable of "thinking about thinking." They should therefore be exposed to the contrast between thinking Christianly and thinking relativistically and anthropocentrically in tune with the spirit of the age. A real danger lurks for Christian high schoolers who *only* know what they believe and what they are supposed to do in obedience to those beliefs.[17] Without knowing why, they have committed themselves to these beliefs, never understanding how their faith makes meaning in response to life's questions—whether of medical ethics or the environment or sexual orientations or political agendas. Without learning how to dialogue intellectually with postmodern moral thinking, these students are prone to either retreat from the world or involuntarily acquiesce under the weight of its immense social pressure.

A number of adolescents actually avoid engaging in reflective thinking. One student said to me, "I want noise all the time—that way I don't have to think about how screwed up my life is." Pacing with conflicting emotions while guiding the middle adolescent's process of making meaning in her moral life is thus one of the most challenging and fruitful places of ministry for spiritual caregivers.

4. Provide feedback, support and challenge as they establish their unique identities as men and women of God. An early adolescent longs to discover how he can make a contribution to others' lives. A middle adolescent longs to discover who he is in relationship to others' lives. The need to make an impact with one's unique self continues, but it expands into a more intensely interpersonal process. Feedback, support and challenge in response to the adolescent's unique self are among the spiritual caregiver's most precious gifts.

"You did a good job." "Thanks for helping." "I enjoyed reading your essay." Unfortunately, each of these words of encouragement fall short. In what way did he do a good job? What about his work was most helpful? What kind of impact does the essay make on the reader? The more specific, accurate and personal the feedback, the more powerfully it shapes the middle adolescent's sense of identity.

The most meaningful, personally potent feedback speaks to a point of choice. To say, "You are really smart," can be accurate but lacks an affirmation of the deeper sense of personal identity students crave. Contrast the external observation "You are really smart" with "You are naturally smart. I respect that talent. What I really appreciate the most, however, is the way you use your intelligence to think seriously about the life choices you make. I believe God is honored by your attitude." This feedback communicates, "I have watched you closely. I like who you are and who you are choosing to become."

Feedback to high school students should include specific observations such as, "I have seen God use you to make a difference in . . ." or "I sense God is at work in your life in the area of . . ." or "I am not sure you realize how people are perceiving you. Let me share some insight on how I see them responding to you." Each of these ways of offering feedback could contain words that are fun to hear or words that would be hard to hear. However, if spoken in the context of relationship, with a sensitivity to the person and a commitment to speak in love, these are words that need to be heard.

Accurate, loving feedback encourages healthy identity formation and affirms mature responsibility-taking. High school students who hear specific, personal feedback about their choices play the words over and over in their head, like their favorite song on their newest CD. Even when the feedback includes challenge, I have found that students become more connected to me and more open to my influence. Because I have taken the time to observe and relate truth about who they are and the choices they are making, they feel respected and valued.

What high school students most want to hear from their spiritual caregivers is "I will be there for you." By pacing with students' feelings and thoughts, attending their sporting events or activities, and planning time just to enjoy their company, caregivers communicate that message. In contrast to early adolescents' focus on doing, being with middle adolescents literally means *being with*. They crave relational time and respond most warmly to those who take the time to be their friend.

As with feedback, the more personal the support the more meaningful it is. Until we have paced with a student to know his heart, we can't offer meaningful support at the point of his heart's longings. Moreover, until we have given relational support at the point of his heart's longings, our role as God's conduit of love is extremely limited. We are not truly perceived as joining him on the Jacob's Ladder of life unless we have come in contact with the places where he feels the need to be affirmed as lovable and worthwhile.

Over the years I've learned how critical is high schoolers' need for specific, personal support. One of the central themes of my teaching of middle adolescents is "You are who you are by the grace of God." When speaking at high school retreats I repeat that message and revisit its truth from every angle. I know that the audience is filled with fragile internal selves that remain unconvinced of their worthiness, value and significance in the world. Comparing themselves in every way and sure that others are making similar comparisons, high school students struggle to receive God's embrace of grace assuring them of their worth, value and significance to him.

One evening, after sharing this message of God's unconditional love and acceptance, I was approached by a student with tear-filled eyes. A beautiful girl who would have been noticed by every high school guy and envied by every high school girl in the crowd, Kim-Li told me how ugly she felt. She acknowledged spending hours on her hair and trying on multiple outfits every morning, only to feel that she never measured up. While the whole world took note of Kim-Li's attractiveness, her idealized image of beauty eluded her no matter how much effort she expended.

God had used his word in my message to unlock the doors that imprisoned Kim-Li's self-acceptance. What she need now was a spiritual caregiver to lead her into the freedom of God's view of her. Only someone who took the time to see the inside of Kim-Li would have ever known how she saw herself on the outside. Like many of her peers, she had accepted God's generic love. But also like many of her peers, she lacked a deep grasp of the personal embrace of grace God wants to share *with her.* Only a spiritual caregiver, not a retreat speaker, could become a consistent reflection of God's view of Kim-Li.

Feedback and support speak to the adolescent in the present. They encourage him to see himself as God sees him. Challenge leads the student toward the preferred future God has for him. Envisioning where God desires the student to go and then challenging him toward that goal fosters the growth of a healthy sense of identity.

Blessing a student with a challenge for God's calling in his life should parallel the specificity of feedback and support. Generic challenges to "serve God" provide little impetus or direction for a young person's life. Pacing must precede leading in this area as well. A challenge not based on an accurate understanding of a student's created self and redemptive calling from God can be confusing at best, oppressive at worst.

An excellent example of a meaningful challenge based on the individual person can be found in *The Blessing:*

> Marcia struggled throughout her years in school. If it took her classmates a half hour to do an assignment, you can bet Marcia would only be halfway through the same project an hour later. Her parents even received the disturbing news from her teacher that she was being placed in the "slow learners" group. However, even this news did not discourage Marcia's parents from picturing a special future for her. While they knew she was struggling in school, they also knew that their daughter had many positive characteristics.
>
> Rather than pushing Marcia to "hurry up" or read faster, her parents would praise her for being methodical and for staying with an assignment until she finished it. They also noticed that Marcia had an obvious gift for verbally encouraging her younger sisters and the neighbor children and for explaining things to them in a way they could understand. They began to encourage her to use these talents by letting her help them teach the young children in Sunday school and use her gifts in serving these little ones.[18]

Marcia later became an elementary school teacher. Her parental spiritual caregivers did not gauge who their daughter was in comparison to others; had they done so, Marcia's life would have been dominated by academic underachievement. Her parents rather chose to pace with the unique creation God had made in Marcia. In doing so they discovered an extraordinary gift that the school system could not recognize and affirm. By challenging Marcia to use that gift, they ignited a dream within her, the dream of using her gifts of teaching to help others learn.

Note the intersection of feedback, support and challenge in Marcia's life. Too many of our Christian high school students fail to make an impact on their world because we fail to empower them to do so. Generalized approaches to identifying spiritual gifts, mobilizing students for ministry and providing opportunities for kingdom service show a disregard for God's creative work and a disrespect for the potential that lies within high school students.

Robert Laurent's research on why adolescents leave the church confirms that too often adult communities fall into the trap of undersupporting and underchallenging their teenagers. According to Laurent's findings, the number one reason teenagers left their churches was " a lack of opportunity for involvement."[19]

High school students should not be viewed within adult Christian communities the way they are in the culture: as passive consumers. These students should be seen as young evangelists, teachers, shepherds, missionaries, servants in the home, leaders in the community and the next leadership generation for the body of Christ. The infusion of adult caregivers' feedback, support and challenge should compel these called, gifted students to be faithful stewards of God at work in and through their lives.

Between Two Times, Between Two Worlds

Over the years I have often presented an embarrassing childhood experience as a metaphor for the tension felt by students crossing the bridge of adolescence. Given that twenty-first-century middle adolescents not only are feeling torn between childhood and adulthood but are also being stretched between their postmodern culture and the modern culture of their parents, the illustration seems particularly appropriate today.

The humbling encounter with an escalator occurred during a Christmas shopping trip with my mother. While walking through a department store, I decided that I wanted to go upstairs to the sporting goods department. I confidently placed my left foot on the escalator, and then it happened—my mother asked me where I was going. This would not have been a problem except for the fact that I had not yet placed my right foot onto an upwardly mobile step. As I turned to hear what my mom was saying, her eyes got very wide and she pointed toward my steadily ascending left foot.

At this point I knew I was in trouble: I was headed toward the same fate as the wishbone from last Thanksgiving's turkey! By the time I fully grasped the situation, the opportunity to recover was long gone. I was being played like an accordion as each successive step stretched my body to its limits and then dropped my foot down again. As a crowd gathered (as I recall, my mother pretended not to know whose twelve-year-old was providing the Gumbyesque performance), I realized that saving my pride was beyond hope. The best I could hope for is that I would escape with no long-term physical damage.

With one foot still rooted in the Judeo-Christian world that includes childhood dependence and the other foot aggressively yanked by the postmodern, sensate world into which they are about to walk as independent adults, middle-adolescent Christians face few easy options. Asking, *Who am I?* they turn to their peers and the youth way, only to find that the answers they receive often contradict what they learned as a child about God, truth and love. They cannot turn back to childhood; the created natural forces of puberty have closed the door on that option. Yet they cannot figure out how to relate their childhood beliefs to the complex world that they are beginning to call their own.

How do I reconcile "Jesus loves me, this I know" with my Christian girlfriend's continued sexual advances? What do I do with "Jesus loves the little children, all the children of the world" when my closest friend comes from a Buddhist family? What does it mean to respond to the Great Commission when I spend every night of the week trying to keep up with a part-time job, advanced placement courses and basketball practice? What does "in the world, but not of it" mean when I feel more accepted by the externally rebellious but embracing crowd at school than by the externally Christian but exclusive group at church? Such are the real-life contexts of twenty-first-century middle adolescents between the times, between two worlds.

In these contexts they cry out *Whose am I?* In the midst of tension, confusion and hurried schedules, one thing is certain: high school students will soon grow up to become young adults. The role of the parental or pastoral spiritual caregiver is not to control the process but to pace with and then lead the adolescent to reflect beyond the question *Who am I?* to the foundational question *Whose am I?* A fully formed Christian adult self will be realized only to the extent that the young man or woman is able to hear the heart of the Father saying, "You are mine." The spiritual caregiver therefore listens closely to the Father's heart and just as closely to the adolescent's heart, looking for real-life opportunities to communicate, "You are his."

Reflecting on Your Journey

☐ Does the Monroe High School story bring back memories of your own high school experience? Do you find it an accurate or inaccurate representation of what middle adolescents you know experience day to day?

☐ Recount your own process of differentiation and integration as a high school student. How successful do you believe you were at individuating as a self separate from parents and peers?

☐ Describe yourself as a tenth grader. What did you look like? What mattered to you the most? When did you feel excited? When did you feel scared? What were your family relationships like? your peer relationships?

☐ What do you think you needed most from others (parents, mentors, peers) when you were in high school? What would pacing-then-leading relationships have looked like for you during that time? Were you or would you have been receptive? Why or why not?

☐ Given what you are learning about postmodern sensate culture, how are today's middle adolescents' challenges similar to and dissimilar from your experiences of growing up?

☐ Identify stereotypes and myths some Christian adults hold concerning high school students. How would you help these adults overcome those faulty mental pictures? How can you become an advocate for middle adolescents in the Christian adult contexts within which you live?

☐ What have you read in this chapter that will shape your future relationships with middle adolescents? Pray for discernment and wisdom as you consider how to pace with more attention and lead with more accuracy in their lives.

Pressing In

☐ Sit with God for a while and reflect on the individual middle adolescents in your past and present world. What new perspectives or attitudes does God seem to be birthing in you? How does he want to transform you so that your relationships with middle adolescents are being transformed?

☐ Ask parents or peers from your high school era to help you remember. Take a journey through yearbooks, scrapbooks and other "artifacts" of those years. What do you see? Where do you see God at work? What does this reflective stroll teach you about God's work in your life? How does this shape your view of your role in partnering with God in middle-adolescent lives?

☐ Watch a movie targeted to high school students. (If you need help identifying one, just ask a student. Note: many of these movies are intentionally filled with explicit language and sexual content. It is not necessary to watch the "worst-case scenario." Aim for a movie that will not be too offensive. Checking the ratings will help but is no guarantee.) Ask yourself, *How does this movie play to middle-adolescent questions, emotions and needs? How would the content and images of this movie be effective in reinforcing the thoughts, feelings and experiences of life as a middle adolescent?*

☐ Watch a television show whose target audience includes middle adolescents. Look for examples of middle-adolescent thinking, feeling and experiencing.

☐ With the help of a schoolteacher or coach, arrange a time to dialogue with middle adolescents who are not involved in churches and do not profess formal religious faith. Ask these students to articulate their thoughts on God, life, family, sex, morality, money, marriage and other important life stuff. Look for ways to understand the searching minds and receptive hearts of these young lives. Ask God for insight into your role as a caregiver to those whose spiritual pilgrimage is an unconscious wandering along the road to Emmaus.

☐ With a Bible, pen and journal, spend several hours in pacing prayer concerning the middle adolescents in your life. Listen for God's heart, let him pace with you, and follow his leading into the real world of high school students for whom he died.

I craved answers, rules. A code. So by my junior year, I was spending part of every week, sometimes every day, watching The Godfather *on videotape. The thing that really attracted me to the film was that it offered a three-hour peep into a world with clear and definable moral guidelines; where you know where you stand and you know who you love; where honor was everything; and the greatest sin wasn't murder but betrayal.*

SARAH VOWELL, *TAKE THE CANNOLI*

Daniel should be happy, must be happy. I'm not. Why not? I'm not supposed to be here. First came anger. Anger swells up greater than life. One person with anger like mine could take on ten men without. It's an inner anger. Makes me quiet. Makes me slow, makes me blank, with an expressionless expression. Loss of motivation. I lost it, can't find it. Feel like I don't need it. People say work hard, try hard, fight for right. End result for everyone: death. Everyone gets there eventually. Life's hard.

On and off depression, total lack of motivation and inability to try is all part of my life right now. How long will it last? I know it won't last forever. And I know God has a perfect plan set up in the long run. I guess that's the answer.

DANIEL, IN TODD HAHN & DAVID VERHAAGEN'S *GenXERS AFTER GOD*

Our deepest calling is to grow into our own authentic self-hood, whether or not it conforms to some image of who we ought to be. As we do so, we will not only find the joy that every human being seeks—we will also find our path of authentic service in the world. True vocation joins self and service, as Frederick Buechner asserts when he defines vocation as "the place where your deep gladness meets the world's deep need."

PARKER PALMER, *LET YOUR LIFE SPEAK*

Be happy, young man, while you are young,
and let your heart give you joy in the days of your youth.
Follow the ways of your heart
and whatever your eyes see,
but know that for all these things
God will bring you to judgment.
So then, banish anxiety from your heart
and cast off the troubles of your body,
for youth and vigor are meaningless.

ECCLESIASTES 11:9-10

11

Late Adolescence

The Final Frontier

*L*auren, my best friend's daughter, graduated from high school this spring. Lauren is mature, poised and well prepared to move beyond the high school world of middle adolescence. Yet as I faced this young woman adorned in cap and gown, I saw a little girl on a wobbly bicycle with her dad running alongside. In her hands she carried her diploma, but in my mind's eye I could see the myriad poems and paintings that once covered my refrigerator door, each bearing the crayon inscription "Love, Lauren."

I can only imagine the images and emotions flooding her parents' thoughts as Lauren closed the middle-adolescent chapter of her life. Even as they celebrated with pride the person their daughter had become, they embraced the sobering significance of the moment. Lauren was graduating *from* high school and childhood; she was graduating *into* college and young adulthood. On graduation day Lauren's world consisted of (a) the house and neighborhood she grew up in, (b) the friends at school and church with whom she has shared everything from giggling seventh grade crushes to grievous betrayal in trusted relationships and (c) a family whose depth of relationship with each other and God has provided eighteen years of immediate, daily security and support. In a matter of a few weeks Lauren's world would consist of (a) a dorm room and campus that she had visited only twice, (b) peers with whom she has had no relational history and (c) a family whose love, while continuing to deepen, must adjust to her increasing absence and growing independence. Nothing for Lauren would ever be the same—including her relationship with God.

Like a pilot-in-training practicing for her first solo flight, Lauren will increasingly assume command of her life journey.[1] Building with great anticipation toward the day when she will truly be on her own, she is already sensing how her life's social, economic and educational responsibilities are shifting away from her parents' locus of control.[2] In the next few months and years (a season Sharon Parks has aptly labeled "the critical years")[3] Lauren will gradually come to terms with who she is as an individuated adult.[4] On the path toward this adult destination of mature psychological independence, she will choose for herself the values, beliefs and relational commitments that will shape the rest of her life's course.[5] Four years from now when I attend her college graduation, I will be watching Lauren flying solo—a flight that neither her dad nor her mom will be able to run alongside as they have before.

Down the Runway

Whether the next step is a full-time job, vocational training for a career, entrance into military service or college enrollment, the late adolescent faces the full force of *What am I going to do with my life?* Never before has he encountered such a breadth of possibilities or such a depth of responsibilities. Moving down the runway to one's solo flight as an adult can be both daunting and exhilarating. The high school graduate finds himself or herself torn between *it feels great to be on my way to choosing my own life* and *what if I'm not ready and I crash this thing called my life?*

Students approach the late adolescent runway in ways as diverse as the individuals themselves. Plagued by social and academic failures, some wilt under the internal pressure of the challenges of the late-adolescent passage. Feeling relationally or vocationally inadequate, these young people choose a path of least resistance. They get a job or go to school but never really engage the process of moving toward the future. Directionless and unmotivated, these late adolescents feel increasingly marginalized from the mainstream of their peers.

Other students, carrying the baggage of painful early- and middle-adolescent experiences, approach this age as a time to distance themselves from the past. These late adolescents become highly motivated in academic, vocational or social pursuits. A burning desire to succeed in order to shed the past often leads to very high productivity. Left unchecked, however, the productivity can mask underlying hurts that later manifest themselves in unhealthy and even destructive adult lifestyle choices.

Many others, like my friend Lauren, move down the runway undergirded by the maturity that was formed powerfully throughout the previous eighteen-plus years. These late adolescents have a growing sense of personal value and efficacy and are increasingly secure in their hope in God. They discover that even their struggles and failures lead to deepening awareness that God is working to transform them into the likeness of Jesus. Life becomes an experience to be embraced for its gifts, not avoided for its threats. The purpose becomes soaring, not avoiding crashes.

Critical components of personal growth must be integrated into a late adolescent's inner world before she can feel enough wind under her wings for a successful takeoff: *intimate companionship, a compelling life vision, a coherent worldview and a composition of commitments.* Young adults cannot, of course, expect to be perfectly formed in these areas. Without these basic elements, however, the late adolescent will find young adulthood a daunting experience. Those who are chronologically young adults yet have failed to gain this growth will find themselves, at best, unable to take flight. At worst, they will become crash victims due to severe turbulence. Moral failures, relational fractures, emotional fragility, vocational flops and spiritual falls are among the adult symptoms of an incomplete maturing process in late adolescence.

Spiritual caregivers can pace with and then lead the late adolescent through her journey toward successful integration. For the deeply wounded, the process may include revisiting missing pieces of early and late adolescent maturity. The runway may have to be lengthened for these injured souls in order to provide space for redemptive healing of broken places. For all late adolescent/young adult pilgrims in progress, however, spiritual caregiving by mentoring adults is indispensable. One cannot take flight as a fully mature Christian adult without heading down the runway alongside mature Christian adults.

Intimate Companionship

Teresa majored in Social Life her first year in college. Her primary courses of study were Dating 101, Hanging Out with Friends 101, Getting Involved on Campus 101, Cheerleading 101 and Getting Involved in Ministries off Campus 101. As an afterthought, she also took a number of academic courses officially offered by the faculty. Not surprisingly, this high school valedictorian accumulated very few points on her grade-point average. A first-year college student is not, however, a finished product. Today Teresa is an accomplished therapist, respected in her community and by her colleagues for her excellent work. She is an intelligent, strong leader who makes a difference in every realm of her life, especially in her home and church. Teresa is also my wife.

Teresa's first year of college was less about a momentary lapse in responsibility-taking and more about a driving need to find social connection. Hundreds of miles from home, feeling the need of a sense of identity in a new environment and growing in her sense of personal independence, Teresa longed to connect in meaningful ways in friendship and dating. As one taxies onto the late-adolescent runway, intimate relationships with peers bring reassurance that it is safe to leave the hangar.

The intensity of the pursuit of intimate relationships can be traced to several sources. First, *late adolescents are trying on adult roles.* No longer satisfied with the level of social clustering they experienced in high school, they want relationships that are more permanent and more deeply personal. They have lived through enough change by now to know that they are moving past the days when a group could satisfy their deep needs for relationship. Moreover, late adolescents enter into dating relationships with the very real awareness *I could marry this person if this relationship continues.* The stakes are therefore much higher in opposite-sex relationships.

Second, *a growing capacity for self-awareness prompts a desire to connect more intimately.* True intimacy results from mutual self-disclosure in a trustworthy relationship. As late adolescents encounter new layers of themselves, prompted by cognitive growth and changing circumstances, they long to be known and accepted on these levels. Middle-adolescent levels of relationship begin to feel shallow and inadequate. Late adolescents love to stay up late talking about their lives, their dreams, their most meaningful relationships. In a very short time late-adolescent relationships take on an increasingly young-adult orientation. To observe this phenomenon one has only to watch a college freshman return to visit friends who are still in high school: everyone knows something has changed, no matter how close the friendship has been.

Third, *the growing dependence on themselves for their lives compels them to pursue intimacy with others.* Sensing new needs for support and sharing the load of their lives, late adolescents reach out for interdependent relationships.[6] Parents no longer serve as the primary relational support base. Yet the establishment of the adolescent's independent single or family life remains in the future. Interdependent relationships thus become like oxygen for a high-altitude mountain climber. For this reason late adolescents thrive in environments where they receive spiritual caregiving not only from older adults but also in supportive relationships with their peers. In "mentoring communities" students process spirituality in real life with a real God at a more intimate level than they would have even with a single spiritual caregiver.[7] Intimacy in these relationships fosters intimacy with God.

Fourth, *late adolescents are completing their path of foundational self-definition.* New ingredients have been added to the identity-formation mix. There is an urgency to affirm one's place in this brave new world, whether college or the marketplace. And connecting intimately with others provides consistent, authentic feedback on where one fits in the complex mosaic of a diverse postmodern world.

One final significant source of the need for intimacy should not be overlooked. For Teresa, like many other recently launched high school graduates, there was also the factor of *experiencing her parents' divorce.* Adolescents who seemingly adjusted well amid the initial pain of divorce often manifest latent elements of loss and abandonment in early adulthood. Having had their sense of security torn apart (in some cases the divorce signals that security never existed in the parental relationship), their first journey down the runway toward adult intimacy looks frighteningly lonely. Many college students cling to dating relationships or friendships as lifelines to a sense of security.[8] Seeking security from insecure others, these relationships are disillusioning and dissatisfying, leaving the person distrustful of lasting commitments. Unless maturity and spiritual healing bring freedom from these hurts, the late adolescent may never be fully able to participate in deeper intimacy. He simply does not trust that the love he receives will last.[9]

Without intimacy, the late adolescent becomes relationally anorexic, isolated from the nourishment of connection God created him to experience. Isolation from human connection affects intimacy with God and results in aberrant strategies to assuage cravings that can be satisfied only in intimacy with God and his people. Consequently, choosing well in human relationships during the young adult years is one of the most important choices one will make in a lifetime.[10]

A longing for intimate companionship drove my own unconscious relational patterns in college. I had always been popular among my peers but felt woefully insecure, particularly in relationship to females. I felt inferior and inadequate, seeing myself as everyone's "brother" but no one's potential boyfriend. When Teresa and I became friends through ministry partnership, I was enthralled with her but held little hope of dating her. Anyway, she was in a serious dating relationship with a very striking, successful senior on campus.

While Teresa worked the social scene, I worked the spiritual scene. I was the chapel speaker, Bible scholar and ministry leader hoping to communicate "I am a guy worth getting to know." Coming out of a family background laced with generations of relational fear and distrust, I did not know how to connect intimately. I succeeded at Christian leadership with the hope that it would attract others to me. I did not know how to nourish my soul with intimate love in relationship with God and others. I medicated my pain with escapist tactics and performance strategies—which gave me a growing sense of being a failure. As I experienced an increasing sense of inadequacy, I also felt a widening gap between my self-knowledge and the person others thought me to be. The stress caused me to lose seventeen pounds my freshman year of college.

I did not gain intimate companionship easily. A period of brokenness in my sophomore year led me to realize that I had to open up more. My best friend, Teresa, became the person God used to build trust in my self-disclosure. The combination of my sense of inferiority and her fear of abandonment made for a difficult relational journey. Along the way, a few key spiritual caregivers and friends provided the intimacy I needed to at least begin to acknowledge and embrace my hunger for God's grace in my layers of self-protection. Teresa's unconditional acceptance of what lay behind those walls enabled me to hope for a life beyond the internal isolation I had come to accept. Without addressing the life question *Can I love and be loved well?* as a late adolescent, I would never have been able to take steps toward learning to love and be loved well as an adult friend, husband, father and pastor. To this day, my journey continues along the path set by those who paced with me when I was nineteen and a relational mess.

A Compelling Life Vision

My whole body responds to the passion of Dr. King's eloquent "I Have a Dream" speech. I experience goosebumps and tears as I feel the courage of convictions resonating in his voice. More significant, my soul is profoundly moved by his compelling vision for racial equality and reconciliation.

We were all created to respond to a vision greater than ourselves. We were designed to follow the Creator's call to live out his vision for life. As a result, each of us hungers for a vision that calls us to make a meaningful mark in the world. During late adolescence the appetite is almost insatiable. Eighteen- to twenty-two-year-olds want to embark on a life journey that will one day make a lasting difference. As a generation, they want to correct the errors of the past and demonstrate that a world under their care can be a better place. As individuals, they want to discover a life dream that will be their own and uniquely meaningful in their life context.[11] They search, consciously and unconsciously, for a compelling vision of who they can become and what they can contribute. History records multiple examples of revivals and revolutions fueled by the late-adolescent quest for bigger-than-life dreams of spiritual and political freedom.

A crucial crossroads. The significance of birthing a life dream in late adolescence has its genesis in the challenges of the passage into novice adulthood.[12] To understand how it feels to stand at this critical life juncture, one need only consider what happens when someone in a tense organizational meeting says, "Call for the question." After much bickering and multiple exchanges of point and counterpoint, someone seeks to force a resolution of the issue. The time of reckoning has come. You can choose one of three responses: yea, nay, abstain. You must make a decision—even if it is to abstain from making another decision.

In the same way, the late adolescent must make a decision. School? Military? Vocational apprenticeship? The best-paying available job? If school, another question quickly follows: what major? The military and marketplace likewise require further decisions about career paths. All these decisions are forced on the front end of adulthood—not after these men and women have had actual adult experience for making such life-altering choices!

Ann and Nate encountered brick walls at their crucial crossroads. Ann, a talented eighteen-year-old with a world of opportunities, felt overwhelmed by the pressure to choose God's will for her future. Her parents and friends constantly praised her giftedness as a student and leader; now she feared greatly disappointing them by making a poor choice. Nate was overwhelmed as well. A sensitive twenty-year-old, he was barely passing his courses. To make matters worse, his introverted personality and low self-esteem motivated him to retreat into relational isolation. Nate felt no hope for the future and wondered if God even had a will for him to choose.

At first glance Ann and Nate have little in common. One is a high achiever, the other a chronic struggler. One sees too many options in her future, the other cannot identify a single option for his. Closer examination reveals that they do have in common one very important characteristic. Each lacks a defined, compelling life vision. Ann is constrained from seeing a compelling vision by the tyranny of opportunities. Nate is blinded by the tyranny of limitations.

Spiritual caregivers face the temptation to "fix" Ann and Nate by giving them immediate solutions for what to do next. This may please them both in the short-term but fails to enable either of them to prepare for a successful takeoff. Simply to tell them what to do would be akin to grabbing the flight controls and saying, "Here, let me fly this thing—you don't know what you're doing." Reacting by taking control may relieve the stress temporarily, but it circumvents the vital process of pacing with and then leading Ann and Nate as they develop their own personally meaningful life visions.

To be sure, these two students would benefit from practical advice from the voice of an experienced spiritual caregiver. To withhold that from them would be unwise. Alongside this input, however, they have a deeper need for a life vision that transcends majors, vocations and peer evaluations. Fostering a sufficient vision for their Christian adult lives includes helping them envision (1) the internal character God has called them to develop, (2) the stewardship of the gifts his grace has creatively and redemptively deposited in them and (3) a movement toward a life that will maximize the intersection of who they are and what they choose vocationally and relationally. Ann runs the risk of erroneously assuming her life will be meaningful *because her life is externally successful* by the culture's standards. Nate risks falsely concluding that his life cannot be meaningful *because his life is externally unsuccessful* by the culture's standards.

Steven Garber, in his definitive work *The Fabric of Faithfulness*, calls college teachers to "understand how to more faithfully and effectively nurture in [students] a vision of being 'the presence of God in the midst of the world and the creation.' "[13] What a beautiful picture of the role of all spiritual caregivers of late adolescents! Ann's and Nate's caregivers have the priceless opportunity to enable them to discover God's vision for being his presence in a way that only they, Ann and Nate, can be.

Biblical examples of compelling life visions. Scripture provides multiple perspectives on the significance of a compelling life vision with its sources in the will of God. Paul envisioned such a dream for his beloved friends in Ephesus: "For we are God's workmanship, created in Christ Jesus to do good works, which God prepared in advance for us to do" (Eph 2:10). To Timothy Paul wrote, "For this reason I remind you to fan into flame the gift of God, which is in you through the laying on of my hands. For God did not give us a spirit of timidity, but a spirit of power, of love and of self-discipline" (2 Tim 1:6-7). Jesus envisioned spiritual fruitfulness for his disciples when he told the parable of the talents. He expected the resources he provided by his grace to be invested so as to be reproducing according to his will.

The Old Testament contains powerful images of the impact of late-adolescent lives yielded to God. A slave, a shepherd and a POW in their adolescent years, Joseph, David and Daniel respectively seemed unlikely candidates for making a meaningful impact on their world. Yet each was compelled by God's vision for his life.

Perhaps the most poignant portrait of an adolescent's obedience to a compelling vision from God is found in the life of Mary, mother of Jesus.[14] Mary's response to the awesome calling God had placed on her life is recorded in Luke. To the angel Mary replied in simple obedience, "I am the Lord's servant. . . . May it be to me as you have said" (Lk 1:38). Responding to her relative Elizabeth's joyous greeting "Blessed is she who has believed what the Lord has said to her will be accomplished!" (Lk 1:45), Mary sings a song of praise bearing an incredible vision for humbly living in the goodness of God's work:

> My soul glorifies the Lord,
>   and my spirit rejoices in God my Savior,
> for he has been mindful
>   of the humble state of his servant.
> From now on all generations will call me blessed,

for the Mighty One has done great things for me—
holy is his name.
His mercy extends to those who fear him,
　from generation to generation.
He has performed mighty deeds with his arm;
　he has scattered those who are proud in their inmost thoughts.
He has brought down rulers from their thrones
　but has lifted up the humble.
He has filled the hungry with good things
　but has sent the rich away empty.
He has helped his servant Israel,
　remembering to be merciful
to Abraham and his descendants forever,
　even as he said to our fathers. (Lk 1:46-56)

On the road to Bethlehem, when there was no room at the inn, and when her beloved son was spat upon, Mary must have returned to that vision. Only God's call could have provided the comfort and hope required to parent God's Son.

Ann and Nate are likewise called to catch God's vision for their lives. They are to become living models in the postmodern world, joining the elders of Ephesus, young Timothy, Jesus' disciples, Joseph, David, Daniel and Mary as parts of God's redemptive work in salvation history. Ann and Nate need to change their questions; instead of *What am I supposed to do now? How can I make a choice that will lead to success?* they need to ask, *Who has God made me to be? How can I respond to his grace in order to best experience and express my uniqueness for his glory?* The answers to the latter questions will provide the criteria for discerning their first young-adulthood steps in their journey with God.

A Coherent Worldview

Neal's intellectual world had been turned upside down. So had his faith in God. Neal had arrived at the large, private university with a desire to make an impact for Christ. He visited the introductory meetings of various campus ministries to invite new students into their fellowship. He remained faithful in reading from his devotional Bible, and though he had not settled into regular attendance at one church, he went to church at least twice a month during his first semester. Neal had prepared himself to fight against the tendency of many students to slip away from Christian faith during their college years.

What Neal had not prepared himself for was the intriguing course in comparative religions he took his second semester. Dr. Harken, the instructor, was a brilliant scholar who respected and valued the faith statements of all religions. Dr. Harken's father had been a seminary professor and Old Testament scholar. Like his son, the elder Dr. Harken appeared to have been gracious, tolerant and interested in the diverse religions of the world. Dr. Harken was the most intelligent, witty, compassionate and fatherly professor on the campus.

Intrigued by the man, Neal became intrigued by the ideas of the man. He joined Dr. Harken's group of "disciples," as they were referred to on campus, and joined a Tuesday evening discussion group in the student center. There he met Jennifer, a lovely and brilliant young woman who, like him, had grown up in the Christian faith. Jennifer, however, had been in the Peace Corps the previous two years and had experienced a spiritual awakening in Asia. Her beliefs were a synthesis of Eastern mystical religions and the early church fathers' spirituality. Neal was attracted not only to Jennifer but to her spiritual freedom and ease. She seemed to have gained a sense of spirituality that transcended doctrines and belief systems. Neal found in Jennifer an understanding of life that seemed less restrictive, naïve and judgmental than the Christian environment in which he had been raised.

Neal's spiritual journey led him to new territory at a time when he was attempting to bring coherence to his way of thinking. Moving past childhood and childishness, the late adolescent struggles to synthesize past beliefs and present learning. In his encounters with Jennifer and Dr. Harken, Neal saw the "certainties" of his early- and middle-adolescent framework of faith collapse. Seeking to reconcile his new relationships, ideas and life dreams with the past became a painful experience. Reality had penetrated the prepackaged neatness of the faith Neal once articulated with such clarity and conviction.[15]

The challenges of integrating one's faith do not present themselves only in state universities. Dave Veerman, in *The Passages of Parenting*, reflects on his experiences as a late adolescent struggling to own his faith in the expanded world of college life.

> I thought I had all the answers when I left for college. But there I encountered students much more devoted to Christ than I who believed differently

in some areas. From other students and in various classes, I heard questions for which I had no answers. And what was even more disconcerting, I discovered that I had answers for questions that no one was asking.

Suddenly my faith began to seem irrelevant and childish, and I began to struggle with doubts. I had been an *environmental Christian*. My Christianity had come from my own environment, had been given to me by others; it wasn't my own. So when I had left my home and Christian environment, in effect I had left my faith. I doubted everything: the truth of the Bible, whether Jesus Christ is divine, and even the existence of God. But through the next couple of years and by the grace of God and help of dedicated Christian professors and friends, I was able to believe again, but this time my faith was my own.[16]

Dave found mature pacing-then-leading Christians to lean on as he sought to own his faith. Neal and Jennifer needed the same.

Late adolescents, even those who do not leave their hometown to attend university or enter the military, enter into a restructured social environment that pushes against conventional approaches to their prior faith commitments.[17] In the midst of these changes, the adolescent is also maturing in her conceptual abilities.

Confronting social changes and maturing conceptual sophistication would be enough to create a challenging intellectual environment for late adolescents. Add to this a sensate culture that regards intellectual commitments to absolute truth as naïve and intolerant, and one can see the difficulty in owning a coherent Christian worldview. As Garber observes, "The challenge for the contemporary college student—especially the Christian student whose creedal commitments are rooted in the possibility and reality of truth—is to form a worldview that will be coherent across the whole of life because it addresses the whole of life."[18]

Doctrinal commitments isolated from life meaningfulness and fragmented bits and pieces of a Christian thought are insufficient to address the postmodern context of this generation's future adult lives. Without a disciplined, integrated, intentionally crafted, coherent worldview, emerging Christian adults are left vulnerable to being tossed about by the whims of the spirit of the age.

In the final analysis everyone has an operational worldview, whether it is consciously reflected upon and coherently formed or not. But with the goal being a coherent worldview and the obstacles so great, spiritual caregivers can ill afford to neglect fostering coherence in late adolescents' worldview development. Garber reflects on the process of forming a "vision for a coherent faith":

> Why do you get up in the morning? What happened during your college years to shape your understanding of the world and your place in it? What do you care about and why? Over the course of hours of listening to people who still believe in the vision of a coherent faith, one that meaningfully connects personal disciplines with public duties, again and again I saw that they were people (1) who had formed a worldview sufficient for the challenges of the modern world, (2) who had found a teacher who incarnated that worldview and (3) who had forged friendships with folk whose common life was embedded in that worldview. There were no exceptions.[19]

The spiritual caregivers' role in all three of these elements is key. Without caregivers who help late adolescents face the reality of their world's challenges, who embody the "live theology" of a Christian worldview and who facilitate environments enabling intimate fellowship with others seeking to live out Christ's vision, our students would be left to fend for themselves in a world where the enemy seeks to devour them (1 Pet 5:8). Crafting a coherent worldview requires spiritual caregivers who are willing to pace and then lead through example and guidance. An internalized coherent worldview is not something students must "get"; it is something that has to be formed as they mature.

A Composition of Commitments

Larry is a professional surveyor in the rural South. Occasionally he needs to survey a farm that has been passed down through one family for several generations. One such farm had a deed that was sealed in beeswax and dated in the mid-nineteenth century. Like all property descriptions, there was a fixed point from which the original survey had been taken. That was the good news. The bad news was the starting place that was chosen. The property's fixed starting point was "the big oak down by the stream where Joe's horse died last winter." Joe's horse had been dead for about 150 years, and the stream had dried up decades before Larry visited the farm. The oak tree had likely disappeared as well. Larry was left to choose a new starting point, one that he would identify with a permanent stake in the ground and with clear coordinates in the deed.

Late adolescents are completing the process of composing their long-term ethical, relational and spiritual commitments. In order for a coherent worldview with *deeply owned life commitments* to emerge, late adolescents must critically examine both the content and the source of the commitments they internalized as children. They must be guided in their quest to firmly establish a "permanent stake in the ground" for their new adult lives. Gary L. Chamberlain describes the process:

> Especially in relation to moral issues, students may look for a place to stand, a way of composing truth that is more adequate to their lives than other possibilities are. Here, students take self-responsibility for their own knowing while, at the same time, remaining aware of the finite nature of all judgments. This emerging commitment first takes the form of a tentative, or . . . "probing," commitment. The student explores possible forms of truth and their fittingness to the student's experience of self and world. At this stage, even deeply felt affirmations have a tenuous, exploratory, and divided quality.[20]

Late adolescents encounter competing structures of commitments that can be persuasive and attractive. This was Neal's experience with Dr. Harken and Jennifer. It is not that commitments are casually considered up for grabs. During this time, however, commitments are open to evaluation to discern their integrity in the new internal and external world of emerging adulthood.[21] Until a student has questioned commitments for herself, they are not truly owned. Asking the questions can be scary, as Mark Rutledge notes: "During experiences of failure of intimate relationships or in the classroom where authority-bound beliefs are criticized, the student suffers not only the obvious loss but also a sense of the unraveling of self, world, and God. These can be painful times for many students."[22]

Preparing students for and guiding them through this process is a critical task for spiritual caregivers during these years. Pacing and then leading provides a safe environment to ask scary questions. Only after the late adolescent has scrutinized past commitments does he possess the maturity to compose with creativity and clarity his adult life commitments.

Creating time and space for owning life commitments. Composing takes time. Composing takes space. Composing this book has been a process of months of writing and years of learning. The greater part of this book has been composed in a very quiet, beautiful room overlooking the Tennessee River. Without significant quantities of time and space, I could never have partnered with God in putting together the ideas and choosing the words.

Without substantial amounts of time and space, late adolescents will never be able to partner with God in owning their life commitments. Composing life commitments requires enormous stretches of time and space. Spiritual caregivers can foster the creating of that time and space in late adolescent lives in a number of practical ways. Among the most important strategies for empowering ownership are *leading, congruent with pacing, toward an experience of life as a sacred conversation with God.*

When the weighty issues of the faith are being examined, spiritual caregivers face the temptation to listen and then ignore what has been heard. We hear the dissonance or doubt and then rush in to save the day. Like theological superheroes, we feel called upon to fix the situation before it gets out of control.

Choosing not to fix does not mean we withhold insight, answers and guidance. Leading congruent with our pacing does mean we should not attempt to steer the late adolescent's journey toward our own comfort zone. We must not shut down tough questions or painful emotions. Rather, effective caregiving embraces the necessity of the occasionally faltering steps the late adolescent takes in her attempts to take ownership of her becoming. We must restrain ourselves from grabbing the controls and taking the student by force to a place where we feel more in control.

Leading congruent with pacing thus demands an intentional commitment not to rush the student's process of owning his life commitments. On one occasion, after several others had made attempts to get through to a spiritually struggling young man, I was asked to speak with him. I met with him to talk—but not very much. Mostly I just listened. In fact, after the initial greetings were exchanged, for an hour I said little more than "I want you to walk me into what is going on internally with you right now. Several people have told me that you are feeling troubled, but I want to know what *you* think is going on." For about five minutes we sat in silence, me beside him, staring ahead and waiting. With tears, confusion and frustration, he then invited me into his current view of reality. After an hour of listening, I had input to offer—input that connected with the pain of his journey. The pacing had set the table for leading him forward in his personal composition of life with God.

Spiritual caregivers are not responsible for convincing or cajoling late adolescents into adopting a certain set of life commitments. Neither do they have the authority. The Holy Spirit is the one who guides, convicts, confirms and seals late adolescents in their adult faith. Critical to effective caregiving for late adolescents is the recognition that this life passage has been designed by God to teach genuine spiritual dependence. The props of early and middle adolescence in the home and community have been removed. Belief in God becomes more real, more frightening and more awesome than one could ever have imagined. Adult ownership of life with God demands that he be encountered in these terrifyingly wonderful places. Spiritual care-givers create time and space for these encounters by praying for, praying with, worshiping with, sharing their life with God and waiting for God as he unveils his gracious love.

Spiritual caregivers also create the environment for intimate encounters with the Spirit of God by guiding late adolescents into critical reflection. Critical reflection is the process of examining the *why* behind the *what* of one's life.[23] Late adolescence should be considered the prime time for the for-mation of critical reflection skills and habits. Garber writes of this age: "The years between adolescence and adulthood are a crucible in which moral meaning is being formed, and central to that formation is a vision of integrity which coherently connects beliefs to behavior personally as well publicly."[24]

The route to integrity in one's convictions, commitments and behaviors is the path of critical reflection in dialogue with the Holy Spirit. Critical re-flection questions include

- Why am I making the choices I am making?
- What unconscious beliefs are controlling my behaviors?
- What internally hinders me from actualizing my beliefs?
- What commitments need to change?
- What behaviors need to change?

Learning to live in these questions as a *sacred conversation* with God represents the greatest competency to be learned in the young adult years.[25] Critical reflection facilitated by the spiritual caregiver enables the late ado-lescent to initiate dialogues with the Holy Spirit in the deepest chambers of her heart.

"Flight Attendants, Prepare for Takeoff"

Jim, a pilot, once told me that the most critical moments in flight are during takeoff. The engines are at full throttle, the flight path is not conducive to altering one's course for landing, and the senses are heightened by the flight demands of takeoff combined with the external presence of air traffic. Without takeoff, however, there would be no soaring.

Adolescence is a risky passage in a postmodern world. The final process of entering the skies of the adult world may be the most intense moments of the entire journey. If soaring is defined as religious successes by "good Christian kids," few could be considered adequate for the flight. Soaring, however, is to be measured by one's authentic engagement in sacred conversation with God. Given his character and commitment, even young adults like Teresa and I used to be can look toward the horizon with anticipation of an adventurous journey into the heights of his love. The likelihood of finding that hope increases exponentially as a spiritual caregiver in sacred conversation with God shares the runway and the dialogue of life with the late adolescent.

Reflecting on Your Journey

☐ What was or is your personal story as a late adolescent? Reflect on the process of preparing to "fly solo" as a young adult, and describe the important relationships and experiences along the way.

☐ Critique your preparedness at the age of twenty-two in terms of intimate companionship, a compelling life vision, a compass of commitments and a coherent worldview. Where were you the strongest? the weakest? How has that level of preparedness helped or hindered your growth from that point forward?

☐ Who, if anyone, paced with and then led you spiritually as a late adolescent? What impact did that person—or lack thereof—have on your journey?

☐ How do you understand the author's description of life as sacred conversation with God? In what ways do you experience life this way? In what areas do you long for a deeper experience of that life?

☐ What have you read in this chapter that will shape your future relationships with late adolescents? Specifically, how do you see yourself learning to model and mentor sacred conversation?

☐ What would you say is your most significant challenge in your role as a spiritual caregiver to late adolescents? Pray for discernment and wisdom as you consider how to pace with more attention and lead with more accuracy.

Pressing In

☐ Sit with God for a while and reflect on the late adolescents in your past and present world. What new perspectives or attitudes does God seem to be birthing in you? How does he want to transform you so that your relationships with late adolescents can be transformed?

☐ Take a journey through yearbooks, scrapbooks and other "artifacts" of those years. Call an old friend from late adolescence and share the journey. Listen to what your friend says that can help you reenter the life you lived at that time. What do you see? Where do you see God at work? What does this reflective stroll teach you about God's work in your life? How does it shape your view of your role in partnering with God in late-adolescent lives?

☐ Spend time on a college or university campus. Sit in the student center, eat in the cafeteria, or attend a sporting event where most of the fans are students. What do you observe? How does this inform your relationships with students?

☐ Get to know a late adolescent who has either chosen not to go to school or been prevented from doing so for financial reasons. Spend time listening to the feelings and experiences of a person who has not taken the standard "go straight to college" path.

☐ Invite a campus ministry leader over for dinner. Ask him or her to describe the challenges he or she faces day to day. Pray for the leader and the ministry, engaging the heart of God for the lives on that campus.

☐ With the help of someone who works on a college campus, arrange a time to dialogue with late adolescents who are not involved in churches and do not profess formal religious faith. Ask them to tell you their thoughts on God, life, family, sex, morality, money, marriage and other important life stuff. Look for ways of understanding their searching minds and receptive hearts. Ask God for insight into your role as a spiritual caregiver to those whose spiritual pilgrimage is an unconscious wandering along the road to Emmaus.

☐ Read Steven Garber's *The Fabric of Faithfulness* to understand in greater depth the process of late adolescent moral and spiritual maturation.

☐ With a Bible, pen and journal, spend several hours in pacing prayer concerning the late adolescents in your life. Listen for God's heart, let him pace with you, and follow his leading as you walk into the real world of the post-high school men and women for whom he died.

Section 4

Spiritual Care for
    Spiritual Caregivers

Preparing for Your Journey

As you prepare to read chapter twelve, ask God to move the learning through your mind and heart into the very depths of your soul. Pray that God will speak truth and grace into your life concerning the following questions:

☐ What are my next steps on my spiritual journey?

☐ Where have I "dehydrated" my inner self? How will I move to replenish these parched areas?

☐ How can I learn to lead increasingly from deep wells of spiritual, emotional and personal resources?

☐ How does God want me to relate to him when I feel ineffective in my spiritual pacing and leading? What does success look like to God?

☐ Where is life beating me up? What does it mean to be in sacred conversation with God in those times of pain and brokenness?

☐ Who are the adolescents in my life who seem to need much more than I have to give? How can I be honest to God with my feelings while continuing to choose to love those students?

☐ Who will pace and then lead with me? To whom will I turn for my own spiritual care?

The soul is like a wild animal—tough, resilient, savvy, self-sufficient, and yet exceedingly shy. If we want to see a wild animal, the last thing we should do is to go crashing through the woods, shouting for the creature to come out. But if we are willing to walk quietly into the woods and sit silently for an hour or two at the base of the tree, the creature we are waiting for may well emerge, and out of the corner of an eye we will catch a glimpse of the precious wildness we seek.

PARKER J. PALMER, *LET YOUR LIFE SPEAK*

If your eye is single, God is in all your thoughts. If you are constantly aiming at Him who is invisible, if it is your intention in all things small and great to please God and do the will of Him who sent you into the world, then the promise will certainly take place: "Your whole body will be full of light." Your whole soul will be filled with the light of heaven—with the glory of the Lord resting upon you.

JOHN WESLEY

As long as ministry only means that we worry a lot about people and their problems; as long as it means an endless number of activities which we can hardly coordinate, we are still very much dependent on our own narrow and anxious heart. But when our worries are led to the heart of God and there become prayer, then ministry and prayer become two manifestations of the same all-embracing love of God.

HENRI NOUWEN, *THE WAY OF THE HEART*

One thing I ask of the LORD,
this is what I seek:
that I may dwell in the house of the LORD
all the days of my life,
to gaze upon the beauty of the LORD
and to seek him in his temple.

PSALM 27:4

Show me your ways, O LORD,
teach me your paths;
guide me in your truth and teach me,
for you are God my Savior,
and my hope is in you all day long.

PSALM 25:4-5

12

Self-Care for
Wick Burners

One more chapter. That's all that stood between me and the manuscript's finish line. The time had been set aside. The ideas had been birthed. All that seemed to be lacking were the necessary internal resources to complete the task. My soul's reservoir had been depleted. I was tired, I was thirsty.

On the way to lunch with John and Sue, I told Teresa about my condition. Recent travels and speaking had taken a greater toll on me than I had anticipated. This was not a time, though, when I felt I could afford to be in a recovery mode. I felt pressure to increase my pace to reach my deadline, not freedom to decrease my pace in order to replenish my soul.

As we talked over lunch, I acknowledged my place of deficit with John and Sue, who noted that I "looked tired." As the conversation flowed, their warm concern and wise words were gifts to Teresa and me. Particularly important to me was Sue's illustration of the contrast between a candle and an oil lamp. A candle, Sue explained, burns its wick as it burns the wax. An oil lamp, however, is designed to burn oil, not wicks. In fact, the wick on an oil lamp begins to burn only when the oil has been used up.

The analogy, aimed I am sure by God, hit the bull's-eye. I saw myself in a new light immediately. I felt as if I should be introducing myself to a twelve-step group, saying, "My name is Rick and I'm a wick burner."

Over the next few days, God's embrace of grace met me in this new metaphor for understanding my condition and its causes. I began to look for every opportunity to replenish the oil in my soul. I restructured my schedule, said no to several pending commitments and redirected my soul toward rest. I began to picture my inner self collapsing into a hammock, soaking in warm rays of sun while a cool spring breeze danced across my face. I spent more time with my children, spoke more honestly with my wife and listened more intently to God's Word. I took a couple of walks, even when I "didn't have time" to do so. I engaged in meaningful conversations with family and friends, realizing along the way that I had failed them and me by not doing so sooner. I prayed more quietly, with fewer requests and more self-disclosure.

I could almost physically feel the oil level rising. I felt more hopeful, less rushed. I also felt full of vision for approaching the blank canvas of a computer screen upon which I would craft the final chapter of my manuscript. I began writing chapter twelve, "Self-Care for Wick Burners."

Thus this book concludes by encouraging and challenging spiritual caregivers to care for themselves as well as their students. As a mentor to students and youth ministry leaders for two decades, I've come to the conclusion that I had little need to worry that these men and women would wipe out in ministry because they didn't know what program to take on next. Nor were they likely to find themselves out of ministry in five years because they failed to keep up with cultural change. Most of the *doing* of adolescent spiritual caregiving can be taught to any person who has relational gifts and a sense of calling. The significant challenges for spiritual caregivers are always ultimately issues of personhood. When life becomes hard—and inevitably it will—*who* one has become internally is destined to emerge. At that crossroads, years of spiritual self-care in relationship to a living God, or years without such care, determine whether there exists enough spiritual vitality to carry us into deeper levels of life.

The depths of spiritual caregiving flow out of wells of deeply lived journeys with God. Those who excel at the external elements of caring for adolescents while neglecting their own spiritual journeys face an impending personal implosion. But adults, young and old, parents or pastors, who have heeded the axiom "I can only reproduce what is real within me" can anticipate a life of increasingly intimate relationship with the God they serve. The same is true for adolescents themselves. Our lives can only be as spiritually fruitful as we are spiritually deep in relationship with God. Furthermore, our own sacred conversation with him is the only means we have for inviting others to join us in dialogue with the God of our spiritual journeys.

Student ministry spiritual caregivers, however, are notorious wick-burners. That busyness drains without replenishing, leaving caregivers with nothing more to share than what they can siphon off a short prayer or a quick lunch meeting for "accountability." Richard Foster notes that youth ministry leaders "should never have a 50- to 60-hour work week. That's sin and we should confess it and cut it back."[1]

Identifying the problem is easy. Actually getting to the roots of our tendency to overplan, overschedule and overcommit is not. The search for self-understanding requires a lifestyle of listening to God pacing with us. As for our students, that type of journey will require participation in a mentoring community where *we* are paced with and then led to deeper spiritual authenticity.

Ironically, what is most needed to correct the busy life is the very thing that is assassinated by the busy life! Initially more effort is required to avoid busyness than to perpetuate its hectic pace. Once one has chosen self-care, though, the energy that comes from a healthier lifestyle fuels the pacing and leading that will shape adolescent spiritual lives meaningfully over the long haul.

When one considers the choice between burning-out wicks and a deep reservoir of oil as a gift to adolescents, the choice is self-evident. To encourage and guide spiritual caregivers to burn the oil, not the wick, four disciplines for nurturing self-care are considered below. Each of these areas represents a place of death and life. To practice these disciplines we must go to the cross to lay down the hindrances that prevent walking in them. Each discipline brings life only as we yield ourselves to resurrected spiritual vitality. The four disciplines are *valuing one's own journey, creating space for one's individual life with God, immersing oneself deeply in community* and *leaning into pain and brokenness.*

Valuing One's Own Journey

Robert succeeded at everything he touched in student ministry. He was equally gifted with junior high, senior high and college students. He could train leaders to maximize their giftedness for ministry. As his groups increased, so did his level of influence among other youth ministry leaders.

I was not surprised to encounter him on the docket of a conference leadership team. What shocked me, however, was how he looked. He had the countenance of a zombie in a late-night horror flick—a shell of the vibrant person I had known. When I asked him how he was doing, he acknowledged being tired but assured me that his ministry was just as dynamic as ever.

A month later I learned that he had left his wife and children to pursue a relationship with a much younger woman in his church. Sadly, I was not shocked.

Jeff Van Vonderen offers a parable for Robert's life in *Tired of Trying to Measure Up:*

> The ancient myths tell of a man who was punished by the gods. They bound him and cursed him with a burning thirst, then held up a cup of cool water before him. But no matter how he struggled, the ropes merely cut deeper into his flesh and the soothing water remained a few tantalizing inches beyond his parched lips.[2]

Robert was an effective leader and a committed disciple of Christ. But he always had to keep doing more and more. No matter how much he accomplished, the thirst for affirmation was never quenched. In the end, dried up from trying, he dug his own cistern instead of drinking from the well God had provided in himself and in Robert's wife (Gen 2:13).

Robert knew how to value the spiritual journey of others; he did not know how to value his own. Lacking a sufficient experience of God's unconditional love for him, Robert failed to place high value on his own physical, emotional and relational needs. He became deaf to the Voice calling God's beloved to the intimacy of whole-person sacred conversation. Consequently, he spiritually imploded and sought refuge in an adulterous relationship.

Van Vonderen suggests that the root of such personal devaluing and "dysgrace" can be found in shame. Shame causes men and women to be driven in vain to find "the one button that's going to make God smile."[3] Symptomatic of this shame is a lack of genuine self-care. Sacrificing quality of life for quantity of achievement in an attempt to earn love, shame-based spiritual caregivers even fool themselves into thinking that ignoring self-care represents a holy sacrifice to God.

The mind, emotions, will and body are integrally connected.[4] In harmony with one another, these distinct yet interrelated components constitute the context within which our souls live with God. To fail to care for any component well while attempting to nurture our spirituality is an exercise in futility. Spiritual caregiving that leaves us with no time and energy to be attentive to our own thoughts, feelings, life choices and physical condition puts us in tension with the work of God to conform us to the image of his Son. Then we are rooting our identity in what we can do rather than in who we are in him. To do this is to practice idolatry. Living to gain approval in order to fight down our sense of shame holds our souls captive. The positive feedback of others rather than the unconditional love of God becomes the true lord of our life. As Robert discovered, the idol of external validation is a cruel taskmaster.

Creating Space for One's Individual Life with God

David, in 1 Chronicles 14, has followed God's commands precisely and thus won a great victory against the Philistines. Now the Philistines are rallying again to raid the valley, and David once again seeks the Lord's will for his leadership. God's unexpected answer comes in verses 14-15: "Do not go straight up, but circle around them and attack them in front of the balsam tress. As soon as you hear the sound of marching in the tops of the balsam trees, move out to battle, because that will mean God has gone out in front of you to strike the Philistines."

I am struck by the imagery of David positioning his army for God to move among them, over them and in front of them as they enter battle. Of all the ways God could have led David, he chooses to have him wait on God to show up.

In the new covenant we recognize that we now have God among us and within us. Our Immanuel, Jesus, left us with the presence of the Holy Spirit so that we do not have to wait for God to "show up." However, having God present and experiencing his presence are vastly different realities. To experience God's presence requires creating space to hear him, to engage in spirit-to-Spirit dialogue and to be yielded to the filling presence of his Spirit, the oil required to avoid burning the wick.

Our culture encourages us to "take the hill," not wait on God to move through the trees. Robert Mulholland observes,

> We are a do-it-yourself culture. We are what I call an objectivizing, informational-functional culture.

An objectivizing culture is one that views the world primarily as an object "out there" to be grasped and controlled for our own purposes. We are the subjects whose role in life is to appropriate the objects in our world and use them to impose our will upon the world. . . . "Being conformed" goes totally, radically against the ingrained objectification perspective of our culture. Graspers powerfully resist being grasped by God. Manipulators strongly reject being shaped by God. Spiritual formation is the great reversal: from being the subject who controls all other things to being a person who is shaped by the presence, purpose and power of God in all things.[5]

Being "shaped by the presence, purpose and power of God in all things" requires the sacred conversation of life with God. The rushed, panicked, overwhelmed lives our culture reinforces leave no margins for waiting under the trees, listening for God to move and learning to trust in his provision.

Life in the twenty-first century promises more immediate rewards to space-fillers than to spacemakers. Spacemaking requires the discipline of delayed gratification. Spacemaking is an intentional act of exchanging one's life for the life God wills to give us. Peterson's *Leap over a Wall,* a reflection on the life of King David, includes these observations concerning the life exchange that results from meeting God in quiet spaces:

When we sit down, the dust raised by our furious activity settles; the noise generated by our building operations goes quiet; we become aware of the real world. *God's* world. And what we see leaves us breathless; it's so much more full of energy and action than our ego-fueled actions, so much clearer an answer than the plans that we had projected. . . .

When David sat down before God, it was the farthest thing from passivity or resignation; it was prayer. It was entering in the presence of God, becoming aware of God's word, trading in his plans for God's plans, letting his enthusiasm for being a king with the authority and strength to do something for God be replaced with the willingness to become a king who would represent truly the sovereignty of God the high King.[6]

Creating space for God thus begins with the discipline of *sitting down.* The choice may be actualized through Christian disciplines of prayer, fasting, extended solitude, Scriptural study, reflective listening or theological reading.[7] Critical to each practice is a commitment to prevent the means from becoming an end. Each must be "offered to God as an exercise of faith and a means of grace."[8] Spiritual disciplines are not a means for us to "get to God." The practices are rather a means for responding to his pursuit of us. Disciplining oneself to make space is the art of yielding rather than the science of attaining.[9]

Without a persistent renewal of yieldedness to God, idolatry resurrects itself in the heart. The old adage is wrong—there is one more certain thing in life, besides death and taxes: every member of the human race inevitably pursues a god. The issue is not whether it is *a* god but whether it is *the true* God. God's child, though directed in his heart toward God and saved by the grace of Jesus, often finds himself living as a practical idol worshiper. Space for God combined with a yielded heart empowers him to experience and express true worship of the true God.

Simple steps are the most effective when discovering or renewing the call to create space for oneself. A quiet place to listen, read, talk, sing and journal with God signals the change to a space-creating pace of life. Cultivating silence and solitude empowers one's choice to exchange one's rush-hour orientation for that of a leisurely stroll. Our twenty-first-century souls have been beaten down by the wear and tear of our "objectivizing culture," so we should not expect these simple steps to be easy. However, like water poured on the cracked soil of a farmer's fields, the living water of God's Spirit soon permeates even the driest of souls. As we enter sacred conversation in our dehydrated inner soil, we are passionately drawn to the Source of living water. We develop "irrigated" lifestyles that weather every season, including the longest droughts.

Immersing Oneself Deeply in Community

"Can't I just go to God to get my needs met?" Josh, a twenty-one-year-old college junior, had been confused by my chapel message. The central theme of my talk had been "We desperately need God *and* we desperately need each other." Josh could resonate with the first point; my latter assertion left him unsettled.

God established community in the creation act. Creating humanity in his own image meant that he could not do otherwise. To be authentically in relationship with God requires being in community. As Gilbert Bilezikian notes, "Community is deeply grounded in the nature of God. It flows from who God is. Because he is community, he creates community. It is his gift of himself to humans."[10]

Having affirmed the necessity of relationships in the adolescent spiritual journey toward wholeness in Christ, we cannot now deny our own need for healthy relationships. Yet I encounter countless spiritual caregivers whose entire experience of community is limited to places where they are in leadership. I confess to my own tendency in this direction. Caregivers can, of course, experience rich community as parents within a family or as a small group leader of fourteen-year-olds. The issue is not quality but sufficiency. To live in the fullness of God's call to life with him, every believer requires authentic Christian community with peers and mentors. Such community has two key aspects:

☐ Authentic Christian community begins when a group of persons commit to the intentional pursuit of whole-person maturity in obedience to God: mutually submissive, sincere communication with one another and redemptive relationships that work through real-life issues as they emerge individually and corporately in the course of walking out life together with Jesus.

☐ Authentic Christian community is characterized by genuine and appropriate self-disclosure of group members' internal selves, acceptance of and support for each person's individual process of growth, redemptive conflict resolution, and grace-based challenges for individuals and the group to move beyond itself as salt and light in the broader world.[11]

Josh was hesitant to consider the role of others in meeting his deep personal needs. He wanted God alone to touch those places. On the one hand, Josh described the human condition accurately. Only God heals the broken places of our being. On the other hand, Josh was avoiding an important component of experiencing the redemptive, healing life Christians are called to live. He pushed away community, preferring to go it alone with God. As we talked further it became evident that Josh had good reason to push people away. He had been burned before. The self-protecting approach he had developed in response had worked—to a point. God had indeed met him in broken places. Now he needed God *and* God's people to grow through the next steps. He hesitated, not out of spiritual vitality but because of fear.

Fear is the greatest threat to community.[12] Fear comes from anticipating how we would feel if others responded hurtfully to the parts of ourselves that already feel unlovable and unworthy. The bigger those parts appear in our inner rear-view mirror, the more threatening are the relationships that could potentially expose them. The longer they stay hidden, the bigger those objects appear in the mirror.

Past relationships filled with shame and rejection created those scary places of internal shame. Engaging in authentic community thus seems too much. We fear others will act as police helicopters flying over dark alleys, shining bright lights on the villains lurking in our dark spaces. So we hide in fear.

Adam and Eve dove behind bushes. We bury ourselves under defense mechanisms and busyness. It did not work for them; it will not work for us.

Leaning into Pain and Brokenness

To overcome the fear attached to shame is an act of faith. I have been working to grow in such faith for years. My sense of personal shame and my fear of rejection by others caused me to be terrified of opening my true self to anyone. I initially chose to be a leader partly because the image projected by leaders is a wonderful form of self-protection. More recently I have recognized the self-deception of my self-protection.

I have always wanted to be a mat carrier, not the guy flat on the mat. Through a series of experiences that were emotionally, physically and spiritually painful, I reached the end of myself. I recognized that I was hiding my wounded self behind the aura of the ministry I performed. God laid me flat on the mat. I had no choice but to depend on others. I could no longer hide my internal weaknesses. I began to see the man in the mirror as a broken man lying lame on his mat. I desperately needed God *and* I desperately needed people.

Only in this place was I ready to begin the deep healing processes the Great Physician had been preparing for me. Only in this place was I prepared to become a true mat carrier for the broken lives around me. I was no longer playing physician ("I'm not a doctor but I play one at church every Sunday"). I began living as a fellow paralytic who had found the Healer.

Pain denied or concealed becomes infected. Brokenness not properly set leads to twisted, limp lives. The church is filled with silent bearers of pain and brokenness.[14] Weeping alone, believers fight off infections of the soul and bravely attempt to provide spiritual care from wounded relational selves.

My own "flat on the mat" experiences reduced me to a daily confrontation of my pain and brokenness. For the first time I experienced what I would call true suffering. I wanted so desperately to perform my way out, but I lacked the necessary strength. I had to lean into my pain and broken-ness; I no longer had the means to avoid myself.

I am instinctively afraid of heights. I have, however, chosen not to be controlled by this fear. I have actually come to enjoy flying, plunging seventy miles per hour down a rollercoaster drop and climbing in the mountains. I even like the exhilaration of ropes courses—everything except the first step. That first step, that moment of letting go of a tree or ladder that I know by a lifetime of experience will hold me, is what really terrifies me.

On a recent ropes course adventure I was teamed with Brad, a twenty-three-year-old lacking any hint of a fear of heights. We were chosen to tackle the most challenging element on the course, highest and hardest. The element could be conquered only through a carefully choreographed part-nership.

Brad stepped onto the thin cable first, hanging precariously to ropes running parallel to the cable. He secured his balance, then turned to me. I wanted to pretend that I was as cool about this as he was, but I could not even pretend. I was seriously committed to accomplishing this task; I was seriously scared about taking the first step.

Standing on a three-foot-square platform, staring at the thirty-five feet of space below the thin cable directly in front of my feet, I had a choice to make. Would I take the step or not? I decided to apply what I had been learning about myself through the painful crucible of suffering—I would face rather than shout down my fears. I would engage them with honesty and vulnerability.

I said to Brad, "I want you to know that I will take this step. But I need to be honest—this first step scares me to death. I am really feeling afraid, even though I know I will be OK. So this may take a minute."

Brad responded with "It's OK, I'll wait. Here, grab my hand to balance your first step."

With that I took my step and gained confidence in the rope—and Brad and I became the only team to conquer that particular element that day. And I had a blast!

My fear was real. I could not talk myself out of it. Rather, I had to face it. Having a partner to listen to, accept and meet me at that place made the first step much easier. It was humbling to tell a twenty-three-year-old that I was scared. I found it even more humbling to have to lean on his sense of confidence to overcome my own deficit. Just as it was humbling for me to go to a therapist to seek counseling for my fears of rejection and worthlessness. Just as it is humbling to reveal to others that I am a naturally fearful, anxious person who wants to hide the real me. Just as it is humbling to write this in a book that will be read by perfect strangers. Being authentic, however, has become my only known path of freedom.

Ray Anderson writes:

> I have attempted to counter this tendency toward denial in the Christian theological tradition by a return to a biblical understanding of the self. The Hebrew view of reality does not split good and evil, happiness and suffering, into separate metaphysical entities. Personal loss and painful grief are part of a larger and longer cycle of the self. Recovery in the form of self-care is more than reduction of pain and the healing of grief.[15]

Leaning into pain and brokenness does not have as its goal immediate relief. Rather, the goal is to acknowledge, experience and grieve through our suffering on the way to a full experience of grace. Anderson challenges, "Through grief we apprehend the grace of God, and by the grace of God we recover the courage to be."[16]

Christians too often attempt to shout down, cut off or gag the pain that wells up within. Anderson's words call us to grieve it with God and his people in order to deepen our experience of grace. June Lewers Terry's inspiring work *When Teardrops Dance* presents a similar vision for embracing the places of suffering in our lives. A South African nurse and servant leader who has ministered the gospel of grace to men and women encountering deep suffering, Terry speaks from her own experiences of God's presence in suffering. For Terry, one of the most difficult aspects of her suffering was the loneliness she felt through years of singleness. But it was that very suffering that produced within Terry her deepest intimacy with God.

> Suffering is nothing compared with the surpassing greatness of knowing God. Count suffering as nothing, knowing God as everything. I am profoundly grateful that God brought me to this convinced position about three years before my marriage. I was able to say that singleness with its distress of loneliness, frustration and apparent rejection was worth it for what I had learned of God by walking alone with him into my forties.[17]

Living as One Being Healed

Leaning into our pain and brokenness constitutes a lifetime journey. In this life we will never be fully healed. To live well with God, however, means to be constantly living as one who is *being healed.*

How do we step forward in this journey? First, we embrace pain as part of our growth in grace. Paul Brand and Philip Yancey open their book *Pain: The Gift Nobody Wants* with the story of Tanya, a child described by her father as "a monster." By age four, Tanya had seriously ulcerated feet from her refusal to wear shoes and mangled fingers from her repeated habit of chewing on and even biting off her fingertips. Her parents, not knowing the source of her behavior and desperate for help, brought her to see Dr. Brand. He discovered that Tanya had "congenital indifference to pain." Simply put, her brain did not register pain. Brand and Yancey record the impact on Tanya's life:

> Seven years later I received a telephone call from Tanya's mother in St. Louis. Tanya, now eleven, was living a pathetic existence in an institution. She had lost both legs to amputation: she had refused to wear proper shoes and that, coupled with her failure to limp or to shift weight when standing (because she felt no discomfort), eventually put intolerable pressure on her joints. Tanya had also lost most of her fingers. Her elbows were constantly dislocated. She suffered the effects of chronic sepsis from ulcers on her hands and amputation stumps. Her tongue was lacerated and badly scarred from her nervous habit of chewing it.[18]

To this horrific picture the authors add this profound observation: "A monster, her father had called her. Tanya was no monster, only an extreme example—a human metaphor, really—of life without pain."[19]

Life includes pain. God's children are called to lean into the places of pain to discover the healing grace of God. God is not a painkiller; he is the disease healer. Those who become busy, avoid God and community, and medicate their pain with escapist activities or ministry experiences, simply ignore the damage being done through a numbed sense of the pain within.

The second step to living as one being healed is the active integration of the first three disciplines: valuing one's journey, creating space for one's life with God and creating space for life in community. Like the adolescents we love, we are whole, integrated persons. Pain and brokenness cannot be addressed as if it were a skin growth. These hurtful places permeate our being. If we treat them as if they lie on the surface, we will fail to engage God in authentic sacred conversation at our points of greatest need. All aspects of self-care are critical to the healing of the broken self.

From a spiritual caregiving point of view, the vitality of pacing and then leading is dependent on such a holistic encounter between us and our Father. Unless God can be seen as real in our moments of loss and hurt, postmodern adolescents will dismiss his reality. Sensate offerings of escape promise more relief than an impotent god who cannot deliver when it counts. Better then to be entertained than to be merely religiously active. Who wants to be carried on a mat up a ladder, through a roof, into a sneering crowd only to find that the religious guy is all talk?

The Lingering Leader

My son Zachary and I had a wonderful walk together once I chose to pace with him on that abandoned railroad bed. To pace with a four-year-old requires patience and a commitment to linger. We were going nowhere fast—physically, that is. Emotionally and spiritually we were rapidly accelerating into each other's interior world. I pray to spend a lifetime cultivating that lingering pace with Zachary, my other two children, Jessica and Benjamin, and my wife, Teresa.

The pacing-then-leading vision calls spiritual caregivers to be lingering leaders who journey with the interior worlds of postmodern adolescents. Ironically, as this chapter has demonstrated, the spiritual caregiver's path to becoming a lingering leader is marked by a great reversal. The true picture of a pacing-then-leading caregiver can be found in Zachary rather than me. Zachary only wanted to be with me that day. My son's deepest desires were for me to see the world he was seeing, to hear his thoughts on the bugs and rocks he touched, and to feel as if nothing else in the world mattered as long as much as being with him. This is my first calling: to be God's lingering child.

The lingering leader is conceived through life experiences as a lingering child. Pacing and then leading gestate as we continually recognize and respond to our pacing Father. Unlike me, he never gets distracted from being present with us. He is focused, patient and committed to lingering. In fact, if you are listening, he is initiating a sacred conversation with you—will you choose to linger?

Reflecting on Your Journey

☐ Where do you see evidences of wick burning in your life?

☐ Looking back at the four self-care disciplines, where do you hear God's voice calling you to deepen your self-care? Describe your emotional response to that voice (guilt, hope, fear, excitement, despair). How can you linger with the Father in that emotion?

☐ What do you think are the roots of your struggles with busyness? What in your external circumstances fuels wick-burning? What within your interior self drives you to wick-burning?

☐ How would living as "one being healed" translate into your everyday life? What are the practical implications of this orientation? What resources will you need in order to cultivate this lifestyle?

☐ How can you linger with God—right now, in this very moment? Recognize and respond to your pacing Father who desires to lead you into the depths of himself.

Pressing In

☐ When, if ever, have you experienced being totally "flat on the mat"? If you have, what lessons did you learn during that season? Identify weeds in your interior garden that have choked some of the life out of what God planted in your time of broken yieldedness.

☐ Purpose to cultivate a deeper relationship with a mentor, a friend, a spouse, a counselor, a small group leader or other safe person. Intentionally invite this trustworthy person into new layers of your hidden spaces.

☐ Covenant with a person or group to learn together how to live as those who are being healed. Read together Philip Yancey's *What's So Amazing About Grace?* Pray fervently for and with one another as you seek to be exposed, embraced and empowered in the spiritual womb of grace.

☐ If you lack authentic community, set your heart to pray for and look for every opportunity to initiate that community. Without authentic connection with God's people, wick-burning is inevitable in the spiritual caregiver's life.

☐ Journal your sacred conversation. Write your fears. Write God's voice. Listen for what echoes through the walls of your interior. With the help of his Holy Spirit and your own authentic community, identify your idolatry. Linger with God in those places. Ask him to help you experience his pacing so that you may follow his leading into the true worship that leads to deeper intimacy with him.

Notes

Chapter 1: The Walk of Life

[1]My use of "pacing, then leading" as a metaphor is ultimately rooted in my theology and the social science arena of communication theory. The theology is self-evident as the book unfolds. The origins of the metaphor are not so apparent. Surprisingly my own journey toward the adaptation of this imagery began with the reading of Paul Hersey and Kenneth H. Blanchard, *Management of Organizational Behavior,* 6th ed. (Englewood Cliffs, N.J.: Prentice Hall, 1983). As I followed the authors' articulation of a pacing-then-leading model of interpersonal communication, I began to resonate with their emphases on rapport, pacing, leading and behavioral adaptability. Years of teaching on the divergent topics of adolescent spiritual nurture and organizational culture ultimately brought the richness of the metaphor into my field of vision. However, it was on a walk with my son, Zachary, that life was breathed into the pacing-then-leading approach to the spiritual nurture of adolescents.

It is appropriate, given the genesis of the terms, to assign credit for the origin of my terminology to Hersey and Blanchard's work. See pages 333-35 of that text for a full development of the model as it was originally conceptualized in organizational theory.

[2]Certainly Jesus had the unique power to pace with a person before even asking the question. Given that knowledge, I find his consistent pattern of providing a pacing experience as an invitation to the truth even more compelling. If pacing were simply a matter of figuring out what will get people to the truth, Jesus would have bypassed the whole process. Pacing is, rather, a means of connecting interpersonally. For us, it provides needed insights as we seek to lead an adolescent to a deeper experience or understanding of the truth. Just as significant, pacing invites the adolescent to participate in our life with God by participating in his life with us.

[3]Jim Wilhoit, *Christian Education and the Search for Meaning*, 2nd ed. (Grand Rapids, Mich.: Baker, 1991), pp. 132-37.

[4]Stephen R. Covey, *The Seven Habits of Highly Effective Families* (New York: Golden, 1997), pp. 223-24.

[5]Ibid., p. 231.

Chapter 2: Postmodern Pilgrims in Progress

[1]For an effective overview of the use of "postmodernity" as it applies to this chapter, see Stanley Grenz, *A Primer on Postmodernism* (Grand Rapids, Mich.: Eerdmans, 1996).

[2]An intriguing, comprehensive critique of the impact of this emerging philosophical frame-

work is found in D. A. Carson, *The Gagging of God* (Grand Rapids, Mich.: Zondervan, 1996).

[3]Ibid., pp. 22-37.

[4]Jimmy Long, *Generating Hope* (Downers Grove, Ill: InterVarsity Press, 1997), p. 192.

[5]Frank McCourt, "When You Think of God, What Do You See?" *Life*, December 1998, p. 64.

[6]Marina Warner, "Wrestling with the Oldest Rules," *Self*, December 1997, p. 136.

[7]Long, *Generating Hope*, p. 192.

[8]Carson, *Gagging of God*, p. 35.

[9]Long, *Generating Hope*, p. 193.

[10]Priscilla Grant, "How Spiritual Are You?" *Self*, December 1997, p. 134.

[11]Cindy Pearlman, "Suddenly Spiritual," *react*, December 28, 1998-January 3, 1999, p. 9.

[12]The significance of the theological message of *City of Angels* was first framed for me by my colleague Chad Ellenberg.

[13]Kenda Creasy Dean and Ron Foster, *The Godbearing Life* (Nashville: Upper Room, 1998), p. 16.

[14]Martin Marty, quoted in Mary Schmich, "Heaven's Gaters May Not Have Been So Strange After All," *Chicago Tribune,* March 30, 1997, sect. 4, p. 1.

[15]As a starting place for articulating a thoroughly Christian worldview in the context of postmodern religious pluralism see Ravi Zacharias, *Jesus Among Other Gods* (Nashville: Word, 2000).

[16]Postmodern spirituality is characterized by a syncretistic approach to theological beliefs. Harold O. J. Brown, *The Sensate Culture* (Dallas: Word, 1996), p. 76.

[17]Dean and Foster, *Godbearing Life,* pp. 16-17.

[18]Long, *Generating Hope*, p. 210.

[19]"Leading people beyond religion and into relationship with Jesus Christ" is the mission statement of Fellowship Evangelical Free Church, Knoxville, Tennessee. All of our ministries, including student ministries, are united in their commitment to fulfill this calling.

[20]Quentin Schultze et al., eds., *Dancing in the Dark* (Grand Rapids, Mich.: Eerdmans, 1991), p. 240.

[21]Quentin J. Schultze, "How Should We Respond to Popular Culture?" in *Reaching a Generation for Christ,* ed. Richard R. Dunn and Mark H. Senter III (Chicago: Moody Press, 1997), p. 442.

[22]Richard R. Dunn and Mark H. Senter III, *Reaching a Generation for Christ* (Chicago: Moody Press, 1997), p. 11.

[23]Roger Lundin, *The Culture of Interpretation* (Grand Rapids, Mich: Eerdmans, 1993), pp. 5-6. Lundin writes, "A *therapeutic culture* is one in which questions of ultimate concern—about the nature of the good, the meaning of truth, and the existence of God—are taken to be unanswerable and hence in some fundamental sense insignificant."

[24]The "youth way" as a powerful shaping influence can be more thoroughly understood by reading Schultze et al., *Dancing in the Dark,* and Walt Mueller, *Understanding Today's Youth Culture* (Wheaton, Ill.: Tyndale House, 1994). For an intriguing case study on the breadth of impact of the contemporary global youth culture, read "Millennium Supplement: Culture," *National Geographic*, August 1999.

[25]The appropriate spiritual caregiver response to the treacherous waters of twenty-first-century

"youth way" enculturation is compassion not condemnation. Rick Lawrence writes, "Eating disorders, sexual addiction, drug abuse, alcoholism, and compulsive shopping—all these demonstrate that the core experiences of pain and sin are interrelated. . . . Psychiatrist Jeffrey Satinover has written that the only way for people to find release from these addictive patterns that entrap us is to find healing for some core experience of pain that the sin has tried to address" (*Trend Watch* [Loveland, Colo.: Group, 2000], p. 35). Pacing with the pain and then leading to the healing and forgiveness of sin is the mandate of postmodern spiritual caregiving.

[26]Brown, *Sensate Culture,* p. 9.

[27]Ibid.

[28]Ibid.

[29]Ibid.

[30]Ibid., pp. 9-10.

[31]Ibid., p. 15.

[32]Carson, *Gagging of God,* pp. 422-23.

[33]Betsy Pickle, "Steamy, Audacious Young Cast Raises Temperature in 'Cruel Intentions,' " *Knoxville News-Sentinel,* March 6, 1999, sect. B, p. 6.

[34]Ibid. Engaging students in a morally confused sensate culture may be the most challenging aspect of the next generation of spiritual caregiving. Caregivers will increasingly be called on to embrace unconditionally students whose moral selves are badly misshapen.

[35]Aleksandr Solzhenitsyn, quoted in Brown, *Sensate Culture,* p. 6.

[36]J. I. Packer, "An Introduction to Systematic Spirituality," *Crux,* March 1990, p. 3.

[37]Mueller, *Understanding Youth Culture,* p. 9.

[38]Ibid., pp. 37-38.

[39]Schultze et al., *Dancing in the Dark,* p. 9.

[40]For more on the bicultural nature of churches with disparate worldviews among their congregations, read Richard R. Dunn and James W. Mohler, "The 'Fourth Wave': A Theological Perspective," *Christian Education Journal,* fall 1999, pp. 47-61.

Chapter 3: A Theology for Pacing, Then Leading

[1]Anthony Hoekema, *Created in God's Image* (Grand Rapids, Mich.: Eerdmans, 1986), p. 28.

[2]Ibid., p. 83-85.

[3]M. Robert Mulholland Jr., *Invitation to a Journey* (Downers Grove, Ill: InterVarsity Press, 1993), p. 11.

[4]Gilbert Bilezikian, *Community 101* (Grand Rapids, Mich.: Zondervan, 1997), p. 60.

[5]Ibid., p. 27.

[6]Larry Crabb, *Connecting* (Nashville: Word, 1997), pp. 5-6.

[7]Henry Cloud, *Changes That Heal* (Grand Rapids, Mich.: Zondervan, 1992), pp. 50-52.

[8]Steven Garber, *The Fabric of Faithfulness* (Downers Grove, Ill: InterVarsity Press, 1996), pp. 35-39.

[9]Mulholland, *Invitation to a Journey,* p. 73: "We are spiritual beings whose emotions, psychology, body and mind are the incarnation of our spiritual life in the world."

[10]Jim Wilhoit, *Christian Education and the Search for Meaning,* 2nd ed. (Grand Rapids, Mich.: Baker, 1991), pp. 132-37.

[11]Note that peer pressure is fueled by the fear of rejection. It is therefore inappropriate to speak of "positive peer pressure" or "Christian peer pressure." The appropriate approach of Christian community is positive peer influence.

[12]Anthony Hoekema, *Saved by Grace* (Grand Rapids, Mich.: Eerdmans, 1989), pp. 5-7.

[13]Dallas Willard, *The Divine Conspiracy* (New York: HarperCollins, 1998), pp. 311-73. Willard develops a compelling vision for cooperating with the redemptive work of the Spirit in chapter nine, "A Curriculum for Christlikeness."

[14]Hoekema, *Saved by Grace*, pp. 199-202.

[15]Kevin Huggins, *Parenting Adolescents* (Colorado Springs: NavPress, 1989), p. 178.

Chapter 4: How to Listen Before You Lead

[1]Stephen R. Covey, *The Seven Habits of Highly Effective Families* (New York: Golden, 1997), p. 216.

[2]The term "Unseen Real" has been borrowed from Leanne Payne. For more on the nature of the unseen reality see her *The Healing Presence* (Grand Rapids, Mich.: Baker, 1995).

[3]For insights on the cultivation of one's listening prayer see Leanne Payne's *Listening Prayer* (Grand Rapids, Mich.: Baker, 1994).

[4]Larry Crabb, *Connecting* (Nashville: Word, 1997), p. 21.

[5]Ibid., p. 207.

[6]Covey, *Seven Habits of Highly Effective Families,* p. 227.

[7]Harville Hendrix and Helen Hunt, *Giving the Love That Heals* (New York: Pocket, 1997), p. 118.

[8]Les Parrot III, *Helping the Struggling Adolescent* (Grand Rapids, Mich.: Zondervan, 1993), p. 31.

[9]Hendrix and Hunt, *Giving the Love that Heals*, p. 111.

[10]Ibid., p. 103.

[11]Ibid.

[12]Ibid., p. 12. Hendrix and Hunt define *symbiosis* as "an inability on the part of a parent to distinguish between himself and his child."

[13]Henry Blackaby's *Experiencing God* stresses joining the Father where he is at work in the world. Pacing prayer seeks to apply that principle to spiritual caregiving in the lives of adolescents.

[14]Only the Spirit of God truly sees into the heart of a student. Our role is to guide students to an authentic life in the Spirit of God, not to usurp the role of the Spirit.

Chapter 5: How to Speak the Truth in Love

[1]Gary Smalley and John Trent, *The Gift of the Blessing* (Nashville: Thomas Nelson, 1993), pp. 27-28.

[2]Harville Hendrix and Helen Hunt, *Giving the Love That Heals* (New York: Pocket, 1997), p. 122.

[3]Kevin Huggins, *Parenting Adolescents* (Colorado Springs: NavPress, 1989), p. 27.

[4]Ibid., p. 95.

[5]Hendrix and Hunt, *Giving the Love That Heals,* pp. 56-61.

[6]Larry Crabb, *Effective Biblical Counseling* (Grand Rapids, Mich.: Zondervan, 1977), pp.

146-60.

[7]Stephen R. Covey, *The Seven Habits of Highly Effective Families* (New York: Golden, 1997), pp. 213-14.

Chapter 6: How to Confront & Resolve Conflict

[1]Condemnation results from humanity's choice to rebel against God. God pronounces judgment in accordance with the reality of our condemnation. God therefore does not condemn us; we condemn ourselves. John 3:17-18 thus teaches that "God did not send his Son into the world to condemn the world, but to save the world through him. Whoever believes in him is not condemned, but whoever does not believe stands condemned already because he has not believed in the name of God's one and only Son."

[2]God provides the lamb (John 1:29; foreshadowed in Genesis 22:13-14).

[3]Withdrawing from the relationship leads to a "shaming" of the student. See Dan Weyerhauser, *But Our Lives As Well*, an unpublished manual on student ministries.

[4]Paul Swets, *The Art of Talking to Your Teenager* (Holbrook, Mass.: Adams, 1995), p. 112.

[5]Swets offers the concept of a "no sandwich" (ibid., pp. 73-76).

[6]Kevin Huggins, *Parenting Adolescents* (Colorado Springs: NavPress, 1989), p. 237.

[7]Henry Cloud, *Changes That Heal* (Grand Rapids, Mich.: Zondervan, 1992), p. 39.

Chapter 7: How to Nurture the Adolescent Moral Self

[1]Catherine Stonehouse, *Joining Children on the Spiritual Journey* (Grand Rapids, Mich.: Baker, 1998), p. 125.

[2]Ibid., pp. 20-21.

[3]Robert Coles, *The Moral Intelligence of Children* (New York: Plume, 1998), p. 58.

[4]Don Postema, *Space for God* (Kalamazoo, Mich.: CRC Publications, 1983), p. 34.

[5]Henry Cloud, *Changes That Heal* (Grand Rapids, Mich.: Zondervan, 1992), pp. 43-64.

[6]One of the most challenging aspects of guiding students is respecting healthy differentiation while recognizing unhealthy rebellion. In many instances, effective pacing is necessary in order to discern what lies in the heart behind the challenging behavior. Differentiation may require little more than further guidance; rebellion may require a confrontation.

[7]Jeff VanVonderen, *Families Where Grace Is in Place* (Minneapolis: Bethany House, 1992), p. 117.

[8]Ibid.

[9]The culture God creates among the Hebrew people (in the Old Testament) and in the body of Christ (in the New Testament) demonstrates his desire for a holistic moral climate (see Deuteronomy 6; Ephesians 4:11-16). Social interaction theory, especially as conceived by Vgotsky (see Anastasia Tryphon and Jacques Voneche, *Piaget-Vgotsky: The Social Genesis of Thought* [East Sussex, U.K.: Psychology Press, 1996]) and the research and writings of Robert Coles, particularly his exceptional work *The Moral Intelligence of Children* (New York: Plume, 1997), contribute to my understanding of "caught" morality..

[10]Sandra D. Wilson, *Shame-Free Parenting* (Downers Grove, Ill.: InterVarsity Press, 1992), p. 78.

[11]Uwe Gielen, "Research on Moral Reasoning," in *The Kohlberg Legacy*, ed. Lisa Kuhmerker with Uwe Gielen and Richard R. Hayes (Birmingham, Ala.: Doxa, 1994), p. 53.

[12]Frank Hajcak and Patricia Garwood, *Quick-Fix Sex: Pseudosexuality in Adolescents* (reprint, San Diego: Libra, n.d.).

[13]Robert W. Pazmino, *Foundational Issues in Christian Education,* 2nd ed. (Grand Rapids, Mich.: Baker, 1997), pp. 203-8.

[14]Guielen, "Research on Moral Reasoning," p. 53.

[15]Ibid.

[16]Ken Gire, *Windows of the Soul* (Grand Rapids, Mich.: Zondervan,, 1996), p. 105. Gire borrows from C. S. Lewis to demonstrate the necessity of living in the good but not "safe" place spiritually.

Chapter 8: How to Create Space for Postmodern Spiritual Journeys

[1]Richard R. Dunn and James Mohler, "The 'Fourth Wave': A Theological Perspective," *Christian Education Journal,* fall 1999, p. 47.

[2]Don Postema, *Space for God* (Kalamzoo, Mich.: CRC Publications, 1983), p. 90.

[3]In addition to Postema, two other sources favor "creating space for God" in ways relevant to this chapter: Kenda Creasy Dean and Ron Foster, *The Godbearing Life* (Nashville: Upper Room, 1998); Mark Yaconelli, "Ancient-Future Youth Ministry," *Group,* July-August 1999, pp. 32-39.

[4]Yaconelli, "Ancient-Future Youth Ministry," p. 34.

[5]Ibid., p. 37.

[6]Ibid., pp. 34-36—a more specific description of these models.

[7]Ibid., pp. 34-35.

[8]Ibid., p. 39.

[9]Ibid., p. 34.

[10]Whenever one encounters anything new in spiritual formation—including something "ancient" and new—it is critical to remember that heart rather than technique is the key to spiritual vitality with God.

[11]Philip Yancey, *What's So Amazing About Grace?* (Grand Rapids, Mich.: Zondervan, 1997).

[12]Jimmy Long, *Generating Hope* (Downers Grove, Ill.: InterVarsity Press, 1997), p. 153.

[13]Brennan Manning, *Abba's Child* (Colorado Springs: NavPress, 1994), p. 26.

[14]The phrasing of this sentence was influenced by the comments of Sally Morgenthaler. For more of Morgenthaler's insights see "Authentic Worship Culture," *Worship Leader,* May-June 1998, pp. 24-32.

[15]Warning: not all people who appear to be safe are truly healthy enough to be entrusted with the spiritual care of students. Caution should therefore always be exercised when bringing adult leaders into relationship with students.

[16]Charles Trueheart, "Welcome to the Next Church," *Atlantic Monthly,* August 1996, p. 16.

[17]John Maxwell, *Developing the Leader Within You* (Nashville: Thomas Nelson, 1993), pp. 2-13.

[18]Hule Goddard, "What Will It Take to Reach Generation X?" January 15, 1998 <www.goodnewsmag.org>.

[19]Ibid.

[20]Manning, *Abba's Child,* p. 137.

[21]Douglas Coupland, *Generation X: Tales for an Accelerated Culture* (New York: St. Martin's

Press, 1991), p. 8.

[22]Ibid.

[23]The book of Ecclesiastes has special relevance for the "been there, done that" generation.

[24]Ron Johnson, quoted in Morgenthaler, "Authentic Worship Culture," p. 32.

[25]D. A. Carson, *The Gagging of God* (Grand Rapids, Mich: Zondervan, 1996), pp. 501-5.

[26]Andrew Dreitcer, "The Art of Spiritual Direction," *Youthworker*, January-February 1997, p. 47.

[27]The absolute tenets of the historical Christian faith must be clung to with a white-knuckle grip. Secondary matters must be identified as such in order for the gospel to be proclaimed in its purest form among this generation.

[28]See Thomas Groome, *Christian Religious Education: Sharing Our Story and Vision* (San Francisco: Harper & Row, 1980), for an excellent development on the relation of story to vision in the educational process. While Groome's theology lacks adequate moorings in the authority of Scripture, his educational approach to nurturing a learning community in dialogue with the Word and each other is an important contribution.

[29]Mike Mozley, quoted in Goddard, "What Will It Take to Reach Generation X?"

[30]Jimmy Long, *Generating Hope* (Downers Grove, Ill.: InterVarsity Press, 1997), p. 162.

[31]Mark Driscoll, quoted in Morgenthaler, "Authentic Worship Culture," p. 36.

[32]Long, *Generating Hope,* p. 152.

[33]Morgenthaler, "Authentic Worship Culture," p. 36.

[34]Postema, *Space for God*, p. 111.

[35]Leanne Payne, *Listening Prayer* (Grand Rapids, Mich.: Baker, 1994), p. 21.

[36]Ken Gire, *Windows of the Soul* (Grand Rapids, Mich.: Zondervan, 1996). Throughout his text Gire demonstrates the diverse means by which the "voice of God speaks" in our daily experiences.

[37]Radio newsman Paul Harvey has immortalized the phrase "the rest of the story."

[38]Andrew Kuyper, quoted in Postema, *Space for God*, p. 104.

[39]Kevin Offner, quoted in Long, *Generating Hope*, p. 200.

[40]Ibid., p. 202.

[41]Kenda Creasy Dean and Ron Foster, *The Godbearing Life* (Nashville: Upper Room, 1998), p. 48.

[42]Tom Mueller, "Eco-Trippers: Surviving the Eco-Challenge Adventure," *Hemispheres*, April 1998, p. 74.

[43]Ibid., p. 79.

[44]The postmodern commitments to diversity, synergy and community make this generation particularly capable of experiencing the richness of the body of Christ.

[45]Dunn and Mohler, "Fourth Wave," p. 49.

[46]Chris Seay, quoted in Trueheart, "Welcome to the Next Church," p. 15.

Chapter 9: Early Adolescence

[1]Les Parrot III, *Helping the Struggling Adolescent* (Grand Rapids, Mich.: Zondervan, 1993), p. 15.

[2]David Elkind, *All Grown Up and No Place to Go* (Reading, Mass.: Addison-Wesley, 1984), p. 70.

[3]Catherine Stonehouse, *Joining Children on the Spiritual Journey* (Grand Rapids, Mich.: Baker, 1998), p. 195.

[4]Mark S. Young, "Nurturing Spirituality in the Matrix of Human Development," *Christian Education Journal,* fall 1989, pp. 87-98.

[5]D. A. Carson, *The Gagging of God* (Grand Rapids, Mich.: Zondervan, 1996), p. 26.

[6]In Wayne Rice, *Junior High Ministry* (Grand Rapids, Mich.: Zondervan, 1987), p. 61.

[7]Most respondents recall the early adolescent years as an awkward, uneven passage of life.

[8]David Veerman, *Reaching Kids Before High School* (Wheaton, Ill.: Victor, 1990), pp. 11-15.

[9]Judy Blume, *Then Again, Maybe I Won't* (New York: Bradbury, 1971), pp. 78-79.

[10]Elkind, *All Grown Up*, p. 24.

[11]Ibid., pp. 28-40.

[12]Ibid., p. 70.

[13]Uwe Gielen, "Research on Moral Reasoning," in *The Kohlberg Legacy*, ed. Lisa Kuhmerker with Uwe Gielen and Richard R. Hayes (Birmingham, Ala.: Doxa Books, 1994), pp. 28-29.

[14]Nina Darnton, "The End of Innocence," *Newsweek*, summer 1991 (special issue), pp. 62-64.

[15]Ibid.

[16]Jerry Johnston, *Who's Listening?* (Grand Rapids, Mich.: Zondervan, 1992), p. 49.

[17]Veerman, *Reaching Kids Before High School,* p. 25.

[18]Ibid., p. 40.

[19]Critical to all relational contexts for early adolescent ministries is a commitment to "zero losers." In other words, every event and experience should be designed to have each person make a meaningful contribution, stressing teamwork and interdependence, and minimizing skills that will create a sense of "winners" and "losers." Competition, therefore, should be fun but not at the expense of the less talented.

[20]Jack Canfield et al., eds., *Chicken Soup for the Teenage Soul II* (Deerfield Beach, Fla.: Health Communications, 1998), p. 314.

[21]Ibid., p. 315.

Chapter 10: Middle Adolescence

[1]Jack Canfield et al., eds., *Chicken Soup for the Teenage Soul* (Deerfield Beach, Fla.: Health Communications, 1997), pp. 266-69.

[2]Mihaly Csikszentmaihalyi and Reed Larson, *Being Adolescent* (New York: BasicBooks, 1984), pp. 123-45.

[3]David Elkind, *All Grown Up and No Place to Go* (Reading, Mass.: Addison-Wesley, 1984), pp. 15-16.

[4]This bridge illustration is adapted from an illustration by Wayne Rice, *Junior High Ministry* (Grand Rapids, Mich.: Zondervan, 1987), p. 84.

[5]Steve Patty, "A Developmental Framework for Doing Youth Ministry," in *Reaching a Generation for Christ*, ed. Richard R. Dunn and Mark H. Senter III (Chicago: Moody Press, 1997), p. 77.

[6]Elkind, *All Grown Up*, p. 33.

[7]I am indebted to Dr. Brian Richardson for this quote in a lecture he delivered during my undergraduate studies at Bryan College, Dayton, Tennessee.

[8]Stephen R. Covey, *The Seven Habits of Highly Effective Families* (New York: Golden, 1997),

p. 203.

[9]John M. Dettoni, *Introduction to Youth Ministry* (Grand Rapids, Mich.: Zondervan, 1993), pp. 33-35.

[10]Judith Rich Harris, *The Nurture Assumption* (New York: Free Press, 1998), pp. 276-78.

[11]Ibid., p. 277.

[12]Elkind, *All Grown Up,* pp. 3-21.

[13]Csikszentmihalyi and Larson, *Being Adolescent,* pp. 160-61.

[14]Ibid., 120-23.

[15]As middle adolescents find themselves in increasingly less protected social environments, the need to nurture the moral self through pacing and then leading reaches a critical peak. Middle adolescents who lack a meaningfully involved spiritual caregiver become morally vulnerable to the cultural ethos of the youth culture.

[16]I was first introduced to this critical concept of thinking Christianly about one's moral self by Perry Downs while I was a graduate student at Trinity Evangelical Divinity School.

[17]Catherine Stonehouse, *Joining Children on the Spiritual Journey* (Grand Rapids, Mich.: Baker, 1998), pp. 112-22.

[18]Gary Smalley and John Trent, *The Gift of the Blessing* (Nashville: Thomas Nelson, 1993), pp. 95-96.

[19]Robert Laurent's research included interviews with four thousand high school students. He reported those findings in *Keeping Your Teen in Touch with God* (Elgin, Ill.: Cook, 1989).

Chapter 11: Late Adolescence

[1]James Fowler, "Perspectives on the Family from the Standpoint of Faith Development Theory," in *Christian Perspectives on Faith Development,* ed. Jeff Astley and Leslie Francis (Leominster, U.K.: Gracewing Fowler Wright, 1992), p. 334.

[2]Sharon Parks, "Young Adult Faith Development: Teaching in the Context of Theological Education," in *Christian Perspectives on Faith Development,* ed. Jeff Astley and Leslie Francis (Leominster, U.K.: Gracewing Fowler Wright, 1992), pp. 212-13.

[3]See Sharon Parks, *The Critical Years: Young Adults and the Search for Meaning, Faith, and Commitment* (San Francisco: Harper & Row, 1986).

[4]Romney M. Moseley, David Jarvis and James W. Fowler, "Stages of Faith," in *Christian Perspectives on Faith Development,* ed. Jeff Astley and Leslie Francis (Leominster, U.K.: Gracewing Fowler Wright, 1992), p. 53.

[5]Fred Wilson, "Adult Development," in *Nurture That Is Christian,* ed. John M. Dettoni and James Wilhoit (Wheaton, Ill.: Victor, 1995), p. 175.

[6]John M. Dettoni and James Wilhoit, "Introduction," in *Nurture That Is Christian,* ed. John M. Dettoni and James Wilhoit (Wheaton, Ill.: Victor, 1995), p. 33.

[7]See Mark Cannister, "A Look at Mentoring Communities," *Youthworker,* July-August 1997, pp. 28-33.

[8]Judith S. Wallerstein, "Divorce: Wounds That Don't Heal," *New York Times Magazine,* January 22, 1989, p. 21.

[9]Ibid., p. 42. Wallerstein described late-twentieth-century young adults as the "first generation of young adults, men and women, so anxious about attachment and love that their ability to create enduring families is imperiled."

[10]For a theological reflection on the importance of choosing friends well, see Bill Hybels, *Making Life Work* (Downers Grove, Ill.: InterVarsity Press, 1998), pp. 98-113.

[11]Wilson, "Adult Development," p. 177.

[12]Fowler, "Perspectives on the Family," pp. 334-35.

[13]Steven Garber, *The Fabric of Faithfulness* (Downers Grove, Ill.: InterVarsity Press, 1996), p. 39.

[14]While my thoughts have developed over time, the genesis of and structure for this reflection on Mary must be credited to Kenda Creasy Dean and Ron Foster, *The Godbearing Life* (Nashville: Upper Room, 1998).

[15]Mark Rutledge, "Faith Development," in *Christian Perspectives on Faith Development,* ed. Jeff Astley and Leslie Francis (Leominster, U.K.: Gracewing Fowler Wright, 1992), p. 360.

[16]Dave Veerman, *Passages of Parenting* (Wheaton, Ill.: Tyndale House, 1994), p. 231.

[17]Fowler, "Perspectives on the Family," p. 335.

[18]Garber, *Fabric of Faithfulness,* p. 124.

[19]Ibid., pp. 110-11.

[20]Gary L. Chamberlain, quoted in Robert Pazmino, *Foundational Issues in Christian Education,* 2nd ed. (Grand Rapids, Mich.: Baker, 1997), pp. 212-13.

[21]Rutledge, "Faith Development," p. 360.

[22]Ibid.

[23]See James Mezirow, "How Critical Reflection Triggers Transformative Learning," in *Fostering Critical Reflection,* ed. James Mezirow (San Francisco: Jossey-Bass, 1991), pp. 1-20.

[24]Garber, *Fabric of Faithfulness,* p. 20.

[25]The concept of life as a sacred conversation emerges primarily from my theological reflection on Scripture and the influences of Christian thinkers Dallas Willard, Eugene Peterson, Henri Nouwen and Ken Gire.

Chapter 12: Self-Care for Wick Burners

[1]Richard J. Foster, "Spiritual Leadership in Youth Ministry," *Group,* April-May 1991, p. 23.

[2]Jeff VanVonderen, *Tired of Trying to Measure Up* (Minneapolis: Bethany House, 1989), p. 13.

[3]Ibid., p. 18.

[4]Jeff VanVonderen, *Families Where Grace Is in Place* (Minneapolis: Bethany House, 1992), p. 64.

[5]M. Robert Mulholland Jr., *Invitation to a Journey* (Downers Grove, Ill.: InterVarsity Press, 1993), p. 26.

[6]Eugene H. Peterson, *Leap Over a Wall* (San Francisco: HarperCollins, 1997), p. 164.

[7]Review chapter eight for creative approaches to developing space for your own spiritual journey.

[8]Mulholland, *Invitation to a Journey,* p. 76.

[9]Ibid., p. 31.

[10]Gilbert Bilezikian, *Community 101* (Grand Rapids, Mich.: Zondervan, 1997), p. 27.

[11]Stanley Grenz, *Revisioning Evangelical Theology* (Downers Grove, Ill.: InterVarsity Press, 1993), p. 160.

[12]My views on the relationship of fear to community are derived primarily from the works of

Henri Nouwen.

[13]Sandra D. Wilson, *Shame-Free Parenting* (Downers Grove, Ill.: InterVarsity Press, 1992), p. 27.

[14]Ray S. Anderson, *Self-Care* (Wheaton, Ill.: Victor, 1995), p. 239.

[15]Ibid., p. 210.

[16]Ibid., p. 214.

[17]June Lewers Terry, *When Teardrops Dance* (Grand Rapids, Mich.: Revell, 1994), p. 157.

[18]Paul Brand and Philip Yancey, *Pain: The Gift Nobody Wants* (Grand Rapids, Mich.: Zondervan, 1993), p. 5.

[19]Ibid.

Bibliography

Anderson, Ray S. *Self Care*. Wheaton, Ill.: Victor, 1995.

Astley, Jeff, and Leslie Francis, eds. *Christian Perspectives on Faith Development*. Leominster, U.K.: Gracewing Fowler Wright, 1992.

Augsburger, Myron. *Caring Enough to Confront*. Ventura, Calif.: Regal, 1992.

Bilezikian, Gilbert. *Community 101*. Grand Rapids, Mich.: Zondervan, 1997.

Blume, Judy. *Then Again, Maybe I Won't*. New York: Bradbury, 1971.

Brand, Paul, and Philip Yancey. *Pain: The Gift Nobody Wants*. Grand Rapids, Mich.: Zondervan, 1993.

Brown, Harold O. J. *The Sensate Culture*. Dallas: Word, 1996.

Canfield, Jack, Mark Victor Hansen, and Kimbely Kirberger. *Chicken Soup for the Teenage Soul*. Deerfield Beach, Fla.: Health Communications, 1997.

—————. *Chicken Soup for the Teenage Soul II*. Deerfield Beach, Fla.: Health Communications, 1998.

Cannister, Mark. "A Look at Mentoring Communities." *Youthworker,* July-August 1997, pp. 28-33.

Carson, Don. *The Gagging of God*. Grand Rapids, Mich.: Zondervan, 1996.

Cline, Foster W. *Conscienceless Acts, Societal Mayhem*. Golden, Colo.: Love and Logic, 1995.

Cloud, Henry. *Changes That Heal*. Grand Rapids, Mich.: Zondervan, 1992.

Coles, Robert. "The Long Obstacle Course Called Adolescence." *Youthworker,* summer 1989, pp. 70-74.

—————. *The Moral Intelligence of Children*. New York: Plume, 1998.

Coupland, Douglas. *Generation X: Tales for an Accelerated Culture*. New York: St. Martin's Press, 1991.

Covey, Stephen R. *The 7 Habits of Highly Effective Families*. New York: Golden, 1997.

Crabb, Larry. *Connecting*. Nashville: Word, 1997.

—————. *Effective Biblical Counseling*. Grand Rapids, Mich.: Zondervan, 1977.

Csikszentmihalyi, Mihaly, and Reed Larson. *Being Adolescent*. New York: HarperCollins, 1984.

Darnton, Nina. "The End of Innocence." *Newsweek,* special issue, summer 1991, pp. 62-64.

Dean, Kenda Creasy, and Ron Foster. *The Godbearing Life*. Nashville: Upper Room, 1998.

Dettoni, John M. *Introduction to Youth Ministry*. Grand Rapids, Mich.: Zondervan, 1993.

Dettoni, John M., and James Wilhoit, eds. *Nurture That Is Christian.* Wheaton, Ill.: Victor, 1995.

DeVries, Mark. *Family-Based Youth Ministry.* Downers Grove, Ill.: InterVarsity Press, 1994.

Dreitcer, Andrew. "The Art of Spiritual Direction." *Youthworker* 13 (1997): 46-49.

Downs, Perry G. *Teaching for Spiritual Growth.* Grand Rapids, Mich.: Zondervan, 1994.

Dunn, Richard R., and Mark H. Senter III. *Reaching a Generation for Christ.* Chicago: Moody Press, 1997.

——————. "What Are the Necessary Competencies to Be an Effective Youth Worker?" *Christian Education Journal* 16 (spring 1996): 25-38.

Dunn, Richard R., and James Mohler. "The 'Fourth Wave': A Theological Perspective." *Christian Education Journal,* fall 1999, pp. 47-61.

Eldredge, John. *The Journey of Desire.* Nashville: Thomas Nelson, 2000.

Elkind, David. *All Grown Up and No Place to Go.* Reading, Mass.: Addison-Wesley, 1984.

——————. "Jumping the Gun on Adolescence." *Youthworker* (winter 1991): 28-32.

Foster, Richard J. "Spiritual Leadership in Youth Ministry." *Group* (April-May 1991): 23.

Fowler, James. "Moral Stages and the Development of Faith." In *Moral Development, Moral Education, and Kohlberg,* edited by Brenda Munsey. Birmingham: Religious Education Press, 1980.

Garber, Steven. *The Fabric of Faithfulness.* Downers Grove, Ill.: InterVarsity Press, 1996.

Gielen, Uwe. "Research on Moral Reasoning." In *The Kohlberg Legacy,* ed. Lisa Kuhmerker with Uwe Gielen and Richard L. Hayes. Birmingham, Ala.: Doxa, 1994.

Gire, Ken. *Windows of the Soul.* Grand Rapids, Mich.: Zondervan, 1996.

Grant, Priscilla. "How Spiritual are You?" *Self* (December 1997): 132-35.

Groome, Thomas. *Christian Religious Education: Sharing Our Story and Vision.* San Francisco: Harper & Row, 1980.

Grenz, Stanley. *A Primer on Postmodernism.* Grand Rapids, Mich.: Eerdmans, 1996.

——————. *Revisioning Evangelical Theology.* Downers Grove, Ill.: InterVarsity Press, 1993.

Guinness, Os, and John Seel. *No God but God.* Chicago: Moody Press, 1992.

Gulley, Philip. *Front Porch Tales.* Sisters, Ore.: Multnomah, 1997.

Hahn, Todd, and David Verhaagen. *GenXers After God.* Grand Rapids, Mich.: Baker, 1997.

Hajcak, Frank and Patricia Garwood. *Quick-Fix Sex: Pseudosexuality in Adolescents.* San Diego: Libra, n.d.

Harris, Judith Rich. *The Nurture Assumption.* New York: Free Press, 1998.

Hendrix, Harville, and Helen Hunt. *Giving the Love That Heals.* New York: Pocket, 1997.

Hersey, Paul, and Kenneth H. Blanchard. *Management of Organizational Behavior.* Fifth edition. Englewood Cliffs, N.J.: Prentice Hall, 1983.

Hirshberg, Charles. "The Face of God." *Life* 13 (December 1990): 47-78.

Hoekema, Anthony. *Created in God's Image.* Grand Rapids, Mich.: Eerdmans, 1986.

——————. *Saved by Grace.* Grand Rapids, Mich.: Eerdmans, 1989.

Huggins, Kevin. *Parenting Adolescents.* Colorado Springs: NavPress: 1989.

Huggins, Kevin, and Phil Landrum. *Guiding Your Teen to a Faith That Lasts.* Grand Rapids, Mich.: Discovery House, 1994.

Johnston, Jerry. *Who's Listening?* Grand Rapids, Mich.: Zondervan, 1992.

Kotesky, Ronald L. *Understanding Adolescence*. Wheaton, Ill.: Victor, 1987.

Laurent, Robert. *Keeping Your Teen in Touch with God*. Elgin, Ill.: Cook, 1989.

Lawrence, Rick. *Trend Watch*. Loveland, Colo.: Group, 2000.

—————. "What Really Impacts Kids' Spiritual Growth." *Group* 21 (February 1995): 18-22.

Long, Jimmy. *Generating Hope*. Downers Grove, Ill.: InterVarsity Press, 1997.

Lundin, Roger. *The Culture of Interpretation*. Grand Rapids, Mich.: Eerdmans, 1993.

Lynn, David. "The New Adolescence." *Youthworker* (winter 1991): 40-43.

Manning, Brennan. *Abba's Child*. Colorado Springs: NavPress, 1994.

Maxwell, John C. *Developing the Leader Within You*. Nashville: Thomas Nelson, 1993.

McCourt, Frank. "When You Think of God, What Do You See?" *Life,* December 1998, pp. 60-73.

McDonald, Gordon. *Ordering Your Private World*. Nashville: Thomas Nelson, 1984.

Morgenthaler, Sally. "Authentic Worship Culture." *Worship Leader,* May-June 1998, pp. 24-32.

Mueller, Tom. "Eco-Trippers: Surviving the Eco-Challenge Adventure." *Hemispheres,* April 1998, pp. 72-79.

Mueller, Walt. *Understanding Today's Youth Culture*. Wheaton, Ill.: Tyndale House, 1994.

Mulholland, M. Robert Jr. *Invitation to a Journey*. Downers Grove, Ill.: InterVarsity Press, 1993.

Nouwen, Henri. *The Way of the Heart*. San Francisco: Harper & Row, 1991.

Packer, J. I. "An Introduction to Systematic Spirituality" *Crux,* March 1990, pp. 2-8.

Palmer, Parker. *Let Your Life Speak*. San Francisco: Jossey-Bass, 1999.

—————. *To Know As We Are Known*. San Francisco: HarperCollins, 1983.

Parks, Sharon. *The Critical Years: Young Adults and the Search for Meaning, Faith, and Commitment*. San Francisco: Harper & Row, 1986.

Parrott, Les, III. "Adolescent Spirituality." *Youthworker* 11 (1995): 32-40.

—————. *Helping the Struggling Adolescent*. Grand Rapids, Mich.: Zondervan, 1993.

Payne, Leanne. *The Healing Presence*. Grand Rapids, Mich.: Baker, 1995.

—————. *Listening Prayer*. Grand Rapids, Mich.: Baker, 1994.

Pazmino, Robert. *Foundational Issues in Christian Education*, 2nd ed. Grand Rapids, Mich.: Baker, 1997.

Pearlman, Cindy. "Suddenly Spiritual." *react,* December 28, 1998-January 3, 1999, p. 9.

Peterson, Eugene H. *The Contemplative Pastor*. Grand Rapids, Mich.: Eerdmans, 1989.

—————. *Leap over a Wall*. San Francisco: HarperCollins, 1997.

—————. *Like Dew Your Youth*. Grand Rapids, Mich.: Eerdmans, 1994.

Pickle, Betsy. "Steamy, Audacious Young Cast Raises Temperature in 'Cruel Intentions.' " *Knoxville News-Sentinel,* March 6, 1999, p. B6.

Postema, Don. *Space for God*. Kalamazoo, Mich.: CRC Publications, 1983.

Rabey, Steve. "Spirituality in the Limelight." *Youthworker,* January-February 1997, pp. 17-19.

Rice, Wayne. *Junior High Ministry*. Grand Rapids, Mich.: Zondervan, 1987.

Roehlkepartin, Eugene. "Helping Faith Mature." *Church Teachers,* September-October 1990, pp. 46-47, 75.

Rowley, William J. *Equipped to Care*. Wheaton, Ill.: Victor, 1990.

Schultze, Quentin J., et al., eds. *Dancing in the Dark.* Grand Rapids, Mich.: Eerdmans, 1991.

Schmich, Mary. "Heaven's Gaters May Not Have Been So Strange After All." *Chicago Tribune,* March 30, 1997, sect. 4, p. 1.

Shelley, Marshall. *Keeping Your Kids Christian.* Ann Arbor, Mich.: Servant, 1990.

Siler, Debi. "Who, What, Where, and Why Am I Looking for . . . God?" *re:generation Quarterly* 3 (winter 1997): 20-21.

Smalley, Gary, and John Trent. *The Gift of the Blessing.* Nashville: Thomas Nelson, 1993.

Steele, Les. "Identity Formation Theory and Youth Ministry." *Christian Education Journal* 9 (fall 1988): 91-99.

Stonehouse, Catherine. *Joining Children on the Spiritual Journey.* Grand Rapids, Mich.: Baker, 1998.

Sweet, Leonard. *AquaChurch.* Loveland, Colo.: Group, 1999.

Swets, Paul. *The Art of Communicating with Your Teenager.* Holbrook, Mass.: Adams, 1995.

Terry, June Lewers. *When Teardrops Dance.* Grand Rapids, Mich.: Revell, 1994.

—————. *The Blessing Workbook.* Nashville: Thomas Nelson, 1993.

Trueheart, Charles. "Welcome to the Next Church." *Atlantic Monthly,* August 1996, pp. 37-58.

Tryphon, Anastasia, and Jaques Voneche. *Piaget-Vgotsky: The Social Genesis of Thought.* East Sussex, U.K.: Psychology Press, 1996.

VanVonderen, Jeff. *Families Where Grace Is in Place.* Minneapolis: Bethany House, 1992.

—————. *Tired of Trying to Measure Up.* Minneapolis: Bethany House, 1989.

Veerman, Dave. *Passages of Parenting.* Wheaton, Ill.: Tyndale House, 1994.

—————. *Reaching Kids Before High School.* Wheaton, Ill.: Victor, 1990.

Vowell, Sarah. *Take the Cannoli.* New York: Simon & Schuster, 2000.

Wallerstein, Judith S. "Divorce: Wounds That Don't Heal." *New York Times Magazine,* January 22, 1989, pp. 19-21, 41-43.

Warner, Marina, et al. "Wrestling with the Oldest Rules." *Self,* December 1997.

Weyerhauser, Dan. *But Our Lives As Well,* seminar manual.

Wilhoit, Jim. *Christian Education and the Search for Meaning,* 2nd ed. Grand Rapids, Mich.: Baker, 1991.

Willard, Dallas. *The Divine Conspiracy.* New York: HarperCollins, 1998.

Wilson, Sandra D. *Into Abba's Arms.* Wheaton, Ill.: Tyndale House, 1998.

—————. *Shame-Free Parenting.* Downers Grove, Ill.: InterVarsity Press, 1992.

Yancey, Philip. *What's So Amazing About Grace?* Grand Rapids, Mich.: Zondervan, 1997.

Young, Mark S. "Nurturing Spirituality in the Matrix of Human Development." *Christian Education Journal* 10 (fall 1989): 87-98.

Zacharias, Ravi. *Jesus Among Other Gods.* Nashville: Word, 2000.